P9-APE-107

SPECIAL EDUCATION SERIES

Peter Knoblock, Editor

(Continued)

On Being L.D.:
Perspectives and Strategies of Young Adults
Stephen T. Murphy

Toward Effective Public School Programs for Deaf Students:
Context, Process, and Outcomes
Thomas N. Kluwin, Donald F. Moores, and Martha Gonter Gaustad, Editors

Toward Effective
Public School Programs
for Deaf Students

Context, Process, and Outcomes

Edited by
THOMAS N. KLUWIN
DONALD F. MOORES
MARTHA GONTER GAUSTAD

**TEACHERS
COLLEGE
PRESS**

Teachers College, Columbia University
New York and London

132048

Published by Teachers College Press, 1234 Amsterdam Avenue
New York, New York

Copyright © 1992 by Teachers College, Columbia University

All rights reserved. No part of this publication may be reproduced or
transmitted in any form or by any means, electronic or mechanical,
including photocopy, or any information storage and retrieval system,
without permission from the publisher.

Library of Congress Cataloging-in-Publication Data

Toward effective public school programs for deaf students : context,
  process, and outcomes / edited by Thomas N. Kluwin, Donald F.
  Moores, Martha Gonter Gaustad.
    p. cm.—(Special education series)
    Includes bibliographical references and index.
    ISBN 0-8077-3160-9 (cloth).—ISBN 0-8077-3159-5 (paper)
  1. Children, Deaf—Education—United States.   2. Mainstreaming in
education—United States.   3. Public schools—United States.
I. Kluwin, Thomas N.   II. Moores, Donald F.   III. Gaustad, Martha
Gonter.   IV. Series: Special education series (New York, N.Y.)
HV2551.T68   1992
371.91′2′0973—dc20   92-2932

ISBN 0-8077-3160-9
ISBN 0-8077-3159-5 (pbk)

Printed on acid-free paper
Manufactured in the United States of America
99 98 97 96 95 94 93 92   8 7 6 5 4 3 2 1

Contents

133048

Part II: The Process and Outcomes of Schooling

Acknowledgments

This is a pleasant and yet demanding task because this book is not the result of the efforts of a single individual but of many, many people all over the United States who contributed in various ways to help provide the authors with the data cited here. Much of the work described in this book represents the midpoint of a five-year study of 15 public school districts around the United States that offer programs for deaf students. The contributions of all of those who have helped in this endeavor need to be recognized.

To begin with, there has been a steady stream of talented people who have passed through Gallaudet University and helped maintain the records of this work. These include Mary Simpson, Elena Jiminez Ulloa, Lucy Trivelli, Kate Tobin, Catherine Sweet, and Arlene B. Kelly.

There has been a faithful group of individuals in different locations around the United States who have helped collect and send us much of the data that are reported in this book: Ann Levis, Jim Newman, Milt Graves, Pam Balkovec, June Kempf, the late Jane Landis, Wendy Gonsher, Susan Steege, Mary Ann Zigler, Mary Lou Casey, Charles Osler, Connie Smith, Tracie Daley, Pat Robertson, Elizabeth Royal, Carrie Perez, Ardalia Idelbird, Cheryl Moses, Harriet Kaberline, Sheila Barnard, Carolyn Rowland, Hartley Koch, Barbara MacNeil, and Candy Schauer. Without their continued assistance, this midpoint presentation would not have been possible.

I would also like to recognize the assistance and cooperation of my coeditors. The process of resolving different perspectives gave us the vision of complexity that this book tries to convey.

I particularly want to mention the contribution of one public school teacher, my wife Bridget Kluwin, who provided me with a continuous perspective on the complexity of public school education. Although she is not listed as an author of any chapter, she contributed intellectually to much of what is in this book.

Finally, this book purposely has no dedication because so many have touched this effort and continue to be involved with our ongoing study of public school programs for the deaf. No single individual is responsible for the totality of this book, but then no single individual represents the peculiarly American ideal of providing an opportunity for all of its citizenry through free public education.

T.N.K.

Introduction

Thomas N. Kluwin

While there is over a century-and-a-half of experience with educating deaf children in residential programs and local day programs, the large-scale education of deaf and hard of hearing children in local public schools is a relatively recent phenomenon. As several chapters in this volume will point out, large-scale public school education of deaf children has really taken place only in the last 15 years. During this time frame there has been a continuous concern for effective public school education. While *A Nation at Risk* and *High School and Beyond* are often cited as banners of this movement, a genuine broad-based concern for the quality of American public school education has evolved. Clearly, the rapid changes in the education of deaf children during the past decade-and-a-half, as well as the rising concern for the quality of all American education, call for an examination of the current situation.

The primary purpose of this book is to define and clarify the issues involved. At the same time, a tradition of research in this area has been steadily accumulating and needs to be brought to light. However, definition and explanation alone are not enough because school personnel require the translation of theory and data into usable recommendations. Consequently, another purpose of this book is to recommend, based on a consideration of general theories of education and an examination in particular of educating deaf children in public schools, possible courses of action for organizing effective public school programs for deaf students. This book establishes the essential questions concerning the public school education of deaf and hard of hearing students, defines the major constructs within these questions or concerns, and either demonstrates what effective education is or should be in this type of setting or explains why it is not possible to adequately do so. This is an issues-oriented book that uses new data to define the parameters of complex issues, with an emphasis on clarification.

This book is intended for school personnel who wish to know what the current practice is in their field and for university faculty involved in teacher training or research who are interested in the present level of scholarship as well as the critical issues. The book will also be of use to graduate or undergraduate students concerned about the education of the deaf.

ONE VISION OF THIS BOOK

While straightforward advocacy or scathing criticism would be a convenient starting point for a "vision" of this book and the topic it addresses, that would not be fair to the reality of the situation, for two reasons. First, American public education is a complex, controversial phenomenon, and, despite its many failings, one of the most successful institutions in the world. Second, deaf education is a very contentious field, a fact that has nothing to do with the deaf but rather has to do with many of those who wish to educate them.

Pick any topic either in American culture or in American education—sex education, textbooks, freedom of speech, equity, justice—and you will immediately find two sides and a variety of splinter groups vying for support from the mass of the population. While we may curse the turmoil, it is both the right and the result of a democracy. To maintain order in schools and get on with what is essentially a conservative function, the education of the young, we have fostered the local school system as a way to allow democracy—through local control of the schools—and national conformity—in the goal of universal literacy—to exist side by side. Unfortunately, local control of schools, both in the form of local choices about schooling and in local control over the shape of school governance, is chaotic and unresponsive to national agendas.

However, this contentious system has produced some amazing results. A century ago, the nation faced massive immigration and called on the school system to solve the three problems of teaching immigrants the English language, American living standards, and the obligations of membership in a democracy. Locale by locale, the schools responded, some with success and others with failure.

Overall, the result was the integration of a foreign population into the nation. In 1954, the schools were again called upon to assist in a national goal: racial integration. This process also was painful and the results were mixed. Legal and structural equity was achieved in the schools for teachers and administrators, with a mixed situation for students. Through it all, while universal literacy has not been achieved, American public school education has remained committed to educating the entire citizenry and not just an elite group.

We have placed the chapter on history at the front of this book because we wanted the reader to have a perspective on the tradition of controversy that is so characteristic of deaf education. Some of the sources of this contentiousness are admirable, beginning with the assertion that deaf children can and should be educated for full participation in American society. Others are venal and range from family recipes for curing deafness to the defense of established "fiefdoms" (Moores, 1987). In between are the misguided notions of various eras, such as the "eugenics" movement of the later half of the last century. Unfortunately for observers both inside and outside of deaf education, it is often difficult to separate the self-serving from the sublime.

If this book has a vision, it is a vision of a complex and fractured field, calling out for order. The first step in establishing order is to step back briefly and view the field. That is the purpose of the first part of this book—to define the limits and contours of the field. In the second part of the book, we take the next step and begin to address some of the issues that have arisen.

The question seems to have become, "Does mainstreaming work?" This book answers that the question itself is too simplistic. Programs are varied; students are selected for placement for specific reasons; success can be defined in a variety of ways and can occur in supposedly competing environments. The answer, from this book, is, "It depends."

If the reader comes to this book demanding "an answer," he or she will go away very disappointed because the purpose of this book is to define how complicated the questions can be. If the reader comes to this book looking for a perspective on the current confusion, then the book will offer a wealth of information: how different deaf constituencies have unique needs; how the family contributes to and makes demands on the school system; how, based on some criteria, deaf children are succeeding; and how, using other criteria, they are losing out. The vision of this book lies in its search for understanding the intricacy of the issues and in the recognition that the effective education of our children has to start this Monday and every Monday as long as we seek to maintain this contentious political system of ours.

REFERENCES

Moores, D. (1987). *Educating the deaf: Psychology, principles, and practices.* Boston: Houghton-Mifflin.

PART I

The Context of the Educational Program

CHAPTER 1

An Historical Perspective on School Placement

DONALD F. MOORES

Since the establishment of education of the deaf in the United States controversies have raged over what, how, and where to teach deaf children, but to date there has been no definitive resolution of this controversy. While answers have varied as the United States has grown from an agrarian confederation of approximately four million inhabitants of 13 eastern states to a postindustrial continental nation of 250 million citizens, three themes seem to recur among the forces that shape educational placements for deaf children. The general social milieu of the nation, changes in the national population, and changes in educational philosophies or theories regarding deafness have repeatedly combined to shape the education of deaf children.

The issue of school placement, that is, the question of what constitutes the most appropriate environment in which to educate children with severe to profound hearing losses, is complicated by the fact that early childhood deafness calls for very special instructional techniques while at the same time constituting a rare condition. Thus, the low incidence of profound early childhood deafness, estimated by Ries (1986) as occurring in one child per 1,000, and the special communication and educational needs of deaf children have led to the establishment of separate schools and facilities. A counteracting force has been the natural desire of parents to keep their children—especially young children—at home and have them educated in local settings.

Uncertainty over school placement, as well as in other aspects of education of the deaf, is understandable in light of the fact that the formal education of deaf individuals is a relatively recent phe-

7

nomenon. Deafness was mentioned as early as in Egyptian papyri of the seventeenth century B.C., and Socrates dealt in detail with the sign language of the deaf in ancient Greece (Moores, 1987). However, there is no record of any attempt to educate the deaf until the sixteenth century, when the Spanish monk, Pedro Ponce de Leon, successfully taught a number of deaf children of the Spanish aristocracy, which, because of generations of inbreeding and the presence of recessive genes for deafness, had produced an unusually large number of deaf offspring (Chaves & Solar, 1974). It was not until two centuries later that the first real school for the deaf was established in Paris in 1755 by the Abbe Charles Michel de l'Epee (Moores, 1987). Thus, the idea that deaf children could benefit from an education and achieve literacy is a recent one.

EARLY AMERICAN PATTERNS OF PLACEMENT

The first school for the deaf in the United States, the American Asylum at Hartford for the Instruction of the Deaf and Dumb, was established in 1817. School placement was not immediately seen as a problem at the American Asylum, primarily because students typically did not begin school until after age 10. Because previous attempts to conduct censuses of the deaf had seriously underestimated the numbers of deaf individuals in the country, it was assumed that one residential facility in Hartford could provide education and vocational training for all the deaf in the nation. The identification of significant numbers of deaf individuals in small towns and in cities quickly dispelled this assumption (Moores, 1987).

The next two schools for the deaf to be established were in metropolitan areas—New York and Philadelphia. Originally established as day schools, they quickly evolved into residential schools serving students from wide geographic areas. From the establishment of the American Asylum for the deaf until the Civil War, education of the deaf was driven by three primary motivations: to provide deaf individuals with religious and moral training, to provide them with vocational skills, and to teach them to read and write.

The curriculum used in the early schools was based on that developed in Paris and modified at the American Asylum. The moral training and religious emphasis were different from those encountered in French schools for the deaf, which were established and run by Roman Catholic clergy. In the United States the predominant religious orientation was Protestant, and schools for the deaf reflected the ethos of early-nineteenth-century New England—a deeply religious society in the first stages of industrialization. In common with schools for the hearing at that time and place, emphasis in the deaf schools was on the five Rs: Reading, Riting, Rithmetic, Religion, and Rules of Conduct (Soltow & Stevens, 1981). The practical nature of training for deaf students is illustrated by the fact that in 1822 the American Asylum instituted one of the first industrial training programs in the United States.

The religious nature of education of the deaf in its early stages reflects the heavy religious orientation of much of the pioneering work in education of the handicapped in both Europe and the United States (Kauffmann, 1980). Ministries to the deaf were considered parts of wider missions to preach to and convert all classes of unfortunates, including the heathen, the handicapped, the orphaned, and the poor. Thomas Hopkins Gallaudet, founder of the American Asylum, had been a theological student and was the author of several children's books that contained religious and moral teachings. He was also active in prison reform and was instrumental in sending missionaries west to combat the influence of the Catholic faith in lands acquired from Spain and France (Boatner, 1959). The second U.S. school for the deaf, the New York Institution for the Instruction of the Deaf, was founded on the work of John Stanfield, chaplain to the almshouse of New York City, who in 1810 unsuccessfully tried to teach a group of indigent deaf children to read and write (Gallaudet, 1886).

From the founding of the American Asylum, later renamed the American School for the Deaf, until after the Civil War, education of the deaf was conducted almost exclusively in residential institutions. There is no evidence before 1867 of any deaf children in school with hearing children with the exception of Alice Cogswell, who attended a private girl's school in Hartford before the establishment of the American Asylum. In the 50 years between 1817 and 1867, 24 residential schools for the deaf came into existence. The schools in Hartford, New York, and Philadelphia were in operation by 1820. During the next two decades, only four schools were added. From 1844 to 1860, 17 schools for the deaf, or an average of one school a year, opened their doors. The geographic location of the later schools may reflect a change during the nineteenth century in public perceptions of deafness (and other disabilities) and of the potential benefits of education for handicapped populations. While the first schools were in metropolitan areas, state legislatures placed later schools in rural communities such as Danville, Kentucky; Fulton, Missouri; Staunton, Virginia; and Delevan, Wisconsin, away from large urban population centers. Many states also placed schools for the blind and/or the retarded in the same towns and placed schools for the blind and schools for the deaf under the same administration in combined or adjacent facilities (Jones, 1918).

The first long-standing day schools for the deaf, in which children commuted to school on a daily basis, were not established until 1867, when the Pittsburgh Day School and the Boston Day School came into existence. Because of a small population base, the Pittsburgh Day School later evolved into the predominantly residential Western Pennsylvania School for the Deaf; the Boston Day School, now known as the Horace Mann School, has continued to the present.

THE GENERAL CULTURAL CONTEXT

The trend toward isolation and segregation of the deaf that occurred throughout the nineteenth century took place, of course, within a broader cultural and historical context. Educators of the mentally retarded and other handicapped populations have described similar developments (Dworkin, 1976; Kauffman, 1980). These movements were small parts of even greater changes in American society as the boundaries of the country expanded and demographic composition of the population underwent fundamental changes.

The situation was complicated by massive immigration that started with the influx of German and Irish-Catholic groups following the failure of the liberal revolutions in Europe and profound agricultural disasters in Ireland and Germany, and continued with waves of immigration from central, eastern, and southern Europe through the early part of the twentieth century (Dworkin, 1976; Kamin, 1974).

Until 1840 the majority of Americans were still of English and Scotch-Irish stock. With some variation, there was a commonly shared language, religion, and set of values. Although blacks made up an estimated 20-25% of the population, much higher than at present, they were almost totally subjugated (Dworkin, 1976).

By 1850 the United States had conquered the part of Mexico

stretching from Louisiana to California (approximately one-third of the present contiguous United States), which included a Native American, and a Catholic, Spanish-speaking population. In addition, the Louisiana Territory (stretching from Louisiana north to Minnesota and west to the Pacific) had been acquired from France, and the Florida Territory from Spain.

By 1870 blacks were theoretically free, and large numbers of Jewish immigrants had arrived from Poland and Russia. In the 1890s, Poles, Czechoslovakians, and Hungarians were working in the mines and factories, and by 1900 Italians had replaced the Irish as the largest ethnic group in many northeastern cities (Dworkin, 1976; Kamin, 1974). The United States was being transformed from a relatively homogeneous culture to a society of almost overwhelming ethnic, cultural, racial, linguistic, and religious diversity—a transformation that continues today.

Industrialization of the United States and western Europe caused a change in educational emphases. The evolving industrialized societies required universally trained, educated workers to form components of a complex mechanical system. Such societies are concerned with identifying individuals who might not be capable of benefiting from mass training and education techniques (Wines, 1888). To this end, the major thrust of the mental-testing movement, beginning with the work of Binet in France around the turn of the century, was to identify and remove children of limited intellectual ability from the regular educational program (Kanner, 1967).

Programs for the handicapped (the blind, the retarded, and the deaf) that were developed in the early and middle nineteenth century essentially reflected an optimistic view of the potential benefits of education and training. They were humane and had educational orientations. The goal was to prepare handicapped individuals to function in society at large (Kanner, 1967; Kauffman, 1980). The outstanding early educators of the handicapped—such as Thomas Hopkins Gallaudet, Laurent Clerc, Samuel Gridley Howe, and Edouard Seguin—were firm believers in educability. Seguin, who came to the United States after the French Revolution in 1848, was especially effective in popularizing this philosophy.

Different attitudes were apparent by the latter part of the nineteenth century. First, evidence began accumulating that not all handicapped individuals could be educated to take their place in society, especially a technical society. Second, the expansion of schools and institutions was seen more and more as a drain on the treasuries of the various states. Third, the conviction grew that many handicapped individuals, especially the retarded, constituted a threat to society. Residential institutions became less educational and more custodial in nature, with the expectation that many individuals would stay in them for their entire lives. This trend was accompanied by the previously noted tendency to build facilities away from population centers.

Increasing credence was given to the belief that heredity was the sole determining factor for human behavior. Studies purported to 'prove" that retardation and criminal tendencies were passed on from generation to generation. This idea was accompanied by a growing fear that the "lower classes" and those of "foreign stock" were outbreeding the original white stock, thus contributing to a degeneration of the United States population.

The surge of immigrants to the United States created a public clamor, and limitations on immigration by retarded individuals were called for (Kamin, 1974). The Immigration Act of 1882 prohibited "idiots" from entering the country (Kanner, 1967). By 1893 James Cattell was advocating the use of mental tests to identify the "feebleminded" in the United States. A student of Galton in England, Cattell had been influenced by Galton's ideas about eugenics and the heritability of intelligence. The ideas about intelligence testing that Cattell brought to the United States were advanced by eugenics advocates as a means to diagnose retardation in Americans and would-be immigrants (Kamin, 1974).

At one time or another, members of almost all immigrant groups were considered to be of inferior intelligence. In 1890 Billings reported that immigrant women from Ireland had a larger proportion of retarded children than did women from England and Wales, Scotland, Germany, Scandinavia, and British North America. By the end of the century, however, a preponderance of immigrants were of Mediterranean and Alpine stock, as opposed to western and northern European origin; thus the focus of concern shifted. At various times, objections were aired regarding immigrants from Italy, Russia, Poland, Greece, Turkey, and the Slavic and Latin countries. It was argued that people from these areas were markedly less intelligent than western and northern European groups and that the Hebrews ranked far below the average in intelligence (Dworkin, 1976). Other groups also fared poorly, as Dworkin (1976) describes the prevailing mood of the country: "Mexicans are flowing into the country [yet] their average intelligence is below that of the Portuguese . . . the increase of French Canadians . . . average Negro. The foreign born have something wrong . . . lips thick, mouth coarse, goose bite noses" (p. 379).

Requirements for entrance to the United States became stricter over time. All immigrants had to pass a physical examination and show no evidence of "mental" problems. Causes for rejection included eye problems, (such as partial blindness and trachoma), senility, lameness, deafness, general weakness, physical deformity, scalp disease, and tuberculosis. After 1917 all adult immigrants had to pass a literacy test either in English or in their native language (Brownstone, Franck, & Brownstone, 1979, p. 10).

Terman (1916) believed that there were genetically determined differences in intelligence across races and that mental subnormality was more common in Spanish-Indian and black populations. He advocated that such children be segregated into special classes. He further believed that from a eugenics point of view those populations presented a grave problem because of "their unusual prolific breeding" (1916, p. 92).

Within this general social milieu, the segregation of handicapped individuals into isolated institutions was seen as reducing the perceived threat to civilization, but the perceived long-term problem with this solution was that it brought the "undesirable population" into closer contact with each other in adult life. Influenced by the impact of the eugenics movement, Americans developed a willingness not only to segregate but also to sterilize larger number of individuals judged "unfit." Laws restricting marriage and calling for sterilization were passed in many states.

The situation was never as grim for the deaf as it was for those with other conditions, but schools for the deaf increasingly were established away from large cities. At times restrictions on marriage and on procreation of the deaf were seriously considered (Bell, 1884; Groce, 1980).

The complex patterns of placement and segregation were further compounded by a brutal system of racial segregation and the establishment of poorly funded, staffed, and housed so-called "separate but equal" programs for black handicapped children. For example, in Washington, D.C., the Kendall School for the Deaf served only white children. Black deaf children from the District of Columbia had to go to an all-black program in Maryland to receive an education, a situation that existed in Washington until the 1950s. Washington, D.C. was not exceptional in that throughout the South and parts of the Midwest, separate residential schools for black deaf children were established, sometimes in the same community as schools for the white deaf and sometimes in physical contiguity.

In some cases there even existed four segregated residential schools under one administration—schools for the black deaf, white deaf, black blind, and white blind (Jones, 1918). In each case the administrator was a hearing, seeing white man. The existence of such clusters raised complex, sometimes ludicrous logistical problems, especially when segregation by gender was also called for in areas such as dormitory space and infirmary services. I had the experience several years ago of visiting the campus of what had been four separate schools for white/black and deaf/blind children and is now two separate schools for deaf students and blind students. The infirmary had been constructed to isolate sick students into eight discrete groups: black blind girls, white blind girls, black deaf girls, and so on.

Education of the deaf during the nineteenth century moved from the establishment of benevolently motivated programs attempting to gather together a sufficient population to a new meaning of the term *asylum*. As the century closed, the increasing social segregation of a rapidly diversifying American population was reflected in the greater reliance on separate educational institutions, not only for the deaf but for other "less desirables" as well. Ironically, this practice raised the spectre of a "deaf race," resulting in a call by A. G. Bell (1884) for educational reforms.

NINETEENTH-CENTURY ATTEMPTS AT INTEGRATION

In Europe, unlike the United States, there were several national movements to integrate deaf children into the public schools. Integration was advocated in the early part of the nineteenth century in England by Arrowsmith (1819), and the practice was widespread for a time in Germany, especially Prussia (Gordon, 1885a). In the middle of the nineteenth century the integration movement was so strong in France that it was predicted that all residential schools for the deaf would be closed (Moores, 1987).

In every case, the national integration movements of the nineteenth century disappeared without a trace and the efforts were written off as failures. From today's perspective it is relatively easy to identify the reasons for the failure of the first "mainstream" attempts. In essence, it was assumed that the very act of placing deaf children in physical contiguity with hearing children in school would have a beneficial effect on the development of the speech, behavior, and academic skills of deaf children. It was believed that, by functioning in a hearing environment, deaf children would absorb the language of the larger community more easily than if they were segregated in residential institutions with other deaf children and used manual languages to communicate. This was a classic example of fitting the child into the environment and expecting the child to adapt, instead of altering the environment to facilitate the child's development. In these movements there were no serious efforts to modify curricula or to provide special instructional support for deaf children. It was a matter of sink or swim, and most deaf children sank.

The United States experienced no widespread integration movement in the nineteenth century. There were some attempts at integration, mostly with younger children, but they did not follow the European mode of placing one deaf child in a class of hearing children. The best, and most successful, example of U.S. programs was a "family school" established by Bartlett in New York City. Bartlett accepted both hearing and deaf children in his school (Bartlett, 1852). He followed a natural language approach, and all modes of communication were used by both deaf and hearing children. He believed that the use of the manual alphabet improved spelling and that signs improved ease and expressiveness in hearing children. Thus Bartlett's program was different from European attempts in that deaf children were not in the minority and hearing children communicated by manual as well as oral means. According to Gordon (1885b), Bartlett's program was a success, but it did not survive its founder.

The single most influential proponent of integrated programs for deaf children in the United States was Alexander Graham Bell, who based his opposition to residential schools for the deaf primarily on genetic, not educational, grounds. Among his numerous interests, Bell was a firm advocate of eugenics and was a leader in the American eugenics movement, carrying out breeding experiments with sheep (Moores, 1987). Like many other eugenicists of that time in Germany, Great Britain, and the United States, Bell was concerned with the proliferation of "undesirable" traits in the human species. Given his interest in education of the deaf, Bell had a special concern for the inheritance of deafness.

Bell initiated a study of the occurrence of deafness in families within and across generations, with special attention to Martha's

Vineyard, an island off the coast of Massachusetts, which throughout most of the nineteenth century had an unusually large number of deaf inhabitants for its small population. The island at that time had a homogeneous population of English, mostly Kentish, stock, with the exception of a small Indian town (Groce, 1980). The presence of recessive genes for deafness combined with the inbreeding of the population to produce an unusually large number of deaf individuals.

Bell discerned that migration from the island to Maine and Massachusetts and then to other parts of New England was accompanied by increases in the incidence of deafness in the newly settled areas. Bell was alarmed at the possibility of a tremendous increase in the incidence of deafness in the country. He could not have known that with the influx of Portuguese fisherman and settlers from the American mainland of various ethnic backgrounds, intermarriage would disperse the recessive genes and, with the exception of one elderly inhabitant, deafness would disappear from the island by the middle of the twentieth century (Groce, 1980).

In a work entitled "Memoirs on the Formation of a Deaf Variety of the Human Race" (1884b), which was followed by an article, "Fallacies Concerning the Deaf" (1884a), Bell raised alarm over what he considered the dangerous marriage patterns of deaf Americans. Bell acknowledged that deaf Americans were better educated and more successful than their European counterparts, but argued that this success was a problem in itself in that it brought deaf people together, who would then tend to marry among themselves. Bell feared that the outcome of this would be the establishment of a new variety of the human race. Realizing the difficulty of enacting legislation to restrict marriages of deaf Americans, he proposed measures that would isolate deaf people from each other. His reasoning was "the production of a defective race of human beings would be a tragedy" and that "intermarriages have been promoted by our methods of instruction" (Bell, 1884b, p. 41). The primary changes that Bell called for were the elimination of educational segregation of the deaf; of "gesture language," which Bell believed caused the deaf to associate with each other; and of the use of deaf teachers. Bell's opposition to deaf teachers was so adamant that he testified before the Senate in 1895 against the establishment of a teacher training program for hearing students at Gallaudet College (now Gallaudet University). He feared that, despite its promises to the contrary, the College would also accept deaf students into the program (Bruce, 1973; Winefield, 1986).

Bell's efforts met with some success in restricting the use of sign language in classrooms and in limiting employment of deaf teachers to vocational education and instruction of older children. Bell realized only limited success in his efforts against residential schools and separate day schools for the deaf. Except for an extensive day class movement in the state of Wisconsin, strongly supported by Bell (Van Cleve & Crouch, 1989), education of the deaf remained primarily in the hands of residential schools or separate day schools for the deaf in large metropolitan areas.

FROM 1900 TO WORLD WAR II

At the beginning of the twentieth century a system of school placements was in existence that would continue with only minor modification through the first two-thirds of the century. In essence, there were three discrete subsystems: public residential schools for the deaf, public day schools for the deaf, and private residential schools for the deaf. Some background information on each of the three is necessary to have a clear picture of the form and function of each.

The term *public residential school* covered a wide variety of school types in the early twentieth century (Day, Fusfeld, & Pintner, 1928). Many such schools had private governing boards, and some owned their land separately. These types of schools were especially common in the eastern part of the country. Typically, they had been established as private schools and over the years had become dependent on state support to the extent that they evolved into de facto state schools. The term *public residential school* also included schools throughout the country that had been established by state legislatures and were operated under the jurisdiction of a state department of education and welfare.

Public day schools, without exception, were situated in large urban areas and, as part of the public school system, were under the control of local boards of education. As such, they were much more closely attuned to public school curricula and to local communities.

Private residential schools, although few in number, had a disproportionate influence on education of the deaf in relation to their size. These schools served a national—even international—constituency and had not come under the control of state systems of education. Like the public schools, their mode of instruction was always oral only. Unlike the public day schools and public residential schools, their student populations were drawn from relatively affluent and highly educated segments of the population. The private schools provided most of the leadership in the development of speech and English language curricula for the deaf and in advances in the use of residual hearing. Along with Gallaudet College, they were the only sources of research on deafness during most of the twentieth century. The Clarke School for the Deaf in Northampton, Massachusetts was particularly noted for its tradition of research in genetics and deafness, and the Central Institute for the Deaf in St. Louis, Missouri for its research on audition. Gallaudet College's research placed a greater emphasis on the education of the deaf, as illustrated by its National Survey, discussed next.

GALLAUDET COLLEGE'S NATIONAL SURVEY

In what has been the largest and most comprehensive in situ study of programs for the deaf in history, Day, Fusfeld, and Pintner (1928) analyzed the governance structure, physical facilities, teacher background, student characteristics, and student achievement scores of 29 public residential schools for the deaf and 13 public day schools for the deaf in a national survey covering the 1924–25 academic year. No private residential schools were included. The differences found between the day and residential schools were fascinating and appeared across all variables studied.

In the public residential schools more than three-quarters of the academic teachers were hearing and more than three-quarters were female, but in the industrial programs in those same schools, more than half the teachers were deaf and nearly half of those were male. In the public day schools the teaching staff consisted "practically entirely of women and there were no deaf teachers" (Day, Fusfeld, & Pintner, 1928, p. 17).

The residential schools obviously functioned more "in loco parentis," than did the day schools. For example, all 29 had courses in moral training and 26 had Sunday school classes taught by teachers, usually male. Only four of the day schools had moral or ethical training courses, and the students were expected to attend religious services with their families.

The mode of instruction in day schools was overwhelmingly oral and was used with 97% of the children, with manual communication permitted in only one school. For the residential schools there was great variability, with many schools offering two or more of four options—oral only, auricular, manual only, or combined. The auricular option, which concentrated on the use of residual hearing, was available in schools with a substantial number of children identified as hard of hearing. The combined mode of instruction—as the name implies—combined oral and manual communication in instruction. Generally, children would start off with oral instruction. Those children who were classified as "oral failures" would be reassigned to either manual-only or combined classes, depending on the philosophy of the school. Overall, 62% of children in residential schools were taught through oral-only means as compared with 97% in day schools.

Differences also existed in child characteristics. On the average, children in public day schools had more moderate hearing losses. Day, Fusfeld, and Pintner (1928) reported average hearing losses of 65–70% for day school students and 75–80% for residential school students. They also tended to have a later age of onset of deafness. For 75% of the residential students, deafness was either congenital or present by age 2. This was true for only 57% of the day school students. Day school students began school at earlier ages, and intelligence scores were higher. As might be expected, measured school achievement also was higher.

The data on family variables reflect fascinating differences, with the day school children more representative of immigrant settlement in the large cities. Only 30% of the day school students had both parents born in the United States; in 57% of the cases *both* parents were foreign born. For 68% of the residential students, both parents were native born. A language other than English was spoken in one-third of the homes of the day school students, with Yiddish (12.4%) and Italian (12.1%) most common. In the residential schools another language was spoken in less than 17% of the homes, with Italian (5.3%) and Yiddish (2.9%) accounting for almost half the cases.

In summary, day schools for the deaf in the 1920s were taught almost exclusively by hearing women using oral-only modes of communication. The residential schools had greater representations of deaf teachers and male teachers, and used a variety of modes of communication. Students in day schools tended to have less severe hearing losses, later onset of deafness, earlier entry into school, higher intelligence, and higher academic achievement. The majority of children in day school programs were children of foreign-born parents and a language other than English, usually Yiddish or Italian, was spoken in 33% of the homes.

Figure 1.1. Change in program placements over a century

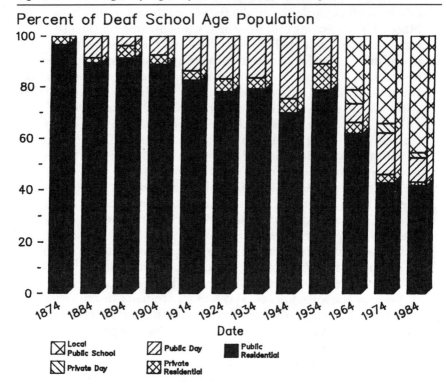

Percent of Deaf School Age Population

Date

Local Public School   Public Day   Public Residential
Private Day   Private Residential

This pattern has been repeated in the current differences between local public school programs and residential schools (Schildroth, 1988), with the tendency of the nonresidential schools to reflect a greater proportion of less severely handicapped students and minorities and a greater likelihood of the use of speech as a mode of communication.

The pattern of placement continued to follow the tripartite breakdown of public residential school, public day school, and private residential school up to World War II, with a slight trend toward increased public day school placement. This was offset in some states during the Depression years of the 1930s, when there was a noticeable increase in residential school enrollment, perhaps related to an inability of families to provide for their children (see Figure 1.1).

DEVELOPMENTS FROM WORLD WAR II to 1975

The patterns of school placement for the deaf, influenced by a number of demographic variables, became much more complex after World War II. The trend of deaf children attending school on a day basis continued, but for the first time significant numbers of day classes for the deaf were established. Unlike the completely separate urban day schools, one or more classes for the deaf would be located within an elementary or secondary school serving a predominantly hearing population. Such classes might be established in either urban, suburban, or even rural areas. In the early years such classes were usually "self-contained," that is, deaf children were taught in separate classes by trained teachers of the deaf. Integration, such as it was, occurred in the lunchroom or playground, and tended to be minimal. In some cases, however, high-achieving deaf children might attend one or more of the hearing classes, usually for mathematics. Such children tended to be hard of hearing, possessing good expressive and receptive oral skills (Day, Fusfeld, & Pintner, 1928).

From 1945 to 1975, as in other periods, trends in placement of deaf students were influenced by developments in general and special education and by societal forces. The most obvious developments after 1945 were the urbanization and suburbanization of the country, accompanied by a tremendous population increase. Because of an extended baby boom, extensive immigration, and increases in life expectancy, the U.S. population became approximately double that of pre-World War II years. There were more people, and they were more highly concentrated in metropolitan areas.

The post-World War II baby boom triggered unprecedented construction of elementary and then secondary schools throughout the country. In many areas, construction of such facilities could not keep pace with the demand. The population increase was most evident in metropolitan areas, especially in the growth of suburbs. Suburbanization itself was related to aspects of the developing federal highway system, which involved construction of interstate routes through and around the cities in the form of beltways. For the first time there were very large concentrations of people in many areas throughout the country with ready intra-metropolitan highway access, thus mitigating the age-old problem of providing educational services to children with a low-incidence condition such as deafness.

When the baby boom was ending in the 1960s, educators of deaf children were faced with the results of the largest known worldwide rubella epidemic, which greatly increased the number of deaf children (Moores & Kluwin, 1986). The appearance of this unusually large number of deaf children in the middle of the 1960s presented unique problems to the field of education of the deaf. As in American society in general, the number of deaf children in the U.S. population and in U.S. schools had been increasing for over a generation; however, starting in 1965 the general preschool and elementary school age population began to decline at the same time educators of the deaf were faced with the problem of moving an unusually large block of children through the educational system. At each step in the preschool, elementary, secondary, and postsecondary school systems this block would present unprecedented challenges to the education of the deaf.

It is to their credit that educators responded quickly and effectively to the challenges presented by these children. One important outcome was that the presence of such numbers substantially altered the ways in which deaf children are educated from preschool through adulthood. In terms of placement, it speeded up the process of public school placement. With the appearance of children deafened as a result of the rubella epidemic, some implicit decisions were immediately made by state legislatures. Of primary importance was the fact that the existing residential schools did not have the resources to handle such an influx of students at one age level, especially the younger ages. In most residential schools, preschool programs themselves were relatively recent phenomena, and there was a scarcity of teachers of the deaf trained to work at the preschool level. Also, many children deafened through rubella had secondary handicaps, and not all schools were equipped to deal with this type of student. Except for a few states, little or no consideration was given by state legislatures to the construction of additional residential facilities. The children were seen as a one-time-only educational problem, and there was a reluctance to invest in construction that would be underused after they left.

Concurrently, because of the birth rate decline, schools built to accommodate a burgeoning population had empty classrooms for the first time. It was clear that in many towns and cities elementary and secondary schools eventually would be closed. Thus, the presence of children deafened by the rubella epidemic coincided with the appearance, for the first time since the Depression, of unused classroom space.

PUBLIC LAW 94–142

Beginning in the 1960s, some special educators began to question the efficacy of residential or special class placement of handicapped children (Dunn, 1968). It was at this time that the term *mainstreaming* came into popular use. Several court cases regarding educational treatment and placement of handicapped individuals established precedents. The most well known of these were *Pennsylvania Association for Retarded Citizens* v. *Commonwealth of Pennsylvania* (1972) and *Mills* v. *Board of Education of the District of Columbia* (1972). In both cases it was ruled that exclusion of retarded individuals from a free public education was illegal. In both cases regular classroom placement was judged to be preferable to special class placement, which in turn was preferable to placement in a residential school or institution. The implication was that, to be acceptable, placement of a particular child in a residential school or institution should be demonstrably superior to placement in a special class or regular class.

These concerns about educational placement were related to a growing awareness of—and sensitivity toward—institutional abuse of severely retarded and emotionally disturbed individuals of all ages. To a great extent, in the public's mind the line between institutionalization and residential schools was blurred.

In the fall of 1975 President Ford signed into law U.S. Public Law (PL) 94–142, the Education for All Handicapped Children Act. This legislation represented a shift toward direct federal involvement in special education and fundamentally altered the relationship between the federal government and state and local agencies educating handicapped children. The basic thrust of the law was a mandate for a free appropriate public education for all handicapped children in the least restrictive environment appropriate to an individual child's needs (Harvey & Siantz, 1979). The law stipulated that handicapped children should be educated with nonhandicapped children to the greatest appropriate degree. Because many of the key terms in the law—including least restrictive environment and free appropriate public education—have not been operationally defined, there has been controversy regarding federal regulations written to implement PL 94–142. The mandate for least restrictive environment is subsumed under that of appropriate public education, which is interpreted as meaning that placement cannot be limited to one type of setting; alternatives may include instruction in regular classes, resource rooms, self-contained classes, and special schools and institutions. Bersoff and

Voltman (1979), in a review of educational placement, summarized the impact of PL 94–142 as follows:

> Despite the preference for mainstreaming in Public Law 94–142, placement of handicapped children in regular classrooms may be inappropriate, as recent judicial decision had held. . . . it seems that although placement in regular classes is viewed as desirable under PL 94–142, such a placement will still be open to challenge as being inappropriate for a particular student's educational needs. (pp. 19–20)

The U.S. Supreme Court, in *Rowley* v. *the Hendrick Hudson Board of Education and the Commissioner of Education of the State of New York*, decided that in its enactment of PL 94–142 the U.S. Congress did not impose on the states any greater substantive educational standard than would be necessary to make access to education meaningful, declaring that "the intent of the Act was more to open the door of public education to handicapped children on appropriate terms than to guarantee any particular level of education once inside" (p. 14). The U.S. Supreme Court further declared that PL 94–142 imposes no clear obligation on recipient states beyond the requirement that handicapped children receive some form of specialized education: "To require . . . the furnishing of every specialized service necessary to maximize each handicapped child's potential is, we think, further than Congress intended to go" (p. 22). The U.S. Supreme Court interpreted PL 94–142 as offering only a "floor of opportunity" for handicapped children, as opposed to maximizing the potential achievement of each handicapped child. The implication is that the legal mandate for extensive special services is limited.

CHANGES IN SCHOOL PLACEMENT: 1975 TO THE PRESENT

There has been a significant increase in the placement options for deaf students in recent years, and there is a resultant confusion of terminology, with different school districts using a variety of terminologies. Moores (1987) identified five basic classifications, with as many as 12 modifications in any one state. The five basic classifications are residential schools, both boarder and commuting; day schools in larger metropolitan areas that do not enroll hearing children; day classes for the hearing impaired established in public school buildings in which the majority of children have normal hearing; resource rooms planned so that children spend most of their day in regular classes; and itinerant programs where children attend regular classes full time and receive support services from an "itinerant" teacher who may work with children from several different schools (Moores, 1987, p. 18).

Many school districts now centralize their programs in order to consolidate resources and support services. It is not uncommon to have services on a day class, resource room, and itinerant basis all in one building with a majority of hearing students. Given the requirements of an annual individualized education plan and the possibility that a child will require different types of placement over a period of years, the concentration of programs in one location reduces the need for frequent school changes.

In the past, only the children with the most residual hearing and the best oral communication skills tended to be placed in resource room and itinerant settings. The use of manual interpreters in regular classrooms in the past several years has led to an increase in the number of children with profound hearing losses in regular classrooms for at least some academic subjects (Schildroth, 1988). Integration tends to be higher for mathematics than for other subjects (Moores, Kluwin, & Mertens, 1985).

One way to understand the impact of PL 94–142 on placement is to compare enrollment for fall 1974 (the year before PL 94–142 was passed) with data for fall 1986. The 1975 edition of *American Annals of the Deaf* (Craig & Craig, 1975) has enrollment data for October 1974, and the 1987 directory (Craig & Craig, 1987) has similar data for 1986.

As shown in Figure 1.2, there was an overall decline in enrollment for the 12-year period of 10.9%. This is consistent with a decline in the general public school enrollment over the same period. From 1974 to 1986 public residential school enrollment declined by 6,945 students, while public day class enrollment increased by 8,163. Of the seven types of programs listed in Figure 1.2, all but public day classes experienced a decline in enrollment of 35% or more over the 12 years.

Although enrollment dropped over the 12-year period, public residential schools still enrolled approximately one-fourth of all deaf school children in the United States. An interesting feature of the residential school population is that 4,616, almost 40%, were day students and commuted to school from home (Craig & Craig, 1987, p. 124). The sizable enrollment in residential schools so

Figure 1.2. Change in enrollment patterns, 1974–1986

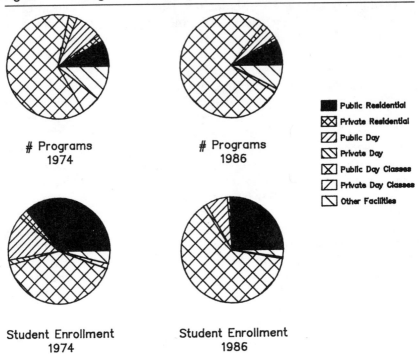

Programs
1974

Programs
1986

Legend:
- Public Residential
- Private Residential
- Public Day
- Private Day
- Public Day Classes
- Private Day Classes
- Other Facilities

Student Enrollment
1974

Student Enrollment
1986

many years after the enactment of PL 94–142 suggests that large numbers of deaf children will be educated in these facilities for the foreseeable future.

From Figure 1.2, it appears that PL 94–142 and societal trends in general have had a greater impact on private programs and public day schools than on public residential schools. Enrollment in public day schools declined more than 50%, falling from 7,269 students in 1974 to 3,271 students in 1986. The drop reflects the tendency in large metropolitan areas to move from separate day schools for the deaf to day classes for the deaf within schools in which the student body is predominantly hearing.

The most startling changes have been associated with the decline in private residential schools and private day classes (Figure 1.2). Only 10 private day classes, with a total enrollment of 186 students, were identified in 1986, a decline of 70% from 1974. The drop in private residential school enrollment is as dramatic. Enrollment in 1986, 409 students, was about one-fourth of that in

1974 (1,501 students). By 1986 fewer than 1% of deaf children attended private residential schools. Several private residential schools historically served a national and even international constituency, drawing students from many geographic areas. The data indicate that the remaining private residential schools now serve students on a regional basis: Approximately 40% of the students at private residential schools in 1986 were day students (Craig & Craig, 1987, p. 132), similar to the percentage of day students in public residential schools.

The precipitous declines in enrollment in private residential schools, combined with the erosion of private day classes, suggest that the free appropriate public education stipulations of PL 94–142 have had an enormous impact on private programs. In 1974 almost 6% of deaf children were educated in private schools and classes; by 1986 private enrollment had declined to a negligible 1.5% of the total.

The evidence suggests that by 1986 education of the deaf had become almost exclusively a public school responsibility, probably largely because of the free appropriate public education requirements of PL 94–142. There was also a movement away from residential school placement and toward enrollment in day classes. To some extent this was probably an effect of the least restrictive environment requirements of PL 94–142. Substantial numbers of deaf students, however, continue to attend residential schools, which enroll approximately one-fourth of deaf students in the United States. One significant change from the past is that approximately 40% of residential school students attend school on a day basis, that is, they commute to school from home.

SUMMARY

Patterns of educational placement of deaf children have undergone significant changes from the beginnings of education of the deaf in America in 1817. Over the past several generations there has been a trend toward educating deaf children in public school programs on a commuting basis, a trend that was accelerated by the rubella epidemic of the mid-1960s and the passage of Public Law 94–142, the Education for All Handicapped Children Act of 1975. At present more than 60% of deaf children are educated in public school day class programs, with opportunities for academic integration on a class-by-class basis. A little more than 25% of students are educated in public residential schools, meaning that almost 90% of deaf children are in one of two settings—public day classes or public residential schools. The only other significant enrollment is in separate public day schools, which enroll almost 7% of deaf students. Enrollment in private day and residential programs had declined significantly and now constitutes a negligible part of the deaf school enrollment.

REFERENCES

Arrowsmith, J. (1819). *The art of instructing the infant deaf and dumb*. London: Taylor and Hessex.

Bartlett, D. (1852). Family education for young deaf-mute children. *American Annals of the Deaf, 5*(1), 32–35.

Bell, A. G. (1884a). Fallacies concerning the deaf. *American Annals of the Deaf, 28*(2), 124–132.

Bell, A. G. (1884b). *Memoirs on the formation of a deaf variety of the human race*. Washington, DC: National Academy of Science.

Bersoff, D., & Voltman, E. (1979). Public Law 94–142: Legal implications for the education of handicapped children. *Journal of Research and Development in Special Education, 12*(1), 10–22.

Boatner, M. (1959). *Edward Miner Gallaudet: The voice of the deaf*. Washington, DC: Public Affairs Press.

Brownstone, D., Franck, I., & Brownstone, D. (1979). *Island of hope, island of tears*. New York: Rawson, Wade.

Bruce, R. (1973). *Bell: Alexander Graham Bell and the conquest of solitude*. Boston: Little, Brown.

Chaves, T., & Solar, J. (1974). "Pedro Ponce de Leon: First teacher of the deaf." *Sign Language Studies, 5*(1), 48–63.

Craig, W., & Craig, H. (1975). Directory of services for the deaf. *American Annals of the Deaf, 120*, 125–221.

Craig, W., & Craig, H. (1987). Directory of services for the deaf. *American Annals of the Deaf, 132*, 81–127.

Day, H., Fusfeld, I., & Pintner, P. (1928). *A survey of American schools for the deaf, 1924–25*. Washington, DC: National Research Council.

Dunn, L. (1968). Special education for the mildly retarded: Is much of it justified? *Exceptional Children, 35*(1), 13–20.

Dworkin, G. (1976). *The IQ controversy: Critical readings*. New York: Pantheon.

Gallaudet, E. (1886). History of the education of the deaf in the United States. *American Annals of the Deaf, 32*(3), 110–147.

Gordon, J. (1885a). Deaf mutes and the public schools from 1815 to the present day. *American Annals of the Deaf, 30*(2), 121–143.

Gordon, J. (1885b). Hints to parents. *American Annals of the Deaf, 30*(4), 241–250.

Groce, N. (1980). Everyone here spoke sign language. *Natural History, 89*(6), 10–19.

Harvey, J. & Siantz, J. (1979). Public education and the handicapped. *Journal of Research and Development in Education,* 12(1), 1–9.

Jones, J. (1918). One hundred years of history in the education of the deaf in America and its present status. *American Annals of the Deaf, 63*(1), 1–43.

Kamin, L. (1974). *The history and politics of IQ.* New York: Halstead.

Kanner, L. (1967). *A history of the care and study of the mentally retarded.* Springfield, IL: Charles C. Thomas.

Kauffman, J. (1980). Historical trends and contemporary issues in special education in the United States. In J. Kauffman & D. Hallahan (Eds.), *Handbook of special education* (pp. 3–23). New York: Prentice-Hall.

Mills v. *Board of Education of the District of Columbia,* 348, F. Supp. 866, 868, 875, D.D.C. 1972.

Moores, D. (1987). *Educating the deaf: Psychology, principles, and practices.* Boston: Houghton Mifflin.

Moores, D., & Kluwin, T. N. (1986). Issues in school placement. In A. Schildroth & M. Karchmer (Eds.), *Deaf children in America* (pp. 105–123). San Diego, CA: College-Hill Press.

Moores, D., Kluwin, T., & Mertens, D. (1985). *High school programs for deaf students in metropolitan areas* (Monograph No. 3). Washington, DC: Gallaudet Research Institute.

Pennsylvania Association for Retarded Citizens (PARC) v. *Commonwealth of Pennsylvania,* 343, F. Supp. 279, E.D. Pa., 1972.

Rehnquist, J. (1982). Majority Opinion. *Hendrick Hudson Board of Education* v. *Amy Rowley.* Case No. 800–1002, Washington, DC: Supreme Court of the United States, June 28, 1982.

Ries, P. (1986). Characteristics of hearing impaired youth in the general population and of students in special education programs for the hearing impaired. In A. Schildroth & M. Karchmer (Eds.), *Deaf children in America* (pp. 141–163). San Diego: College-Hill Press.

Rowley v. *the Hendrick Hudson Board of Education and the Commissioner of Education of the State of New York,* 79 Civ. 2139 (VLB) (S.D.N.Y. 1979).

Schildroth, A. (1988). Recent changes in the educational placement of deaf students. *American Annals of the Deaf, 133*(2), 61–67.

Soltow, L. & Stevens, E. (1981). *The rise of literacy and the common school in the United States.* Chicago: University of Chicago Press.

Terman, L. (1916). *The measurement of intelligence.* Boston: Houghton Mifflin.

Van Cleve, J. & Crouch, B. (1989). *A place of their own: Creating the deaf community in America.* Washington, D.C.: Gallaudet University Press.

Winefield, R. (1986). *Never the twain shall meet.* Washington, DC: Gallaudet University Press.

Wines, F. (1888). *Report on the defective, dependent and delinquent classes of the population of the United States as returned in the tenth census (1880).* Washington, DC: U.S. Government Printing Office.

132048

CHAPTER 2

What Does "Local Public School" Program Mean?

THOMAS N. KLUWIN

It is not as easy to describe public school programs for the deaf as it is to describe the traditional, residential school programs. Because the public school programs are, for the most part, of relatively recent vintage, they do not have the structural stability of the state residential schools. This situation is further complicated by the fact that public school governance structures are themselves subject to changes in political or legislative interests, particularly with regard to special populations. As the availability of external funds waxes or wanes, as public interest moves from one issue to another, and as federal legislation or particular litigation impinges upon the public school district, responsibilities within the governance structure are redefined and organizational charts change. Nor are programs for the deaf immune from the usual turf battles that are waged within any human organization. Consequently, public school programs for the deaf cannot be readily categorized. At present, a flexible definition with several components is needed to capture the range of existing programs.

TOWARD A WORKING DEFINITION

Based on my recent experience with a number of local public school programs for the deaf, the required definition will vary along four parameters:

1. Communication philosophy,
2. Type of governance structure,

3. Level of services, and
4. Size of student population.

Because of the continuing pedagogical debates within the field of the education of the deaf, communication philosophy will define several distinct styles of programs, including oral only, total communication only, dual track oral/total communication, and triple track oral/total communication cued speech programs.

Since not all public school programs are integrated into the structure of the school district in the same way, the key to understanding the relationship of the program for the deaf to the entire school system is to look at the individual who has supervisory authority over the teachers of the hearing impaired and that individual's position within the system. This approach will define three types of governance structures: separate, integrated, and special. Mixed systems of governance occur when there are different levels of services provided within a school district at different sites, resulting in unique patterns of building-by-building governance systems.

Level of services defines a range from itinerant teachers of the deaf to freestanding programs for the deaf that offer all of the conventional audiological and counseling services of the better residential schools, with interpreters, notetakers, and tutoring for students who are mainstreamed.

Program size is also an important parameter in describing a public school program for the deaf. Program size ranges from local school programs that service student populations as large as or larger than the typical state residential school for the deaf, to those that have only a few students scattered throughout the system.

It is not possible to pigeonhole local school programs for the deaf. The use of multiple criteria reveals both the complexity and diversity of the various directions that public school programs have taken. For example, there are the "regional" day schools for the deaf in Texas, such as the Dallas Regional School, which at the time of this writing consists of four sites:

1. A contracted preschool program,
2. An elementary school program,
3. A junior high school site, and
4. A senior high school site.

Since there are several hundred children in this configuration, it would have to be categorized as a large, total communication, structurally integrated, but freestanding program, particularly at the high school level.

The Jackson-Mann School in Boston presents a different organizational picture. It is a preschool through secondary level, total communication program that mainstreams students through fourth grade at the primary site. Older students who are mainstreamed are sent to one of three separate sites in the Boston metropolitan area. In these settings they are mainstreamed around a resource room model. At Jackson-Mann the head of the deaf program is given the title of principal. The Jackson-Mann program would be best described as moderate sized, using total communication, with a mixed governance structure in a freestanding program with ancillary sites.

In Fairfax County, Virginia, the "classic" public school model exists. It is classic in the sense that it has a range of sites and organizational structures within the program. It has a triple track communication philosophy, with each element housed at a special site through eighth grade. At the high school, oral-aural students and cued speech students are at one site, and total communication students are at another. In addition, there are itinerant services for less severely impaired students who remain in their home schools. It is a large program serving over 350 students countywide.

The above three examples do not begin to cover the diversity of program options; however, they do illustrate the difficulty of categorization. Given the multitude of factors that go into the creation of a local school program for the deaf, we cannot expect to be able to type them quickly or simply.

In this chapter we will explore each of the parameters in greater detail, propose some questions about their efficacy, and try to arrive at a clearer sense of what "local public school" program means for the deaf student.

COMMUNICATION PHILOSOPHY

The first step in defining the type of program is to define the communication philosophy that the program uses. Traditionally, three primary modes of communication with deaf students have evolved: total communication, oral-aural, and cued speech.

Moores' (1987) textbook on the education of the deaf explains these philosophies in greater detail.

Dual Track Oral/Total Communication Programs. In the competition for the deaf school age population, a number of school districts have opted to be pragmatic rather than dogmatic, that is, they maintain two separate systems within their program for the deaf. Essentially, there are two variants on this approach.

In one approach the school district maintains separate total communication and oral programs in different sites from pre-school through grade 12. For the oral program this usually involves an increasing degree of mainstreaming as the child becomes older. By the time the student is in secondary school, he or she is completely mainstreamed, with resource room or itinerant support. The alternative system maintains separate programs at separate sites through the elementary grades, but mixes both types of students at the secondary level. Under this alternative system, if an orally trained student is able to function with itinerant support, that individual may be at a different site; however, orally trained students requiring resource room support and total communication students may be housed at the same location.

Triple Track Programs. Triple track systems have been a response to requests for the use of cued speech in educational programs. With the exception of Montgomery County, Maryland and the Houston Regional Day School for the Deaf, there are very few of them; but they do seem to be organized like the dual track systems in that there are separate sites for each communication mode.

What Communication System is Actually Used?

Woodward (Woodward, Allen, & Schildroth, 1985) reported on a study of the classroom communication practices of 1,760 teachers of the deaf around the United States. The study used a 9% stratified random sample (about 4,500 students) of the 1984 Survey of Hearing Impaired Children and Youth population. Questionnaires were sent to the teachers of these children. Because some teachers responded to the communication questionnaire for more than one child and because of missing or incomplete data, the final sample of teachers was only 1,760.

Based on the results of the survey, only about 1% of all teacher–student communications can be identified as American

Sign Language (ASL) communications, which makes ASL, along with cued speech, the least frequently used form of communication with deaf students in schools. Spoken English as a primary communication form was reported in about 32% of the cases, while some form of signing was used in about 66% of all communications. The vast majority of teachers reported that when signing, they either mouthed words or spoke at the same time. It is difficult to categorize programs because of the designations for school types used by Woodward and his associates (1985). However, it appears that in what would be loosely termed "public school" programs, about 43% of the communications between teachers and students are signed and 57% are not.

Earlier, Jensema and Trybus (1978) had reported on communication practices using the 1973 Annual Survey mailing list as the population and a random subsample of all programs. They concluded that, at the time of their study, substantial differences in communication practices existed among program options. Essentially, residential schools used some form of manual communication, and public school programs were almost totally oral. While the results of the Woodward (Woodward et al., 1985) and the Jensema and Trybus (1978) studies are not comparable, it is interesting to note in the earlier study that as the degree of special programming decreased, the use of speech as a mode of communication increased. The same trend exists today, but the use of manual communication in less specialized settings in public school programs is more widespread than it was 12 to 15 years ago.

We could estimate that the most likely form of communication in a public school classroom would be spoken English, followed by manual communication of some sort, followed very distantly by cued speech or ASL. Unfortunately, the sampling procedures and methodology of Woodward's study (Woodward et al., 1985) failed to deal with the classroom use of interpreters. For example, when a mainstreamed child's teacher uses speech with that child, is that a regular class teacher communicating through an interpreter, an orally trained teacher of the deaf, or a mildly impaired child in a regular classroom with very good compensatory amplification? As a result of this limitation, the estimates of "speech" use may be inflated.

Speech appears to be the dominant form of communication in most public school programs for the deaf either as part of an oral-only program or in a total communication context, but manual communication is a close second with an expanding acceptance. In the past, individual student characteristics within programs had been the primary determinant of a program's communication philosophy in that less severely impaired children were more likely to be taught orally (Jensema & Trybus, 1978). However, that appears to be changing with the greater acceptance of manual communication.

GOVERNANCE STRUCTURE

The first parameter to be considered in describing a deaf program's governance structure is the status of the highest ranking individual within the school building who is identified as a deaf specialist. This parameter can range from individual resource room teachers to members of the administrative team for the school. The second parameter is the position of the individual who evaluates the classroom teachers of the deaf, and the third parameter is the highest ranking individual in the system who is identified as a deaf specialist. Teacher evaluators can be differentiated on the basis of their physical and political location in the system, that is, are they part of the within-school administration or of the district office administration? Since most American public school systems have a superintendent who has a number of deputies reporting to him or her, the defining point for the deaf program will be the existence of a central administration figure who is uniquely a deafness specialist, as opposed to someone who combines hearing impairment with another category of disability such as blindness or speech pathology. Two basic governance structures for public school programs are illustrated in Figure 2.1.

The most common governance situation, separate governance, occurs when the only deaf specialist in a regular school building is a single resource room teacher or itinerant teacher. This individual essentially only occupies space within the building. He or she is not evaluated or even directly supervised in any fashion by the building principal but is evaluated instead by a district office specialist. If there are two or more teachers of the deaf within the building, then one may have seniority and may function as the liaison with the district-level specialist, but this individual rarely has any evaluative authority. An extension of this situation occurs when the program within a building is large enough to have support staff such as a counselor, speech therapist, or audiologist. Be-

Figure 2.1.   Governance structures for public school programs

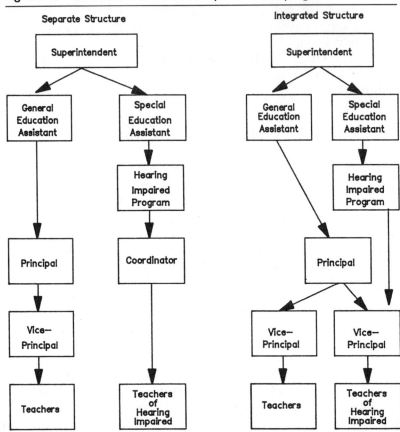

cause of their additional training and experience as well as the fact that these individuals tend to have fewer time constraints, they become de facto program coordinators, although they have no evaluative or budget authority.

Another situation arises when there are sufficient numbers of deaf children in the building to warrant a number of support staff and possibly secretarial support. In this kind of system, there is an in-building supervisor who functions much like an assistant principal.

The integrated governance structure occurs when the degree of integration of the supervisor into the overall school management becomes more specific. In some instances, the supervisor is accorded the status and even the title of assistant principal with responsibility for the deaf program only. In this situation, the in-building supervisor coordinates with the building principal day-to-day issues involving the physical operation of the program such as transportation and classroom space. Discipline involving deaf children is often referred directly to the supervisor. In matters of curriculum and teacher evaluation, the in-building supervisor reports to a district-level specialist.

There are seldom pure structural types within a school district. At the district level, particularly for larger programs, there is a "mix" of governance structures depending on the size of the staff. For example, for a large program with itinerant teachers as well as special sites, the itinerants will be supervised centrally, the resource room teachers will be supervised centrally or by an administrator within the building, and the special sites may have any of the three governance structures. Describing and categorizing the governance structure of programs for the deaf require both district-level and building-level information.

SERVICE OPTIONS

The different levels of service options can be summarized as:

1. Itinerant services,
2. Resource room, and
3. Full service program. (see Jensema, 1975; Wolk, Schildroth, & Karchmer, 1982)

Itinerant services must of necessity cover a range of situations because in practice this format means audiological and educational services on a rotating schedule, where the service provider—teacher, speech pathologist, or audiologist—goes from one site to another. In practice it covers both organized systems of service delivery to mildly impaired older children or severely impaired preschoolers and default systems, in which the primary service is to another group, such as those with speech impairments, and is provided almost incidentally to the hearing handicapped.

Resource rooms represent a clear step in an attempt to provide direct services to deaf children. These service configurations involve a specialized teacher of the deaf who provides a multitude of services, including instruction, tutoring, monitoring of hearing aids, personal counseling, and interpreting, depending on the situation. This system can expand almost to the point at which true staff differentiation begins to take place. In these situations, more than one classroom is devoted to the program for the deaf, with at least one teacher identified as the senior person, but the program provides only instructional support for the deaf children. All other services are provided on an itinerant basis or through the regular school program.

In a full service program, a member of the instructional staff is identified as administrator and has additional permanent noninstructional staff such as audiologists, counselors, vocational evaluation specialists, psychologists, and so on. The full service program generally shares a building with a general education program. Sometimes, particularly at the elementary level, there may be several handicapped populations at the site. Such a program regularly includes a number of segregated classes for the deaf, and its purpose is to provide services to a broad range of hearing handicapped students. In such an environment, individual programming can range from students who are totally segregated academically to students who are totally integrated academically; generally all students are integrated for physical education and for lunch. Frequently, such a program also includes facilities for the deaf with additional handicaps. An example of this type of program would be some of the larger regional day schools for the deaf in Texas.

PROGRAM SIZE

While size alone is not a necessary indicator of program efficiency or effectiveness, as Walberg and Fowler (1987) have pointed out, some observations can be made about program size in programming for the deaf. In the absence of a benchmark, let us first look at the size characteristics of residential programs to gain a basis for comparison.

According to Karchmer and Hotto (1987), the median enrollment for residential early childhood through secondary programs is 155 students, with a mean of 207. The discrepancy between the median and the mean represents the existence of a few very large programs and a number of small to medium-sized programs. The terms *large* and *small* are, of course, relative to the low incidence of the condition. A preschool to grade 12 general education program of fewer than 500 students would be considered tiny in the American educational system where some school districts have populations larger than some member countries of the United Nations. The majority of the residential programs have between 103 and 276 students, again pointing up the skew in the distribution. Median elementary enrollment is 55 students with a range of 1 to 281, while median secondary enrollment is 88 with a range of 14 to 334. This range should be considered in light of the variation in general education programs, which can vary within a state by an order of magnitude (Walberg & Fowler, 1987).

Student–teacher ratios for all residential schools average 5.1 with a median of 5 students to 1 teacher. The range, however, is from 1.8 to 8.2 students per teacher. The majority of programs have ratios between 4.0 and 6.1 students per teacher. While the smallest class size tends to be between 3.2 and 3.8 students per teacher, there is considerably more variation at the high end, with between 6.5 and 8.9 students per teacher. Generally, as the children become older, the high end of the class size range becomes the norm. As far as other staff at residential schools are concerned, there is, on the average, one school psychologist for every 139 students; one audiologist per 164 students; one speech therapist per 62 students; one counselor per 118 students; and one social worker per 153 students.

One cannot use these numbers to argue for an optimal or even a minimal system, but it appears that to have a full range of support personnel, a program would require at least 150 students. To obtain comparable data, I analyzed the April 1984 issue of *American Annals of the Deaf,* which is a compilation of information on all the programs that serve deaf youngsters across the United States. Like the Annual Survey of Hearing Impaired Children and Youth conducted by Gallaudet University each year, the *Annals* survey captures the vast majority of programs and children in the country. Since not every program responds to the survey, however, accessing this database yields information on about 90% of the population. While the depth of the information is not great and the reporting reliability is limited because of the absence of validity information on the reporting system, some useful data can be retrieved.

A total of 665 programs that identified themselves as being "public" and not residential were differentiated into five categories.

Figure 2.2.   Distribution of programs by size and grade span

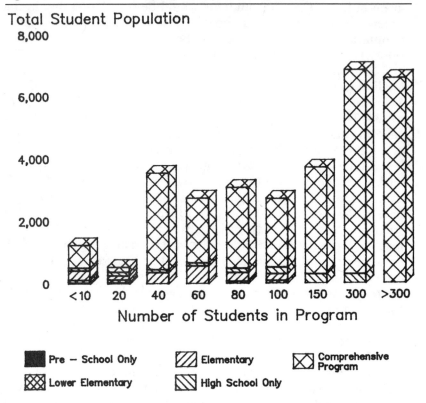

Total Student Population

1. *Preschool only*—programs whose students were in the preschool to kindergarten age range.
2. *Lower elementary only*—programs with students in the preschool or kindergarten to grade 3 range.
3. *Elementary*—accepting children in several of the school
   years between kindergarten or first grade and ninth grade.
4. *High school only*—programs that served students in the seventh through twelfth grade.
5. *Comprehensive*—programs that might start at preschool,
   kindergarten, or first grade and continue to, if not completely through, high school.

Figure 2.2 presents the distribution of those programs in the five
categories.

As is apparent from a consideration of Figure 2.2, there is a considerable degree of discrepancy between the number of service providers and the location of the students in those programs. While preschool only programs accounted for 2% of the total number of programs, they served only 0.3% of the children. The same degree of discrepancy can be seen with the lower elementary programs, which served only 1.1% of the population but accounted for three times that percentage of the programs. The same trend holds for elementary only and high school only programs, in that they account for twice the percentage of programs as of students served. In the case of elementary only and high school only programs, the larger programs, while fewer in number, served twice the number of students; that is, 20% of the programs served two-thirds of the children.

The discrepancy is also apparent in the comprehensive programs, where two-thirds of the total number of service providers served only slightly more than one-third of the total number of students. Ten percent of the programs, comprehensive programs with more than 100 students, served 50% of the deaf school age population. In overall terms, that means slightly more than one-quarter of all deaf students were served in residential schools, slightly more than one-third were served by larger comprehensive programs, and the remaining third were in all the other service configurations combined.

Figure 2.3 presents the distribution of the staff for the different program types.

The *Annals* survey defines support staff to include audiologists, interpreters, psychologists, home-school visitors, social workers, rehabilitation counselors, researchers, and library staff. If those individuals who function as interpreters are so designated by the program, they would be listed as support staff; however, in some programs where they are not formally listed as educational interpreters, they might be listed as teacher aides and not counted as interpreters (Moores, Kluwin, & Mertens, 1985). The role of interpreters is quite important in many of these programs, but it was not possible, given the limitations of the data set, to include them as a separate category. The point is that in programs with interpreters and with large numbers of mainstreamed students, the student–teacher ratio may be higher, but it is not possible to clearly disentangle the reasons for different staffing ratios.

As can be seen in Figure 2.3, preschool only programs tend to be top-heavy with support and administrative staff and short on

Figure 2.3.   Student-staff ratios by program type

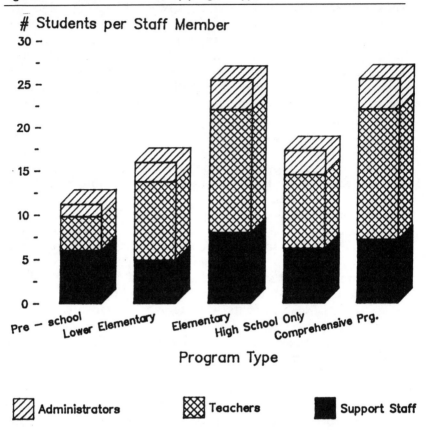

teachers. This is to be expected since a major purpose of preschool programs is to diagnose handicaps as well as provide service to both the families and the children. Similar staff distributions can be seen among lower elementary, elementary only, and comprehensive programs. About 40% of the total staff are teachers, while 25% are support staff. The high school only programs show the greatest divergence in staffing proportions in that a large percentage of the staff are support individuals, about the same as for the preschool only programs. Several factors might create this distribution, including a greater use of interpreters as well as specialized kinds of vocational counselors or guidance personnel.

Preschool only programs are small in number, as measured both by the total number of programs and by the number of students. Nonetheless, they have a high support staff–student ratio. The average number of children in these programs is small, an average of 7.6, reflecting the attempt to provide home-based or home-proximity services for a low-incidence handicap.

Lower elementary programs represent the middle ground between the preschool programs and the elementary and comprehensive programs, based on the student–staff ratios. Almost all of these programs have fewer than 20 students. They represent a peculiar group in that they do not seem to have the clear mandate that a preschool program has. Their function in the total service system should be clarified, but given the small numbers their impact is probably not great.

Most elementary only programs are small; over half have 10 or fewer children enrolled. They tend to be thin on staff in relation to the other types of programming, with the highest student–teacher ratio, almost 8:1, and almost the highest student—support staff ratio, 14:1. However, they serve only a small fraction of the total population. The largest proportion of the population is served by a handful of the largest programs.

There are marked differences between the smaller—fewer than 40 students—and the larger elementary school programs. Compared with the larger elementary school programs, the smaller programs tend to have smaller student–staff ratios, 2.2:1 versus 4.5:1; smaller student–teacher ratios, 5.5:1 versus 10:1; and smaller student–support staff ratios, 8.1:1 versus 21.1:1. These differences do not necessarily reflect improvements in service quality but more likely reflect the fact that a minimum number of functions must be accounted for in the operation of a program, regardless of the number of students. What the differences probably reflect are increased costs for the smaller programs without necessarily an improvement in service delivery.

The modal deaf child is served by a comprehensive program of more than 100 students. These programs have a larger student–teacher ratio, 8.2 students per teacher, than is typical of the residential programs. With a student–support staff ratio of 26:1, they appear, however, to have more support staff than the residential programs. The larger student–teacher ratio may reflect the number of mainstreamed students who would not use a teacher of the deaf and at the same time require an interpreter, thus changing that ratio as well. It was not possible, with the available database, to assess the impact of mainstreaming on staff ratios, but it is probably a factor in the differences.

EFFECTIVENESS OF THE PROGRAM PARAMETERS

Jensema (1975) attempted to answer the question of the efficacy of different service configurations by first correcting for the students' degree of hearing loss, age at onset, number of additional handicaps, presence of mental retardation, and ethnicity across four measures of academic achievement: vocabulary, reading comprehension, math concepts, and math computation. All of his measures were SAT–HI scaled scores for a sample of 6,871 deaf children. The sample was a carefully constructed stratified random sample used for the purposes of norming the 1974 edition of the SAT–HI. He found that the various program types used in his analysis were clearly different. Students in resource rooms or full service programs fell into the middle of the achievement range, with itinerant-served students and residential school students defining the high and low ends, respectively. The age deviation score that Jensema (1975) used represents the average for a service configuration of the deviation of the students from their expected age norms. Essentially, there was no difference among the major public school service systems. The types of students entering the programs account for more of the difference than the outcomes of the different configurations.

Wolk, Karchmer, and Schildroth (1982) report a strong relationship between the degree of academic integration of a child and type of service configuration that the child is in. Previously, Jensema and Trybus (1978) had reported the same general finding; however, the more powerful statistical analysis employed by Wolk and his associates (1982) revealed some striking differences. As the governance structure of the school system came more under the purview of the general education system, it was more likely that a student would experience some form of academic integration. Patterns of nonacademic integration are similar to those for academic integration, according to Wolk and his associates (1982). The exception to this are those students in self-contained classes in public school programs, who were much less likely to have meaningful interaction with hearing peers than would be expected. There are clear differences among service configurations as measured by the degree of academic integration of the children, but initial student differences contribute heavily to decisions about the degree of academic integration.

A third source of the difference in integration patterns is the systems themselves. In service configurations where options are available, students will be either more or less integrated because there is provision for more or less restricted placement. Some children happen to be in itinerant programs because that is the limit of the school district's resources. Other children are placed in itinerant settings because it has been decided that they have the necessary skills to function in that less restricted setting. This pattern of educational placement further complicates any discussion of what an effective program would look like.

Research on effective school programs suggests that moderate-sized programs are more efficient. Walberg and Fowler (1987), in a study of school districts in New Jersey, reported that in general education programs, districts with fewer than 2,600 students on average performed better than predicted given the socioeconomic status of their student population. Districts with enrollments greater than 3,900 students tended to perform less well than would be expected. Among districts with enrollments above 7,500 students, achievement fell off dramatically. These findings were consistent over several measures of achievement, including reading, writing, and mathematics.

Simply increasing the size of a school district does not necessarily mean that the quality of the program will be improved. The problem for someone planning a public school program for the deaf is that the district size that is most effective for students in general education is too small to run a practical program for deaf children. Not enough deaf students would be found in the smaller and more effective districts for a within-district program.

An alternative to the problem of small numbers of deaf students within a single school district has been the creation of "regional" programs or "super-districts." The goal of the two approaches appears to be the same, but the impact on the students can be quite different. Regional programs tend to be multidistrict programs with a single site for each educational level. These programs then operate in some kind of direct relationship with the site's program. Services to the students tend to parallel those found in the regular school program. Super-districts, on the other hand, are often collections of local programs scattered across a wide area. Children are as likely to attend a local school as a central school. What is generally pooled under a single, central administrator are personnel resources for the deaf such as audiologists or speech therapists.

The downside of the regional program is that many of the children can spend nearly as much time on a bus as in school. Because of the extensive transportation requirements, the opportunities for the social integration of the deaf students is reduced; their other educational opportunities are also limited, and the per pupil budget is higher. However, the super-district does not do much for the social integration of the deaf child because of his or her relative isolation. Since there are no large, concentrated numbers of deaf children at any one site, other educational opportunities for the deaf child must be provided on an individual basis and may not include adequate communication support. The greatest advantage of the super-district would appear to be budgetary, since travel costs are spread out over itinerant support staff.

CONCLUSION

To fully differentiate one local public school program from another, four parameters are required:

1. Communication philosophy,
2. Type of governance structure,
3. Level of service provided, and
4. The size of the program.

These parameters are not completely independent of each other. Size of the student population is the primary influence over the other three parameters. For example, small, oral, preschool programs are probably more common than large, triple-track programs. As the size of the student population increases, the level of service generally increases, which in turn increases the complexity of the governance structure. While the debate over the mode of communication to be used in educating deaf children continues, larger programs are more likely to ignore the strictures of any particular philosophy and select an eclectic communication philosophy that will permit the inclusion of even more children.

The available information on programs for the deaf suggests that some kind of minimal floor of between 125 and 150 students is required for a 12-year program to have adequate staff to provide the special support services needed by deaf children. To operate a program specifically for deaf children, several categories of specialists are required, based on current educational thinking. For a 12-year program, a speech therapist, an audiologist, a counselor or psychologist, and a social worker would appear to define a minimal set of special service providers. Given these individuals' workloads, between 25 and 30 students are needed for each additional specialist added to the program, thus yielding a number between 125 and 150 students as the minimal number required to operate a program.

The ultimate test of the effectiveness of any system, no matter how we choose to define it, is the quality of the service it provides to the child. Subsequent chapters will generally treat the question of effectiveness on an individual basis, but the point needs to be made here that individual deaf students are found in particular service configurations. Before the question of the effectiveness of "local public school" programs can be answered, the types of programs need to be defined specifically. The education of deaf children in local public schools is not a monolithic system; it is sufficiently complex to call for a definition that encompasses all this diversity.

REFERENCES

Jensema, C. (1975). *The relationship between academic achievement and the demographic characteristics of hearing-impaired children and youth.* (Series R, No. 2). Washington, DC: Gallaudet Research Institute Center for Assessment and Demographic Information.

Jensema, C., & Trybus, R. (1978). *Communication patterns and educational achievement of deaf students.* (Series T, No. 2). Washington, DC: Gallaudet College, Office of Demographic Studies.

Karchmer, M., & Hotto, S. (1987, April). *Key characteristics of residential/ state-operated schools for the deaf.* Presented at the annual meeting of CEASD, Santa Fe, NM.

Kluwin, T. N., & Moores, D. F. (1985). The effects of integration on the mathematics achievement of hearing impaired adolescents. *Exceptional Children, 52*(2), 153–160.

Moores, D. F. (1987). *Educating the deaf: Psychology, principles and practices.* Boston: Houghton-Mifflin.

Moores, D., Kluwin, T., & Mertens, D. (1985). *High school program for deaf students in metropolitan areas.* (Monograph No. 3). Washington, DC: Gallaudet College, Gallaudet Research Institiute.

Walberg, H., & Fowler, D. (1987). District size and school effectiveness. *Educational Researcher, 16*(8), 17–25.

Wolk, S., Karchmer, M., & Schildroth, A. (1982). *Patterns of academic and non-academic integration among hearing impaired students in special education.* (Series R, No. 9). Washington, DC: Gallaudet University, Gallaudet Research Institute.

Woodward, J., Allen, T., & Schildroth, A. (1985). *Teachers and deaf students: An ethnography of classroom communication.* Proceedings of the first annual meeting of the Pacific Linguistic Conference, Eugene: University of Oregon.

CHAPTER 3

Ethnic and Cultural Considerations

VALERIE J. JANESICK
DONALD F. MOORES

Since the civil rights movement of the 1950s and 1960s, the feminist movement of the 1970s, and the multicultural awareness of the 1980s, educators have been concerned with cultural pluralism in most facets of schooling (see Banks & Banks, 1989; Gollnick & Chinn, 1986; and Sleeter & Grant, 1987). In response to these social movements, the federal government has provided funds for bilingual education programs, multicultural programs, and nonsexist education programs. As a result, there appears to be a growing awareness of cultural diversity in the schools and a genuine attempt to deal with cultural pluralism. However, while many tests and training programs focus on cultural and linguistic diversity, one group, the deaf community, is noticeably absent from the discussion in most cases.

As we attempt to define the effective public school program for the deaf student, it is essential to understand what a deaf student experiences as a member of a cultural or linguistic minority within the American public school system. Essentially the issue is framed in terms of the extent to which deafness per se confers minority status upon an individual in present-day American society. Further, if deafness confers minority group membership, should it be considered a linguistic minority, an ethnic minority, or some complex combination of the two? Finally, what might be the implications of this status for deaf individuals who may already be identified as minority group members, for example, black deaf Americans or Hispanic deaf Americans?

If deafness does in any way imply membership in an identifiable culture, we should consider ways in which cultural issues might be addressed in educational programs for the deaf. As we come to understand the implications of minority status, we may come closer to defining what an effective public school program entails. Furthermore, by understanding the layers of complexity involved in students' understanding of deafness and cultural identification, we can begin to think about how to shape a public school program for deaf students through a cultural lens.

This chapter responds to three questions. First, what is deaf culture? Second, are there other cultural or ethnic groups that intersect with the deaf culture? Third, how can public school programs for deaf and hard of hearing students respond to deaf and other cultural, ethnic, or linguistic demands?

Padden and Humphries (1988) have described deaf culture in terms of the sociocultural life of deaf people. They describe a community of Deaf (with a capital "D") people who share a language, American Sign Language (ASL), and a culture. Padden and Humphries focus on how deaf people *live* their lives, rather than on disability or the medical/audiological/physical condition of deafness. In other words, members of the deaf culture reject the pathological or deficiency model of deafness, which treats it as a sickness or disease. In place of this model they view deafness as a social condition that has unique and valuable linguistic and behavioral attributes. Being Deaf means a person has a certain degree of loss of hearing, but the physical condition of hearing loss is not the sole criterion for membership in the Deaf community. Instead, the criterion is whether a person identifies with other Deaf people and behaves like a Deaf person (see Padden & Markowicz, 1976; Padden & Humphries, 1988; Reagan, 1985, 1988).

In a treatment of the cultural aspects of deafness, Reagan (1990) concluded that cultural deafness is defined by six major components that serve both to identify the deaf community and to establish the parameters that delimit the community. He identifies these components as linguistic differentiation, attitudinal deafness, behavioral norms, endogamous marriage patterns, historical awareness, and voluntary organizational networks.

Linguistic differentiation, of course, involves the use of ASL by the deaf community. Reagan (1985) categorized the American Deaf community as bilingual in nature, with language usage falling along two overlapping linguistic continua ranging from pure ASL to English. Attitudinal deafness, as opposed to audiological deafness, refers to the self-identification of a person as deaf. An individual with a mild hearing loss, for example, may be accepted as deaf while another with a profound hearing loss might not think of himself or herself as deaf, at least in a cultural context. Deaf individuals also have behavioral norms for eye contact, physical touching, conversational turn taking, and facial expression that are different from the general hearing population. Perhaps the strongest argument in addition to the use of ASL, for the existence of the deaf as a cultural or ethnic group lies in the endogamous marriage patterns of deaf Americans, with estimates of in-group marriage ranging to over 90% (Schein & Delk, 1974), much higher than most contemporary American ethnic groups. There is also a strong historical awareness of deafness, transmitted through books and an active "oral" (ASL) tradition. Finally, there are deaf ethnic organizations, many with their own publications, such as the National Association of the Deaf, World Games for the Deaf, the National Fraternity Society of the Deaf, and many others.

The complex nature of language in the deaf world is described by a number of authors (Kannapell & Adams, 1984; Reagan, 1985; Woodward, 1982). Some of the major factors involved in understanding the deaf world can be found in sign language itself. ASL, the everyday vernacular language of the deaf, is historically, formally, and pragmatically different from English and possibly from other Indo-European languages (Kluwin & Woodward, in press). Historically, ASL has not had English roots. The core vocabulary is largely drawn from French school signs brought by Clerc when Gallaudet invited him to teach at the American School for the Deaf (Moores, 1987). Since that time, the influence of English on ASL has been sporadic as the use of "natural signs" has been supported or rejected in the education of the deaf the past 170 years (Stedt & Moores, 1990). This separation from English is reflected in the syntactic forms of ASL.

There are a number of features of ASL that make it different from English (Kluwin & Woodward, in press). Stokoe (1979) made the point that speech and sign differ in that speech is unidimensional (temporal), and ASL is multidimensional (temporal and spatial). ASL employs a radically different medium from spoken English and as a result uses quite different forms to mark similar grammatical functions or does not use the same grammatical functions as spoken English. For example, plurality in ASL is marked by reduplication of the sign; the relationships between elements of the sentences can be marked spatially; and adverbial functions are marked on the verb instead of as separate units (Kluwin & Woodward, in press).

There is voluminous information about language features, such as discourse marking rules (Baker, 1977), that shows that the pragmatic functions of ASL are quite different from English. In addition, the process of language acquisition by deaf students learning ASL is unique. Since most deaf students are born to hearing parents—in fact, fewer than 4% of deaf children are born to deaf parents who sign (Moores, 1987)—the acquisition of ASL must take a different form from language learning by hearing children. To complicate the language acquisition process, until recently most hearing parents of deaf children were not encouraged to learn either ASL or a sign system based on English. Therefore, deaf children typically learned to sign from deaf peers in residential school dormitories (Gannon, 1981). During the period from 1880 to 1970, signs were not used in classrooms before age 12, and deaf teachers were not employed to teach before the secondary level (Stedt & Moores, 1990). As a result, ASL was passed on from deaf child to deaf child, with a later influence from deaf adults.

Kelly (1989) documents the lifelong pattern of social relations within a single deaf community that grows out of the process of enculturation into the adult deaf community. In Kelly's sample, friendship patterns develop early, primarily in the residential schools, and continue through old age. All the participants in Kelly's small study reported that they kept the same friends from residential school through retirement. The only exception was a graduate of an oral, day program. This woman shifted her social focus, through an endogamous marriage to a male graduate of a residential school, away from her friends from the oral program to her husband's circle, thus demonstrating the enculturation process of the deaf community at work on adult deaf individuals.

Endogamous marriage is a long-established pattern within the American deaf community. Bell (1884) documents histories of "deaf families" reaching back several generations, a subject more recently re-examined by Groce (1985), who was able to trace some early American deaf families back to hearing families with medieval roots in England. Fay (1898) reports on the phenomenon at the end of the nineteenth century. Schein and Delk (1974), report on the maintenance of this pattern just before the expansion of public school programs. The preference of deaf individuals for marrying other deaf individuals is a major force in continuing the cohesion of the deaf community.

Stewart (1991; Stewart, Robinson, & McCarthy, 1991), in a series of papers, has documented the extensive role of sports as a foundation for social relations within the deaf community. Participation in deaf sports activities is one of the early experiences with the deaf community. During these events, the deaf child not only meets other deaf peers from outside the residential school, but has the opportunity to interact and develop contacts with adult leaders in the deaf community, thus laying the groundwork for future participation in adult deaf life. In his book, *Deaf Heritage*, Gannon (1981) describes the various functions of this adult deaf support system and other systems, such as adult social clubs, which form the core of the adult deaf community.

In summary, a deaf community exists, as can be seen in its loyalty to a unique language, specific social behavioral forms, and active identification as culturally deaf, expressed through membership in deaf associations and through endogamous marriage patterns.

Not only is there a deaf culture on a macro level, but there is considerable variability on the micro level. For example, writers have described the status of black deaf persons. There are religious organizations for Catholic, Jewish, and Protestant deaf people. It may be said that the deaf community is multicultural internally and bicultural in relationship to the hearing world. The implications for education in a pluralistic society are complex.

MEMBERSHIP IN MULTIPLE WORLDS

It may be asserted that an identifiable subgroup of deaf and hearing impaired Americans forms a highly visible Deaf culture. This subgroup meets many of the criteria for consideration as both a linguistic minority and an ethnic minority. The use of ASL is an obvious linguistic membership marker, and the high rates of endogamous marriages, along with organizations of the deaf and identifiable behavior patterns, are characteristics of ethnic status.

An additional complication may be attributed to the fact that a growing number of deaf school age students are members of ethnic minority groups, as defined by the United States government. Approximately one-third of children in programs for the deaf have minority status, with black children accounting for around 20% and Hispanic children for more than 10% of students in American educational programs for the deaf (Moores, 1987). Historically, blacks have not been accepted as full members of the deaf community, or actually of the white deaf community. In many large

cities there have been, and continue to be, separate clubs and organizations for the deaf based on race. In the past, racial segregation was at least as rigid in the education of the deaf as in general
education. Gallaudet University (then Gallaudet College) did not
accept black students until the 1950s, and as late as 1964 there
were still 13 segregated residential schools for black deaf children
(Babbidge, 1965). Education of the deaf is still dealing with the
legacy of segregation and discrimination.

Even with the elimination of legal segregation in residential
schools, there is evidence that racial segregation may be dividing
the deaf community (Hagborg, 1989). In a limited study of students at a residential school, Hagborg (1989) reported a preference
among white deaf adolescents for other white deaf adolescents,
but no such preference among minority group members. Hagborg
(1989) notes that such preferences are common in situations where
there is a clearly dominant group and further, that the sample is
too limited to generalize from.

The issue of ethnicity is already complex for any member of
the Deaf culture. Deaf people function daily within a hearing culture. Since there are no readily identifiable geographic demarca-
tions, and deaf people patronize the same supermarkets, drug-
stores, service stations, and so on as their hearing neighbors, the
typical deaf American may be thought of as having membership in
at least three cultural groups: the Deaf culture, the dominant hearing culture, and the bicultural community that straddles both.

The situation becomes much more complicated for an individual who is Deaf as well as a member of another cultural group and
who also interacts with the dominant hearing culture. Figure 3.1
is a reproduction of a Venn diagram by Reagan (1990, p. 81) that
represents the possible cultural identifications of such an individual.

From Figure 3.1, we can see that the individual potentially is
a member of seven different cultural groups, each with identifiable
characteristics. Such a person, for example, might live with a deaf
spouse in a racially mixed, predominantly hearing neighborhood
and have hearing children attending public schools. He or she
could have memberships in the Deaf Black Advocates and National Association of the Deaf organizations. The individual might
identify more or less strongly with any one of the seven cultural
groups. Very probably, the sense of identification would vary over
time and depending on circumstances. The situation would be
even more complex if variables such as gender, age, and socioeco-

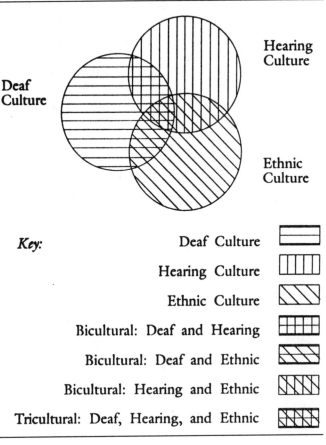

Figure 3.1. Theoretical cultural membership of a deaf individual who interacts with hearing culture and an ethnic culture

Key:

Deaf Culture	
Hearing Culture	
Ethnic Culture	
Bicultural: Deaf and Hearing	
Bicultural: Deaf and Ethnic	
Bicultural: Hearing and Ethnic	
Tricultural: Deaf, Hearing, and Ethnic	

From Brill, 1978, p. 164.

nomic status were factored in. Reagan (1990) sums up the issue of cultural identification for deaf individuals as follows:

> The point of such mapping is really quite simple: The reality facing the teacher is an immensely complex, complicated, and diverse one, and questions of culture and cultural diversity are not amenable to simple or easy resolution. Although this would be true of any target population in contemporary American so-

ciety, it is especially true—and especially complex—in the case
of deaf people. (p. 82)

Given the large numbers of minority children in programs for
the deaf, it is somewhat disconcerting to find almost no information on minority deaf individuals, either children or adults, making it extremely difficult to arrive at informed educational decisions for a significant part of the deaf school age population. Two
important resources, however, are Delgado's *The Hispanic Deaf*
(1984), and *Black and Deaf in America: Are We That Different?* (Hairston & Smith, 1983), written by two successful deaf black professionals.

As Higgins (1980) so well described in his study of the deaf
community in Chicago, there are two major prerequisites to an
understanding of membership in both deaf and hearing cultures:
stigmatization and identity. First, in a world that values physical
ability, deaf people, when counted as disabled, are often discred-
ited. The result of this stigmatization is frequently some kind of
unsatisfactory interaction with the hearing world. Higgins (1980)
calls these people "outsiders" in a hearing world. Second and
equally important, Higgins concludes that deaf individuals' identities arise out of their experiences in the hearing world. Powerful
implications follow from both these conclusions.

As educators, the first implication is the impact of separation
from the mainstream and stigmatization on the development of
the individual's identity. Goffman (1963) in his landmark work describes the social impact and effects of stigmatization. When an
individual or group of individuals possesses a trait that makes
people turn away from them and discriminate against them, both
groups construct a stigma theory, an ideology to explain the individual's inferiority, which uses terms that separate the individual
from whatever is considered "normal." Deaf persons have been categorized as "disabled" or "special students" or "hearing impaired."
The process of educational categorization contributes to the stigmatization process. This contradiction in goals—the desire to integrate deaf students with hearing students in local public schools
and the use of stigmatizing terminology—needs to be recognized
and dealt with. For example, the recent passage of the Americans
with Disabilities Act of 1990 both represents landmark legislation
for the protection of the civil rights of disabled individuals and
also perpetuates the separation of those individuals from the
mainstream by labeling them as disabled.

When members of a group use specific terms in their daily language that stigmatize an individual, the group members tend to impute unreasonable attributes to that individual, such as a "sixth sense" or "understanding" (Goffman, 1963). For example, deaf individuals are sometimes characterized by hearing people as possessing keener eyesight or a better sense of smell. While it may be true that some deaf individuals possess a keen sense of smell or exceptional vision, these attributes are not related to the hearing loss. According to Goffman, the process of stigmatization through verbal labels means that the life of the stigmatized individual becomes defined in terms of being accepted by the mainstream population.

As a result of the stigmatization process, the stigmatized person will go to great lengths to fit in. Goffman (1963) offers this example:

> Miss Peck (a pioneer social worker for the hard of hearing) said that in the early days the quacks and get rich medicine men who abounded saw the League (for the hard of hearing) as their happy hunting ground, ideal for the promotion of magnetic head caps, miraculous vibrating machines, artificial eardrums, blowers, inhalers, massagers, magic oils, balsams, and other guaranteed, sure-fire, positive, and permanent cure-alls for incurable deafness. (p. 9)

In striving to gain acceptance, the stigmatized person often tries to correct the stigma and may spend a great deal of time and effort engaged in an activity to accomplish that objective. Some deaf individuals spend large amounts of time on speech training, although they report that they learn little or nothing from this process (Janesick, 1991).

Other reactions to being stigmatized include attempts to correct the stigma by overcompensating, using the stigmatized condition as an excuse for ill success, viewing the stigmatized condition as a blessing in disguise, and reassessing the "normal" world as not quite so wonderful (see Goffman, 1963). Thus, the stigmatized individual, in trying to maintain membership in the mainstream, can develop a precarious social identity, if the degree of rejection either in terms of the severity of the reaction or the numbers of stigmatized individuals becomes a cultural norm for the stigmatized group. For example, hearing individuals are often the butt of deaf jokes and stories (Holcomb, 1977, 1985; Lane & Ivey, 1985). Humor or parody of the dominant culture is a regular response by the stigmatized group in the formation of its own identity through positive and negative experiences with the mainstream.

This brings us to the second implication of coming to grips with membership in multiple worlds. If as Higgins (1980) concludes, the identity of deaf people develops from their experiences in the hearing world, educators of the deaf need to be aware of the importance of membership in the deaf community. In an ethnographic study with successful deaf adults conducted over a 4-year period, Janesick (1991) found that group solidarity was extremely high in the deaf community. A sense of belonging and a high comfort level with other deaf persons came through as a major theme in the interviews. Even deaf people who worked in bicultural environments said that "they were relieved to leave work and return to their deaf spouses just to feel at home with one's own kind [of person]." As noted earlier in this chapter, there is a pronounced deaf adult community, membership in which is highly prized by deaf individuals.

Regardless of the amount of positive contact a deaf child in a local public school might have with the greater deaf community, there is the strong possibility that the child will form an image of himself or herself as "deaf" from negative contacts with the hearing world. This complicates the task for the public school both in promoting a positive self-image in the deaf child and in appropriately responding to the child's need to be accepted by a nurturing culture. In other words, some deaf children who are not successful in public school programs may attribute their failure to negative forces in the mainstream and shun any contact with hearing people, a result suggested by Gaustad and Kluwin's findings (Chapter 6). Consequently, the task of the public school program is to present not only integration as an option but positive experiences of deafness as well.

CULTURAL ISSUES IN EDUCATIONAL PROGRAMS WITH DEAF CHILDREN

We have developed the argument that deafness itself can assign minority status to an individual and that many deaf Americans identify themselves as members of a deaf culture with both linguistic and ethnic features. Also, we have noted the complexity of deafness and cultural identification, especially when the individual also identifies with other cultural groups and in reality participates in multiple cultural communities. Further, we have pointed out that even in the absence of positive cultural information, a sense of the self as "deaf" will develop. Within this framework, questions of cultural pluralism and cultural particularism take on significance in educating deaf children.

The traditional agent for enculturation into the deaf community has been the residential schools for the deaf, but with the rise of local public school programs, we could question whether deaf children in local public schools are, in fact, becoming members of the deaf community. One essential element of deaf culture, or deaf ethnicity, has been its strong traditional association with residential schools for the deaf. It was at these schools that deaf children became enculturated and were exposed to the language and mores of the deaf world (Moores, 1987). Now that the majority of deaf children are educated in public schools, the implications for the form of deaf society and ASL are unclear. The purpose of this section is to examine the implications of deaf culture and minority group status for deaf students in public school programs.

Returning to Reagan's (1990) criteria, we can consider whether deaf children in public schools are becoming members of the deaf community. According to Kluwin and Gaustad (Chapter 6), most deaf or hard of hearing children in local public school programs fail to meet two of the criteria for membership in the adult deaf community: linguistic differentiation and attitudinal deafness. According to Gaustad and Kluwin (Chapter 6) and others (Woodward, Allen, & Schildroth, 1985), the primary modes of communication of deaf children in public school programs appear to be speech, speech reading, or some form of manually coded English with or without speech. Less than 3%, according to Woodward and his associates (1985), of the communication in local public school classrooms is likely to be in ASL. Further, as we said earlier, the traditional means of learning ASL has been in the dormitories of residential schools. While some students in local public school programs may have acquired ASL through attendance at a residential school, the current level of information does not suggest that there is any widespread use of ASL in local public school programs, and certainly not to the degree that it is found in residential schools.

Attitudinal deafness, according to Gaustad and Kluwin (Chapter 6) as well as Stinson and Whitmire (Chapter 8), is characteristic of some students in local public schools to the extent that they wish to identify with other deaf individuals; however, there is also a group that wishes to identify primarily with hearing persons. A third group, consisting of students who identify with both other groups, is difficult to categorize as attitudinally deaf because we have no direct measure of the students' values on this criterion. Nonetheless, some students in local public schools do show a strong identification with a local peer-group deaf community.

We simply lack information on the behavioral norms of deaf children in local public schools and on the impact of local public school programs on marriage patterns. The first limitation results from the lack of specific research in this area, and the second from the fact that the Schein and Delk study (1974) was done before there was large-scale public school attendance by deaf individuals.

The last two criteria for cultural deafness, historical awareness of deafness and contact with deaf organizations, are probably absent in the local public school program because the primary vehicle for both of these processes has been residential schools for the deaf. Unless the local public school program actively encourages contact with deaf adult organizations, neither the oral traditions of deafness nor membership in deaf clubs will occur during the school years, a point made by Stewart and Stinson (Chapter 7) and Stinson and Whitmire (Chapter 8).

While there is a deaf adult community that is identifiable on specific criteria as a linguistic or cultural minority, the cultural status of individual deaf children educated in local public schools is at best problematical. If these children are to participate in the deaf adult community when they are adults, access to this support system must be provided to them.

There are two reasons why school programs need to attend to concerns of ethnicity and culture. The first relates to the most fundamental role of a school: the transmission of cultural knowledge. The second is a more recent concern. Schools become concerned with culture when children enter the school system without the cultural knowledge the school program expects them to have. For example, during the period from 1880 to 1920, when large numbers of immigrants entered the United States, there was considerable concern with teaching immigrant children "the American way" of doing things.

The problems of responding to cultural pluralism may be addressed in a relatively straightforward manner for deaf students in residential schools. Just as many large cities with predominantly black public school enrollments adopt Afrocentric curricula or add Afrocentric components to the curricula, residential schools for the deaf might adopt deafness-oriented curricula or, more likely, add components to the curricula that concentrate on deaf culture, deaf history, and ASL.

The situation, of course, is far different in local public schools, where deaf children are always a minority of the general school population and the curriculum for deaf children is either dictated or heavily influenced by the general curriculum. Further, most deaf children go home every day to families in which parents and siblings are hearing. Most young deaf children in public schools are not exposed to a deaf community or a deaf culture in the course of their daily activities. Public schools, along with parents, must decide the extent to which they want to inculcate values of deaf culture and prepare deaf students to participate in a deaf community as adults. If the decision is to incorporate deafness-related components into the curriculum, the next question deals with how this might be accomplished. This is far more complex than it might appear on the surface because of the complications surrounding the wide range of placements for deaf students within the public schools, varying from complete integration in the general classroom to assignment to separate self-contained classes for deaf children throughout the school day. Strategies for provision of instruction and information vary depending on placement. Quite possibly, there will be a correlation between class placement and extent of exposure to deaf culture, with children in self-contained classes tending to receive more of a focus on deafness-related concerns. However, given the individual educational program mandates of Public Law 94–142, this will not always be the case. Each school district with substantial numbers of deaf students probably will have to have several service delivery systems.

Logistically, the easiest approach might be to have curriculum components specific to deafness taught to separate classes of deaf children, who might or might not be integrated with hearing students for other subject matter. To some extent this kind of system is in effect today. Many deaf children take classes with hearing children and then receive special additional training in areas such as speech and English. This model would either add deafness-related academic content to the special part of a deaf child's school day or replace the current emphasis on speech and English communication. Thus, theoretically, the child would have the best of two worlds—hearing and deaf. The problem is that if more mate-

rial is added to the special curriculum, something must be sub-
tracted from the general curriculum. It is not reasonable to expect
deaf children to spend more time on academic subjects than hearing children do. In fact, given the demands on visual attention of
a deaf child in classroom learning, it is a strain for the deaf child
to spend equivalent time on academic subjects (Moores, 1987).
Also, state requirements for graduation and college entrance requirements mandate specific credit hours for academic subjects
such as mathematics and science, so flexibility for special topics is
limited.

A second possibility is to have deaf children meet the general
school requirements, but also have sections related to deafness.
For example, Gannon's *Deaf Heritage* (1981) or Bragg's autobio-
graphical *Lessons in Laughter* (1989) might be read by deaf students as part of the requirements for a high school history or social
studies class. This approach would seem to be most efficacious for
large numbers of deaf children in public schools. One drawback is
that it would not provide the same amount of exposure to deaf
culture as would be provided by special classes.

A third alternative would be to add to the general curriculum
components related to deafness. This would be similar to the second alternative, although the amount of material might be less;
but both deaf and hearing students would have access to the material. The problem here, of course, is that with all the identifiable
ethnic, cultural, and linguistic groups in this country, any attention to deafness in the general curriculum would be quite limited.

There are some simple things that any school program can do
to address ethnic and cultural considerations affecting deaf students. Most pressing is the need for good-faith efforts to recruit
deaf teachers and other professionals for the schools. It should be
stressed that deaf professionals should not be restricted to work
only with deaf students. Another strategy is to ensure that deaf
students have contact with deaf adults in their community as part
of the enculturation process. One promising practice, which has
been initiated in some states, is for deaf public school children to
spend time with other deaf children from residential schools. For
example, one state residential school has a program in which public school children spend weekends at the residential school. One
concern was expressed that the public school children, who use
predominantly English-based sign systems, might have difficulty
communicating with the residential school students, whose signing is heavily influenced by ASL. One of the authors of this chapter

interviewed some public high school students who had recently returned from a weekend at the residential school and found them to be quite excited about the experience. They reported no difficulty at all in communicating.

If there is a sufficient number of deaf students, a school district should investigate the establishment of a chapter of the Junior National Association of the Deaf, which is part of the National Association of the Deaf (NAD). The Junior NAD, with its meetings, publications, and activities, is a valuable source of information about and access to the American Deaf community.

In summary, public schools must take into consideration complex issues related to ethnicity and the cultural aspects of deafness in addressing the needs of their deaf students. The form in which these needs will be addressed is not clear at present, and it is probable that schools will have to consider a variety of strategies and materials in providing services and appropriate education to deaf children. The outcomes will go a long way in determining the ultimate success of local public education for the deaf.

REFERENCES

Americans with Disabilities Act of 1990. Public Law 101–336, July 26, 1990, 104 Stat. 327.

Babbidge, H. (1965). *Education of the deaf: A report of the Advisory Committee on Education of the Deaf.* Washington, DC: U.S. Department of Health, Education, and Welfare.

Baker, C. (1977). Regulators and turn-taking in American Sign Language discourse. In L. Friedman (Ed.), *On the other hand: Perspectives on American Sign Language* (pp. 178–203). New York: Academic Press.

Banks, A., & Banks, M. (Eds.). (1989). *Multicultural education: Issues and perspectives.* Boston: Allyn & Bacon.

Bell, A. G. (1884). *Memoirs on the formation of a deaf variety of the human race.* Washington, DC: National Academy of Science.

Bragg, B. (1989). *Lessons in laughter: The autobiography of a deaf actor* (as signed to Eugene Bergman). Washington, DC: Gallaudet University Press.

Brill, R. G. (1978). *Mainstreaming the prelingually deaf child.* Washington, DC: Gallaudet College Press.

Delgado, G. (Ed.). (1984). *The Hispanic deaf.* Washington DC: Gallaudet University Press.

Fay, E. A. (1898). *Marriages of the deaf in America.* Washington DC: Volta Bureau.

Gannon, J. (1981). *Deaf heritage: A narrative history of deaf America.* Silver Spring, MD: National Association of the Deaf.

Goffman, E. (1963). *Stigma: Notes on the management of a spoiled identity.* New York: Touchstone.

Gollnick, D. M., & Chinn, C. (1986). *Multi-cultural education in a pluralistic society.* Columbus, OH: Charles E. Merrill.

Groce, N. E. (1985). *Everyone here spoke sign language: Hereditary deafness on Martha's Vineyard.* Cambridge, MA: Harvard University Press.

Hagborg, W. (1989). A sociometric investigation of sex and race peer preferences among deaf adolescents. *American Annals of the Deaf, 134*(3), 265–267.

Hairston, E., & Smith, L. (1983). *Black and deaf in America: Are we that different?* Silver Spring, MD: T. J. Publishers.

Higgins, P. C. (1980). *Outsiders in a hearing world: A sociology of deafness.* Newbury Park, CA: Sage.

Holcomb, R. K. (1977). *Hazards of deafness.* Northridge, CA: Joyce Publishing.

Holcomb, R. K. (1985). *Silence is golden, sometimes.* Berkeley: Dawn Sign Press.

Janesick, V. J. (1991). Proud to be deaf: An ethnographic study of deaf culture. Paper presented at the Qualitative Research in Education Conference, University of Georgia, Athens.

Kannapell, B. M., & Adams, P. E. (1984). *Orientation to deafness: A handbook and resource guide.* Washington, DC: Gallaudet University Press.

Kelly, A. B. (1989). *Baltimore's deaf senior citizens.* Unpublished manuscript, Gallaudet University, Department of Linguistics, Washington, DC.

Kluwin, T. & Woodward, J. (in press). The problems of describing the syntax of a signed language. In J. Ney & F. Peng (Eds.), *Foundations of syntax: An advanced study of current theories of syntax.* London: Cole and Whurr.

Lane, L. G., & Ivey, B. P. (Eds.). (1985). *A handful of stories.* Washington, DC: Gallaudet University, Division of Public Services.

Moores, D. (1987). *Educating the deaf: Psychology, principles, and practices.* Boston: Houghton Mifflin.

Padden, C., & Humphries, T. (1988). *Deaf in America: Voices from a culture.* Cambridge, MA: Harvard University Press.

Padden, C., & Markowicz, H. (1976). Cultural conflicts between hearing and deaf communities. In *VII World Congress of the World Federation of the Deaf* (pp. 407–411). Silver Spring, MD: National Association of the Deaf.

Reagan, T. (1985). The deaf as a linguistic minority: Educational considerations. *Harvard Educational Review, 55* (3), 365–377.

Reagan, T. (1988). Multiculturalism and the deaf: An educational manifesto. *Journal of Research and Development in Education, 22,* 1–6.

Reagan, T. (1990). Cultural considerations in the education of deaf children. In D. Moores & K. Meadow-Orlans (Eds.), *Research in educational and developmental aspects of deafness* (pp. 74–84). Washington, DC: Gallaudet University Press.

Schein, J., & Delk, M. (1974). *The deaf population of the United States.* Washington DC: Silver Spring, MD: National Association of the Deaf.

Sleeter, C. E., & Grant, C. A. (1987). An analysis of multicultural education in the United States. *Harvard Educational Review, 57*(4), 421–444.

Stedt, J., & Moores, D. (1990). Manual codes on English and American Sign Language: Historical perspectives and current realities. In H. Bornstein (Ed.), *Manual communication: Implications for education.* Washington, DC: Gallaudet University Press.

Stewart D. (1991). *Deaf sport: The impact of sports in the Deaf community.* Washington, DC: Gallaudet University Press.

Stewart, D., Robinson, J., & McCarthy, D. (1991). Participation in Deaf sport: Characteristics of elite deaf athletes. *Adapted Physical Activity Quarterly, 8* (2), 136–145.

Stokoe, W. (1979, November 12). *Syntactic dimensionality: Language in four dimensions.* Paper presented at the meeting of the New York Academy of Sciences, New York.

Woodward, J. (1978). Historical bases of American Sign Language. In P. Siple (Ed.), *Understanding language through sign language research* (pp. 321–353). New York: Academic Press.

Woodward, J. (1982). *How you gonna get to heaven if you can't talk with Jesus: On depathologizing deafness.* Silver Spring, MD: T. J. Publishers.

Woodward, J., Allen, T., & Schildroth, A. (1985). Teachers and deaf students: An ethnography of classroom communication. *Proceedings of the first annual meeting of the Pacific Linguistic Conference* (pp. 83–101). Eugene: University of Oregon.

CHAPTER 4

How Family Factors Influence
School Achievement

THOMAS N. KLUWIN
MARTHA GONTER GAUSTAD

Learning is a lifelong process ranging from the infant's learning to talk to the geriatric's mastery of the social relations within a nursing home. Consequently, the contexts for learning must be understood very broadly to include "families, schools, museums, religious institutions, places of work, hospitals, community centers" (Leichter, 1978, p. 570). Because these contexts for learning are not independent of each other, however, the relationship between the family and the public school must be considered from the perspective of the overall development of the human being (Leichter, 1978).

In this chapter, we will focus on the education of the child from the perspective of the family's contribution to achievement in school. Of course, the ideal from the perspective of the school is a family that supports all the activities of the school without making any demands on it. In the process of answering several seemingly obvious questions, however, we will separate the ideal from the real.

WHAT IS A FAMILY?

There are two ways to approach the question of what a family is. One is to describe the structure of the relationships within a family, and the other is to define the processes that make families unique social entities.

The structural approach would be to build a definition of the family on the basis of the individuals who are considered members of a family. This approach has fueled considerable anthropological fieldwork in the area of "kinship." However, the use of a simple structural description of a family as mother, father, and offspring will immediately founder on the complexities of current American family structures. According to Walsh (1982) three trends have altered the structure of American families in recent years: the rising divorce rate, more working mothers, and a lower birth rate coupled with longer life expectancy. Based on these trends, Walsh (1982) and others offer several current American family configurations that make simple structural descriptions difficult. The range includes:

1. Contemporary, nuclear families,
2. Single-parent families,
3. Recombined families resulting from the remarriage of divorced adults,
4. Two working-parent families in which children are raised by other relatives or by strangers,
5. "Boomerangs" or adult children returning to the homes of their parents, and
6. Various alternative family modes.

The point is that a structural definition of American family life is not easy to develop. The obvious solution is to say that any group that calls itself a family is a family, but that recourse is not very informative.

The second approach to the question of what a family is, is to define a family on the basis of what it does. While this appears to be a useful alternative to the structural approach to family definition, it also has its problems for the purposes of this chapter. The primary source of information on family functioning, the field of family counseling and therapy, has focused on pathologies in families, has been concerned primarily with defining functions that maintain the family in existence, and has generally ignored the education, both formal and informal, of children. One limited definition of the functions of a family is that of Fleck (cited in Walsh, 1982, p. 34), who has defined five family system parameters:

1. Leadership,
2. Family boundaries,
3. Affectivity,

4. Communication, and
5. Task/goal performance.

Unfortunately, none of these attributes of family functioning sheds any light on what constitutes a family. Consequently, we are left without a simple definition of a family.

A compromise can be found by combining some general traits of the failed structural characterization of the family and the functional attributes found in the family therapy definitions. A family, therefore, is a collection of individuals, minimally a parent or parent-surrogate and at least one offspring or dependent, with the parent or parent-surrogate taking primary responsibility for the family functions described by Fleck (Walsh, 1982). For example, an older sibling or grandparent who provides support and affection for a child in the absence of a natural parent would satisfy this definition of a family. Given this kind of procedural definition, we will focus more on family roles being filled than on who fills those roles.

HOW DOES A FAMILY SUPPORT THE CHILD IN SCHOOL?

A survey of the various research traditions related to families and schooling suggests that four general classes of variables have been considered when looking at schooling outcomes such as achievement:

1. Family resources,
2. Family environment,
3. Parental expectations, and
4. Family activities that promote subject-matter learning.

Family resource studies have examined demographic or structural factors such as the impact of teen mothering, the absence of fathers, family socioeconomic status, or parental education level on the child's school achievement. Family environment is a construct that comes primarily from the family therapy tradition and focuses on the capacity of the family to maintain itself as an entity, including concepts such as parenting style, family cohesiveness, or home emotional environment. Parental expectations studies have examined the relationship between what the parent wants for the child and how well the child succeeds in school. Family processes studies have examined specific parent behaviors that promote direct educational outcomes, including how much television children are allowed to watch, children "playing school," and fathers checking mathematics homework. While it is convenient to separate the various predictor variables for school achievement into these four categories in order to describe them, this is not to suggest that the categories or the variables included within each category are independent of each other. A full model of the impact of family input on school achievement will have to include the interrelationships among these variables.

Family Resources

In the tradition of research on family resource variables and school achievement, the two most consistent predictors of school achievement have been maternal education and measures of overall family resources. For example, Stevenson and Baker (1987) studied 179 families and found that higher maternal education levels led to more involvement in school activities. They failed to find a relationship between family demographic variables and achievement, because of their use of an inappropriate predictor, family involvement in the school, as opposed to family involvement with the child at home about school. Taking a different approach to the definition of family resources, Kinard and Reinherz (1987) studied the effects of adolescent childbearing and parenting on academic aptitude and achievement of fourth graders. Maternal education and family structure did affect achievement in that higher levels of maternal education and two-parent families were more predictive of higher levels of school achievement. In other studies, the presence of a father or second parent has been found to be predictive of achievement (Alexander & Entwistle, 1988; Forehand, Long, Brody, & Fauber, 1986). In a re-analysis of data from a large-scale study of school effects, Page and Keith (1981) measured family background, including a combination of parental education level, occupation, income, and various possessions in the home. They found that family background influenced achievement in three ways: directly, indirectly through the selection of the type of school attended, and in connection with the amount of homework done, which is a major predictor of achievement. Walberg and Shanahan (1983), in another re-analysis of the same database used by Page and Keith (1981), also found that home influences, including parental interest, resources in the home, homework, and family socioeconomic status, were positive predictors of several measures of achievement.

The research on family resource variables suggests two conclusions. First, specific variables such as maternal education, socioeconomic status, and the presence of a second adult in the home are predictors of student achievement. Second, the influence of family resource variables on achievement can be both direct and indirect through parental behavior in support of achievement.

Family Environment

The family therapy research tradition has focused, with mixed results, on family environment variables that might predict achievement in school. For example, Forehand and his associates (1986) examined the relationship between home stress and the school performance of 46 young adolescents aged 11 to 15. Home stress factors included a measure of overt parental conflict occurring in the child's presence, a measure of family disagreements over 44 specific issues, and a measure of depression in adults. None of the family stress variables were found to predict school achievement.

Dornbusch and his associates (Dornbusch, Ritter, Leiderman, Roberts, & Fraleigh, 1987) looked at the broad concept of parenting style and its impact on school achievement. They defined parenting style as authoritarian, permissive, or authoritative. In a large study in the San Francisco Bay area (n = 7,836), they reported that both authoritarian and permissive parenting, as opposed to authoritative parenting, resulted in lower grade point averages. Children from pure authoritative families had the highest mean grades, while those from inconsistently authoritative families had the lowest grades. According to Dornbusch and associates, authoritative parenting is characterized by

> an expectation of mature behavior from the child and clear setting of standards by the parents; firm enforcement of rules and standards, using commands and sanctions when necessary; encouragement of the child's independence and individuality; open communication between parents and children, with encouragement of verbal give and take; and the recognition of the rights of both parents and children. (p. 1245)

Bradley, Caldwell, and Rock (1988) reported on a 10-year follow-up study of home environment and school performance.

Examining the home environments of 42 infants and then following up when the children were 10 and 11, they found strong correlations between infant home environment and home environment during middle childhood. However, only the current home environment was a predictor of school achievement. The total home environment described at age 10 included a measure of the responsivity of the parents, parental encouragement of maturity, active involvement of the parents with the child, and a warm emotional climate.

The family environment studies are generally difficult to compare because the definitions of family environments have been quite diverse and factors ancillary to the research, such as family structure, have been predictors of larger amounts of the variance in school achievement. However, like the family resource variables, specific actions by parents, such as consistently enforcing rules, are predictors of higher achievement in school.

Parental Expectations

The third class of variables are those that measure the relationship between parental expectations and school achievement. This is not a simple relationship, as Seginer (1983) points out in a review of 11 studies of the effects of parental expectations on school achievement. Seginer (1983) suggests that three factors are antecedents or mediators of parental expectations:

1. Parental knowledge,
2. Parental aspirations, and
3. Feedback from the school.

Parental knowledge includes the parents' experience in school, their knowledge of the child's capabilities, and their general knowledge of schools and children; parental aspirations involve the parents' desires for their child's level of success as an adult; and school feedback includes things such as report cards and conferences with teachers. Seginer (1983) notes that parental expectations covary with children's success in school, but she argues that the relationship is not necessarily linear because of the impact of the three mediating variables. School feedback alters parental expectations very early in the child's career, some time between first and second grade. Middle class parents with middle ability children are least affected by the school feedback process because they have more accurate assessments of their children's abilities in relation to the academic demands of the school. The most severely affected parents are working class parents whose assessments of their children's academic abilities are often unrealistically optimistic at an early age. The third mediator, parental knowledge, ranges from formal knowledge of school procedures to general folk wisdom. This factor will covary with parental education and experience with schools since the more precise a parent's knowledge of what is required in school, the more appropriately he or she can plan for and respond to the child's situation. It is clear that with this combination of mediating variables, working class and less well-educated parents can be at a disadvantage in responding to the requirements of the school program.

What Seginer's (1983) review points out is that while it is possible to describe many of the components in a family's contribution to a child's success in school, it is very difficult to disentangle the reinforcing effects of parental background factors such as education level or income level on parental expectations. Finally, Seginer (1983) concludes that it is not just parental expectations, but also parental supportive behavior, that influence the achievement of the child in school. This leads us to the fourth general category of research on family effects on schooling.

Parental Achievement-Supporting Behavior

In the educational research tradition, the focus has been on family activities that are either directly instructional or directly supportive of instructional activities in school. For example, Durkin's (1975) study of early readers found that family possessions, such as blackboards, and family activities, such as older sisters playing school with younger siblings, promoted early reading success. A less specific study of early reading success was reported by Alexander and Entwistle (1988), who examined the relationship between household composition, parental expectations, and reading scores for 689 Baltimore area first graders. They reported that the presence of a father in the house improved reading scores, but, more interesting, the presence of a second adult in the house, not just the father, had a positive effect on reading scores. Family effects on reading scores, at the end of the first grade, were generally felt through changed parental expectations for grades. Specific actions, such as checking homework, contributed to the child's success in school.

A MODEL OF FAMILY EFFECTS ON SCHOOL ACHIEVEMENT

From the various research traditions on family effects on schooling, an intriguing model emerges, as shown in Figure 4.1. Our proposed model begins with Seginer's (1983) model but incorporates other information that we have described in this chapter. In the model, academic achievement is directly predicted by the parents' achievement-supporting behavior, while the other variables either alter the capacity of the parents to offer this support or are mediated through another variable. Parents' achievement-supporting behavior is what Durkin's (1975) study described as effective in producing children who read early. It is the direct and specific actions of parents or parental substitutes, such as reading to children, controlling the amount of television watching, or monitoring homework, that affect learning either by supporting school activities or by increasing the time spent on school-related learning.

In our model, parental expectations and their relationship to school feedback, parental aspirations, and parental knowledge are identical to Seginer's (1983) conceptualization, as described above.

Such a model does not eliminate the effects of parental resources, such as maternal education or socioeconomic status, but rather places those factors in perspective with mediating variables. Parental resources are seen as influencing parental aspirations, parental knowledge of school procedures and values, and parental achievement-supporting behavior.

The failure of various family climate measures to demonstrate consistent and direct influence on school performance argues against its designation as a primary influence. Consequently, family environment is a mediating variable in this model. We hypothesize that family environment in conjunction with family structure will condition parents' ability to provide achievement-supporting behavior. Specifically, dysfunctional families, either through the physical absence of a specific role provider (for example, someone who might check homework) or through some dysfunction (such as an alcoholic father who draws resources away from other purposes), will be less productive of the types of behavior that support achievement than families where all parental roles are filled. Again, we wish to distinguish between role and provider. It is possible for a variety of surrogates other than natural parents to provide achievement-supporting behavior (Durkin, 1975).

Figure 4.1. Model of the effect of family factors on achievement

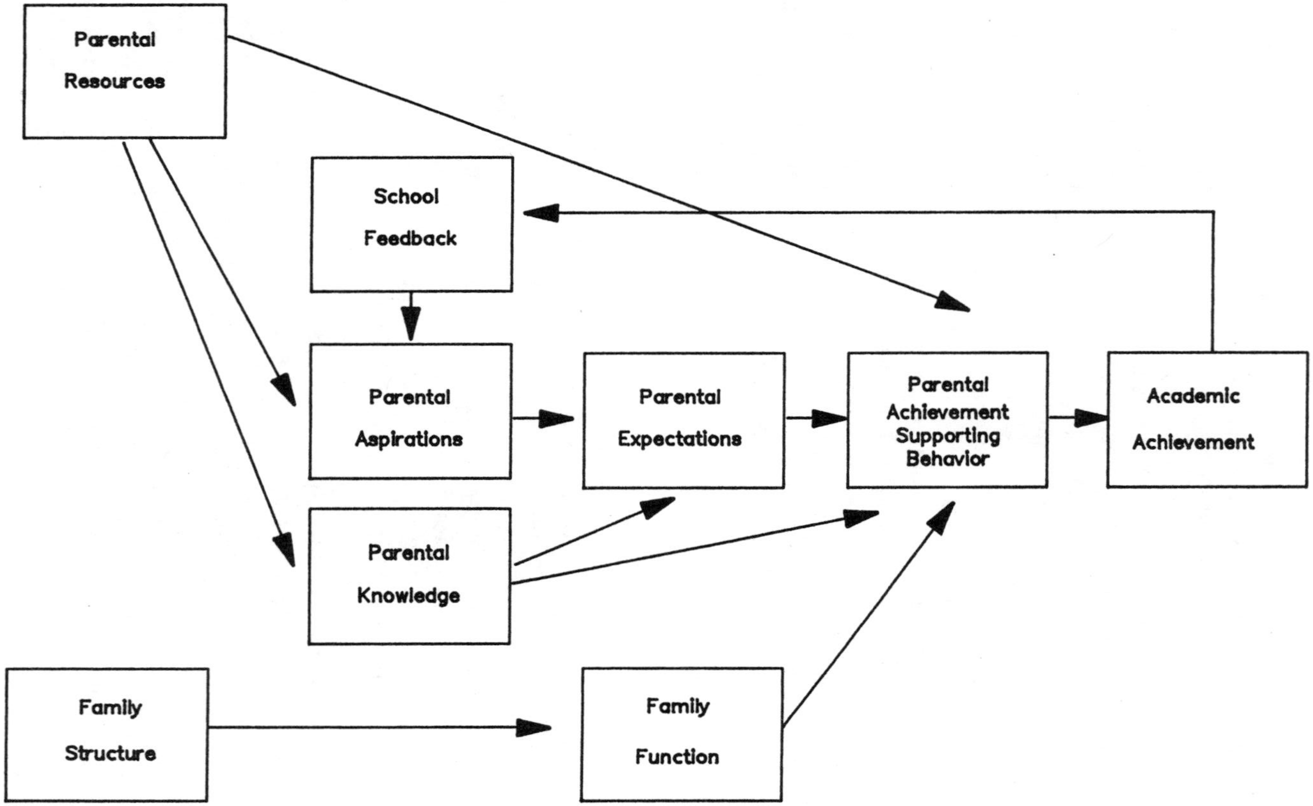

THE DEAF CHILD IN A MODEL OF FAMILY EFFECTS
ON SCHOOLING

Since over 90% of all deaf children are born into hearing families, starting with a model of family function highlights the primary issue of the need for specific family actions to support school achievement. In addition, our model and the research we have reviewed suggest several key points for consideration when including the presence of a deaf child in a model of family effects on schooling. These include family resources, particularly the variables of maternal education and socioeconomic status; the family's response to deafness as a communication problem; and the mediating effects of parental achievement-supporting behavior.

Kluwin and Gaustad (1991), in a study of a national sample of deaf adolescents and their families, report that maternal education has a considerable impact on the choice of a communication mode in the family. Although those results were not tied to school achievement, they do help to establish the link between maternal education, school feedback, and achievement-supporting behavior of parents of deaf children. Higher levels of maternal education resulted in a greater likelihood of the mother's adopting manual communication as a mode of communication with a more profoundly hearing impaired child (Kluwin & Gaustad, 1991). Since the use of manual communication within the family is most likely to come about as the result of a school program's recommendation and provision of services to the family, the higher levels of maternal education suggest that better educated mothers are more responsive to the school program's recommendation for their children. This finding would parallel middle class mothers' abilities to more appropriately respond to school assessments of hearing children.

Socioeconomic status, representing the range of available family resources, may also be a contributing factor in the degree to which families can respond to the special needs of a deaf child, as suggested in a study by Lerman (1984) of Hispanic deaf in New York City. The Hispanic parents in his survey were largely unemployed or working in menial positions, and family size was larger than the national average. In these families, not only the demands of the handicap but the burden of economic survival limited the family's actions in supporting the academic achievement of their deaf children.

There is a fairly complete description of parental achievement-supporting behavior in a study by Bodner-Johnson (1986), who examined family effects on the school achievement of deaf students. Using an open-ended interview technique, she surveyed 125 families with deaf children in the northeastern region of the United States. Using a factor analytic approach, she reduced the contents of her interview protocol to four factors:

1. Family involvement or interaction,
2. Guidance or knowledge,
3. Press for achievement, and
4. Adaptation to deafness.

Family involvement or interaction included items that measured the degree of parental involvement in educational and extracurricular activities as well as the parents' knowledge of the child's school progress. Guidance or knowledge included primarily speech training or English language training activities and a measure of involvement with the school program. Press for achievement included measures of expectations such as those described by Seginer (1983). Adaptation to deafness included learning sign language, family acceptance of the condition, and even-handed treatment of deaf and hearing siblings. All four factors included what other studies had identified as specific educational process variables, such as providing the child with reading materials, checking homework, and free-time involvement with the child.

Bodner-Johnson (1986) used these four factors to predict reading and mathematics achievement for high and low achievers. Adaptation to deafness and press for achievement accounted for 23% of the variance in reading achievement, but press for achievement alone accounted for 6% of the variance in mathematics achievement, with none of the other variables entering the equation. These findings fit in with our proposed model in that family involvement in the school, Boder-Johnson's guidance/knowledge factor, is not a good predictor of student achievement because it may not represent any behavior that directly or even indirectly supports learning.

From our earlier discussion, it is apparent that some of the same factors that influence achievement in schooling, such as family structure and family resources, interact with a family's response to the hearing loss. We suspect that families that are able to bring more resources to bear are better able to respond more appropriately to the requirements of the deaf child. We might expect family resource factors to have a greater impact on the educational achievement of deaf children, since resources affect the quality of both the response that parents can make to deafness and the support the family provides for the child's education. However, both proactive responses to the child's deafness and parental behavior that supports achievement in school should also contribute to higher achievement.

A STUDY OF FAMILIES OF HIGH SCHOOL AGE DEAF STUDENTS

To illustrate the preceding discussion, we would like to describe a study we conducted as part of a larger research project. We mailed a questionnaire about family socioeconomic status, communication practices, and educational values and expectations to the parents of 364 deaf high school students in 16 public school programs around the United States and Canada. At the time of this study the students were in grades 9, 10, and 11. The students were in both mainstreamed and self-contained placements, primarily in central or "regional" programs. The overall response rate was 69%.

Of those families who responded, 65.7% of the parents of the students were currently married, including 5% of the sample who were remarried. Of the parents in the sample, 29.3% were divorced. The average family size was 4.8 individuals, with a standard deviation of 2.6. The average number of years of education for fathers in the sample was 12.6, with a standard deviation of 3.4 years. Mothers had an average of 12.2 years of education, with a standard deviation of 2.6 years. The parents responding to our questionnaire were less wealthy than the national average in that over one-fourth reported incomes of less than $10,000, while only 17.5% of the national population falls below that income level. In addition, nearly twice as many of the incomes of the parents in our study fell in the $10,000 to $15,000 range than would be found in the national population. Of the responding parents, 83.7% identified English as the primary language used at home.

Questions about the parents' desires and expectations for their children's educational level and career goals, parental education, ethnicity, income, and ownership of specific items were factor analyzed to produce three family background variables:

1. Educational expectations,
2. Family resources, and
3. Special adaptations to deafness.

Educational expectations included questions on the parents' expectations for their children's careers, levels of education, and grade point average. Higher scores on this factor meant that parents expected their children to complete more years of schooling, have higher grade point averages, and have more prestigious jobs.

Economic resources included the father's educational level, the mother's educational level, the family's income level, the family's ethnic group, and ownership of a VCR. Higher scores on this factor meant that the father and mother had more years of education, had a higher level of income, and were more likely to own a VCR. Because of the arbitrary values in the coding system used for ethnicity, higher values indicated white or Asian families; middle values, black families; and the lowest values, Hispanic families.

Only two items loaded onto the "adaptation to deafness" factor: ownership of a television decoder or of a telecommunications device for the deaf (TDD). In the construction of the questionnaire, ownership of a VCR was expected to load with other telecommunications devices for the deaf. It was thought that VCR ownership would mean greater access to captioned videotapes. However, VCR ownership turned out to be related to higher income levels rather than to a commitment to supporting the activities of the deaf child in the family.

Ninth-grade achievement was the dependent measure used in this study. Data were obtained from school records that contained the ninth-grade administration of the Stanford Achievement Test Hearing Impaired Version. The reading comprehension, mathematics computation, and mathematics concepts subtests were factor analyzed to produce a single, composite achievement score.

To predict the composite factor, ninth-grade achievement, a multiple regression analysis was computed. The independent variables were the three factor scores from the parent questionnaire—expectations, resources, and adaptation to deafness—as well as the parents' expectation of their child's doing homework on a regular basis, the parents' report of whether they checked the child's homework on a regular basis, and the degree of the child's hearing loss. The results of the study are shown in Figure 4.2.

The multiple regression equation accounted for 32.8% of the variance in ninth-grade achievement ($F = 9.56$ for 5, 98 df; $p < .001$). The largest factor in the equation was whether the families regularly checked the children's homework, which accounted for 10% of the total variance or 30% of the explained variance.

Figure 4.2. Predicting ninth-grade achievement using family
background variables

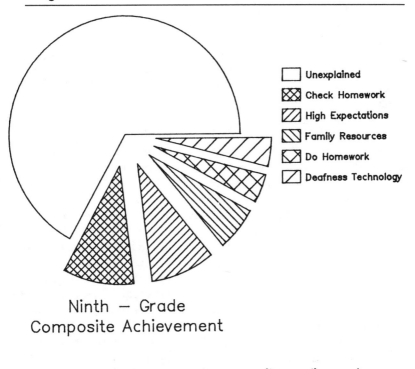

☐	Unexplained
☒	Check Homework
▨	High Expectations
◩	Family Resources
◈	Do Homework
◿	Deafness Technology

Ninth — Grade
Composite Achievement

Dependent measure is composite reading and
mathematics achievement.

Regular homework checking was positively associated with higher
levels of achievement. The second largest factor in the equation
was family expectations for success, which accounted for about
9% of the total variance or 27% of the explained variance. The
children of those families that expressed higher goals for their
children had higher levels of achievement. The third factor that
entered the equation was the measure of family resources. This
factor accounted for 6% of the total variance in ninth-grade
achievement. More affluent and better educated parents had children who achieved at higher levels in ninth grade. The fourth factor in the equation was whether parents expected their children to
do homework. This factor accounted for only 4% of the total vari-

ance in achievement but was also positively related with achievement, that is, parents who expected their children to do homework
had children with higher achievement levels. The last factor to enter into the equation was the use of deafness-related technology in
the home. This factor, which accounted for 4% of the total variation in ninth-grade achievement, was also positively related to
achievement. The degree of the child's hearing loss did not enter
the equation.

Our small study fits well within the other work in this area.
Parental achievement-supporting behaviors, parental expectations, and family resources predict a considerable amount of the
variance. In our study, a simple measure of adaptation to deafness,
the availability of deafness technology, also contributed to explain-
ing the composite achievement measure. However, this may not be
a direct measure of adaptation to deafness; instead, a more complex relationship may exist conditioned by the degree of the child's
hearing loss. In other words, "watching more captioned television"
is not necessarily a way to improve a child's achievement. For children who are moderately skilled readers, access to deafness technology may offer more opportunities to read and write as well as
greater access to a wider range of English vocabulary. For poorer
readers, additional technology may be overwhelming since it taxes
their limited reading skill. For less impaired children with good to
excellent reading skills, additional television viewing might have
a negative impact, just as it does for hearing students.

CONCLUSION

Families affect the achievement of deaf children in local public
school programs in ways that are mediated by a succession of intervening variables. First, the degree of the child's hearing loss sets
the limits for the family's response to the child's deafness. For example, profound deafness requires the use of manual communication for efficient family interaction, while a mild hearing loss
may require special assistive devices and more attention to oral
communication behavior. At the same time, the child's deafness
can place special demands on family resources.

Family resources may be more or less available to spend as
"social capital" on schooling because of other demands related to
the child's deafness. The structure of lower socioeconomic status

(SES) families may be adversely affected by the added financial demands of this handicap (Lerman, 1984). But in a strange twist, some of the assumed benefits of higher SES may be nullified by communication limitations within the family. Access to media, such as books and magazines, that would expand the world knowledge of middle and upper class children are of little benefit if parents, older siblings, or other important adults are unable to read or interpret the complex content for the deaf child. Also, added demands, such as visits to doctors or specialists, can reduce the time that parents have available to promote their child's literacy through both direct instruction and modeling adult behavior such as leisure reading.

Independent of these factors but interacting with them to produce specific achievement-supporting behavior are parental expectations for school success. However, of potentially greater consequence to the deaf child's educational experience is the manner in which schools handle parental expectations. The school can enhance or retard the achievement of deaf children through the school personnel's expression of the child's potential, the explanation of the steps needed to support the child in school, and specific and direct instruction of the parents in how to respond to the child's hearing loss in positive ways that will enhance or support achievement.

Ultimately, this complicated relationship of resources, education, and expectations is affected by the family's response to the communication problems presented by the child's hearing loss. If the parents actively and positively respond to the child's hearing loss and to the input of professional school staff, the child's chances for higher levels of achievement are enhanced. Such responses can range from both parents actively learning sign language as a way to communicate with a profoundly deaf child, to school personnel showing parents how to physically present books to a deaf child so the child can follow the pictures, the text, and the parents' communication.

From our data, it is apparent that more positive parental expectations, an active and positive parental response to the child's deafness, and specific achievement-supporting behaviors will produce greater achievement in deaf students in local public school programs. Theory and data both suggest that the overall system of factors is highly interrelated. In conclusion, a school program that would encourage the achievement of its deaf children must work closely with families in promoting greater ease of communication within the family and in providing information on specific ways that parents can support the learning of their children.

REFERENCES

Alexander, K. L., & Entwistle, D. R. (1988). Achievement in the first two years of school: Patterns and processes. *Monographs of the Society for Research in Child Development, 53*(2), 1–157.

Bodner-Johnson, B. (1986). The family environment and achievement of deaf students: A discriminant analysis. *Exceptional Children, 52*(5), 443–449.

Bradley, R. H., Caldwell, B. M., & Rock, S. L. (1988). Home environment and school performance: A ten-year follow-up and examination of three models of environmental action. *Child Development, 59*(4), 852–867.

Dornbusch, S. M., Ritter, P. L., Leiderman, P. H., Roberts, D. F., & Fraleigh, M. J. (1987). The relation of parenting style to adolescent school performance. *Child Development, 58*(5), 1244–1257.

Durkin, D. (1975). A six year study of children who learned to read in school at the age of four. *Reading Research Quarterly, 10*(1), 9–61.

Forehand, R., Long, N., Brody, G. H., & Fauber, R. (1986). Home predictors of young adolescents' school behavior and academic performance. *Child Development, 57*(6), 1528–1533.

Kinard, E. M., & Reinherz, H. (1987). School aptitude and achievement in children of adolescent mothers. *Journal of Youth and Adolescence, 16*(1), 69–87.

Kluwin, T. N., & Gaustad, M. G. (1991). Predicting family communication choices. *American Annals of the Deaf, 136*(1), 28–34.

Leichter, H. J. (1978). Families and communities as educators: Some concepts of relationships. *Teachers College Record, 79*(4), 567–658.

Lerman, A. (1984). Survey of Hispanic hearing impaired students and their families in New York City. In G. Delgado (Ed.), *The Hispanic Deaf* (pp. 38–57). Washington, DC: Gallaudet University Press.

Page, E. B., & Keith, T. Z. (1981). Effects of U.S. private schools: A technical analysis of two recent claims. *Educational Researcher, 10*(7), 7–17.

Seginer, R. (1983). Parents' educational expectations and children's academic achievements: A literature review. *Merill-Palmer Quarterly, 29*(1), 1–23.

Stevenson, D. L., & Baker, D. P. (1987). The family–school relation and the child's school performance. *Child Development, 58*(5), 1348–1357.

Walberg, H. J., & Shanahan, T. (1983). High school effects on individual students. *Educational Researcher, 12*(7), 4–9.

Walsh, F. (1982). Conceptualizations of normal family functioning. In F. Walsh (Ed.), *Normal family process* (pp. 23–57). New York: Guilford Press.

CHAPTER 5

Issues of Educational Interpreting

JOE D. STEDT

The issues surrounding educational interpreting were of little interest as recently as 20 years ago. At that time, virtually all deaf or hard of hearing students were being educated in either schools for the deaf or self-contained classrooms in public schools, and the need for educational interpreters existed primarily at the postsecondary level. In the 16 years that have transpired since the passage of Public Law 94–142, the demand for and use of educational interpreters have made educational interpreting a growth area (Frishberg, 1986). Rittenhouse, Rahn, and Morreau (1989) have pointed out that in 1973 only about 10% of all hearing impaired children were even partially mainstreamed with their normal hearing peers. Five years later about one-third, or 37%, of deaf or hard of hearing students were at least partially mainstreamed (Jordan, Gustason, & Rosen, 1979), and the number increased to one-half by 1984 (Schildroth & Karchmer, 1986). In 1989, Rittenhouse and his associates found that mainstreamed deaf or hard of hearing students used educational interpreters in 56% of their mainstreamed classes. Unfortunately, our present knowledge concerning educational interpreters and the profession of interpreting in educational settings is not vast (Gustason, 1985); our knowledge simply has not continued to expand as fast as the field itself.

From the deaf student's perspective of this rapidly changing field, the effectiveness of interpreting in the classroom can range on two continua: the informational impact of the message and the social or emotional content of the message. The informational content of the message can range from simply processing input through comprehending content to responding to content. The emotional impact of the interpretation can be gauged as ranging from absent to involved. The precise measurement of the emotional impact of educational interpreting is in its embryonic stages since there are different measurement devices for interpreting skills. Dreadful interpreting would be characterized by the absence of both informational content and affective response. Optimal interpreting would permit participation in a discussion as well as adequate support to allow for the personal involvement with others in the classroom. As we will see in reviewing the available work on classroom interpreting, much of what occurs may in fact fall into the "dreadful" area.

This chapter will investigate several issues in educational interpreting and examine much of the extant data in this field. The main issues regarding educational interpreting to be examined here are professional status, training, the role of the educational interpreter, adjusting to individual learners, and actual classroom practice.

PROFESSIONAL STATUS OF EDUCATIONAL INTERPRETING

Educational interpreting is the process of relaying information to a deaf or hard of hearing student, using some form of manual communication. (Interpreters generally refer to their clients as consumers. In this chapter, the clients served by interpreters will be called either consumers or students, interchangeably.) An educational interpreter is the person responsible for transmitting manual information to the deaf or hard of hearing student. While these definitions may seem simple, their implications are quite complex.

Most educational interpreters are employed by schools or school districts. Should educational interpreters be considered professional staff or clerical staff? This question remains unresolved across the nation, and currently the same person doing the same interpreting may be considered clerical staff in one school district and professional staff in another district (Moores, Kluwin, & Mertens, 1985).

Equally ironic is the fact that an interpreter doing equivalent work in two districts may be paid as a teacher's aide in one district and as a teacher in the other district. As would be expected, some educational interpreters are paid an hourly wage and have no fringe benefits, and others are salaried employees enjoying perquisites such as paid medical coverage. It might be said that everyone knows what an educational interpreter is but there is little agreement about how to classify such personnel (Kluwin & Moores, 1985).

Scheibe and Hoza (1986) have outlined factors that should be considered in setting the pay scale for educational interpreters. Among these are educational background (in both interpreting and education), years of interpreting experience, and certification by the Registry of Interpreters for the Deaf (RID). In addition, it is recommended that educational interpreters be given a fixed number of working hours each week and that there be a separate category for educational interpreters so that their unique skills can be recognized (Scheibe & Hoza, 1986).

The status problem for educational interpreters is not merely one of professional recognition. Other issues, such as training levels and actual roles in the educational system, are equally vague. As this chapter proceeds, the reader will see the repetition of the status question in other forms.

ISSUES OF TRAINING EDUCATIONAL INTERPRETERS

There is currently no consensus concerning the skills needed to be an educational interpreter, including the length of training, signing system to be used, and pacing during interpreting. Some school districts employ people with rudimentary signing skills and no real knowledge of what educational interpreting is. On the other end of the continuum are those school districts that have their own evaluation process for educational interpreters and a graduated pay scale according to skills and qualifications.

Many educational interpreters get their training in a college-based interpreter training program. In a survey done by Gustason (1985) it was discovered that more than one-third (37%) of the graduates surveyed in 45 interpreter training programs had taken jobs as educational interpreters. Some college programs train their interpreters in two-year Associate of Arts programs; other programs require a four-year degree in interpreting. Some states have even instituted programs that can be completed within a semester or shorter time. Concerning the level of training issue, Kluwin (1981) has reported that it may take 3 to 4 years for a hearing teacher to gain relative mastery of an English-based signing system. While there is a difference between signing when teaching and educational interpreting, it still seems that an educational interpreting program of 2 years or less will be hard pressed to train interpreters to a point of fluency in an English-based signing system.

Based on a survey of 40 interpreters who were currently interpreting high school math classes, Kluwin and Moores (1985) reported that most had completed college coursework but few were college graduates. The interpreters' training had varied from programs that took 3 months to programs of 2 years or more. Only four of these interpreters had RID certification. Rittenhouse, Rahn, and Morreau (1989) reported in a nonrandom survey of a handful of public school programs that only 18% of the interpreters were RID certified. The profile of the "typical" interpreter that emerges from the Kluwin and Moores (1985) study is of a high school graduate with some college work and a brief training period, but no certification or other assurance of skill; however, most of the interpreters had several years of experience. These studies suggest that most school interpreters have minimal to no training; of those who have training, only a minority are certified specifically as interpreters.

Dahl and Wilcox (1990) surveyed the directors of 45 interpreter training programs in the United States to determine what classes are offered to the students and what the directors' perceptions are of such issues as certification for educational interpreters. Of the English-based signing systems used, 91% employed a form of Pidgin Signed English (PSE), 29% used Signed English (Bornstein, Hamilton, & Saulnier, 1983), and 13% used Signing Exact English (Gustason, Pfetzing, & Zawolkow, 1972). These figures illustrate one of the biggest problems regarding the training of educational interpreters. The majority of programs in the United States use Signing Exact English, Seeing Essential English (Anthony, 1971), or Signed English (Jordan, Gustason, & Rosen, 1976, 1979). In juxtaposition, most interpreters (91%), according to Dahl and Wilcox (1990), are trained to use a generic PSE type of signing.

Differences in signing systems between the interpreter and the deaf or hard of hearing student can create severe problems for both. Consider the hypothetical situation of a seventh-grade deaf student who attends a junior high school with a deaf education program that rigidly uses Signing Exact English. The student is usually in a self-contained classroom but is mainstreamed apart from her deaf peers for a mathematics class that is interpreted by an educational interpreter who has been trained to use PSE. Bornstein (1973) has pointed out that 61% of the signs in Signing Exact

English are from ASL, 18% are modified ASL signs, and 21% are new signs. Using these figures with the example of the seventh grader, the interpreter would probably have recognition or production problems with somewhere between 21% and 39% of the signs used. The student would likely be confused and frustrated until she and the interpreter found a common ground for communication. It must be emphasized that these communication problems could occur even when the educational interpreter is well trained and competent in PSE but lacking the requisite skills in Signing Exact English.

This discussion leads to a question concerning the training of educational interpreters: In how many systems should an educational interpreter have competence? In the Dahl and Wilcox study, none of the interpreter programs trained their people in Seeing Essential English (Anthony, 1971), yet there are many programs in the United States that use this system (Jordan, Gustason, & Rosen, 1976, 1979).

To argue that interpreters should be trained in several different systems for manually encoding English is probably not a practical solution based on the information gathered by Dahl and Wilcox (1990). The vast majority (69%) of interpreter programs do not even have a course in educational interpreting, and less than one-quarter have a course in tutoring (Dahl & Wilcox, 1990). In addition, only about half (55%) of the directors of interpreter training programs support a specific certification for educational interpreting in the RID evaluation process. Taken together, these data suggest that there is little or no likelihood that interpreter training programs will begin training their students in different English-based signing systems in the near future.

Another training issue to consider concerns lag time during interpreting. Lag time is the length of time between a speaker's voiced information and the signed counterpart produced by an interpreter. It is a popular belief that interpreters should try, as much as possible, to interpret with little or no lag time (Cokely, 1986). In training interpreters, lag time is often one of the factors used for evaluation, with short lag times highly desirable.

Cokely (1986) gathered data from five interpreters who were simultaneously interpreting a presentation given at a national conference. He measured lag time and mistakes (such as omission, additions, substitutions, and intrusions) made by the interpreters. An inverse relationship was found between lag time and errors made during interpreting, that is, when lag time increased, errors decreased. Interpreters with a 2-second lag time made twice as many mistakes as interpreters with a 4-second lag time, who in turn had twice as many errors as interpreters with a 6-second lag time. It appears that the longer lag time is needed for the inter- preters to properly process the linguistic features of one language and transmit them into the second language.

It has been pointed out that this inverse relationship would not continue with extremely long lag times. An interpreter with a lag time of 20 seconds, for example, would most likely produce many errors. As Cokely (1986) explains, "It is likely that for some individuals there is a lag time threshold beyond which the number of omissions would significantly increase because the threshold is at the upper limits of the individual's short-term working mem- ory" (p. 373). The implications of these data are that training edu- cational interpreters to have virtually no lag time may be counter- productive to the goal of training interpreters who are likely to make few mistakes when interpreting.

The issue of optimal lag time, however, involves not only in- terpreting performance but situational constraints as well. As Rowe (1974) pointed out, the wait time between a teacher's ques- tion and the students' responses in a classroom is measured in fractions of seconds. In other words, lag times of 4 to 6 seconds would mean that an interpreter could be starting a teacher's ques- tion by the time the response had been given and the teacher was giving feedback on a specific response. Such discrepancies would produce confusion for the deaf or hard of hearing student in a discussion-oriented classroom.

THE ROLE OF THE EDUCATIONAL INTERPRETER

Zawolkow and DeFiore (1986) describe the rather full role of the educational interpreter in the program for the deaf as including interpreting in classes, reminding students about homework or other responsibilities, facilitating social interaction with hearing students, tutoring both hearing and deaf students, being a class- room aide, being a liaison between the child and the regular class teacher, being a liaison between the regular class and the resource room teacher, and apprising appropriate individuals of problems children are having.

Gustason (1985), in a survey of interpreter training programs, laments the absence of solid information on what interpreters are

Figure 5.1: Educational interpreter continuum

Educator	Interpreter
1. must have degree	1. degree optional
2. certified by state	2. certified by RID
3. paid by school district	3. paid by different sources
4. consults about student	4. never discusses consumer
5. part of school society	5. may be outside school society
6. understands school system	6. may be naive about school system
7. well-delineated role	7. role may vary with school
8. supervisor well-defined	8. may have no supervisor
9. has student teaching experience	9. may have no experience

prepared to do related to these demands. Only a fraction of the respondents in Gustason's survey indicated that any training was provided in educational interpreting, although over one-third of the graduates of these training programs specialize in educational interpreting.

The role that will be assumed by the interpreter in the classroom is perhaps the most confusing of the issues surrounding the use of educational interpreters. It has been found that more than half the program directors surveyed think there needs to be a "clearer definition of the role and responsibilities of the educational interpreter in the public school, with respect to expectation, ethics and job descriptions" (Gustason, 1985, p. 265). Much of this confusion has been created because there are two separate disciplines seeking to define the educational interpreter: the field of education and the field of interpreting.

Perhaps the best way to conceptualize the differences in viewpoint concerning the educational interpreter is by illustration. Figure 5.1 shows a bipolar continuum that illustrates different ways to view the educational interpreter. Obviously, the characteristics of an educator and an interpreter are different. An examination of these differences will clarify why the same position is viewed quite differently by the two professions.

An educator is certified by the state to perform certain duties and activities. An interpreter is traditionally certified by RID, which is a national organization but is not affiliated with any local, state, or national governmental agency. Certification for educators is, in virtually all cases, dependent on matriculation from some institution of higher learning and controlled separately by each individual state. Certification by RID is based on one's ability to use sign language. College level coursework is not needed to become a certified interpreter. States assume that a person is competent to teach after taking a variety of classes, doing student teaching, or in recent years performing activities to earn alternative certification. RID requires a person to prove competency in sign language by passing tests. The result of such different paths of certification is that all educators have college degrees, whereas some interpreters have never attended a college class. (It is ironic to note that some interpreters who work in college settings as interpreters have never themselves taken a college level class.)

There is a methodical process that is required to become an educator (taking classes, observing in schools, doing student teaching, tutoring). By the time a person is a certified teacher, he or she has at least a rudimentary understanding of the procedures of a school. An educational interpreter, however, may not have had these socializing experiences and will act and look like an "outsider" in the school.

Another factor relating to the socialization of teachers has to do with role. Upon certification, a teacher virtually always understands his or her role within a school system. An educational interpreter may have no idea of his or her role upon arriving at a given school. For example, what is expected when interpreting duties are finished, but the school day is not yet over? Who does the interpreter report to when there are problems? The answers to these questions remain vague among interpreters because there may be great variability among school districts or even among individual schools within the same district. When a person's role in an organization is poorly defined, morale is likely to be poor (Getzals & Guba, 1957), making the importance of role clarification critical.

Another area of difference between educators and interpreters concerns respective codes of ethics. Scheibe and Hoza (1986) compared the RID Code of Ethics with school district policies to illustrate how the two may be in conflict. Their comparison is shown in Figure 5.2. In summary, the differences between interpreters and educational interpreters lies in the areas of confidentiality, impartiality, skill, and mode. An interpreter for an adult situation such as a courtroom or medical examination room is expected to

Figure 5.2: RID code of ethics versus school practice

RID Code of Ethics	*School District*
Everything that is said must be confidential.	Educational interpreter is part of a team and must share information on the student during an IEP meeting.
During the interpreting process, it is important to remain as impartial as possible.	Educational interpreter must help the student find additional support services (or in some cases the interpreter may be the tutor).
Interpreter takes on only those interpreting jobs that are appropriate to his or her skill level.	Educational interpreters are required to interpret in all content areas.
Interpreter interprets in the manual expression most readily understood by the consumer.	Educational interpreter uses a specific English signing system.

be a component of the service: impartial, discrete, skilled for the particular situation, and presenting the information in the most comfortable mode for the consumer. The educational interpreter may, on the other hand, be expected to be part of the educational system (Moores, Kluwin, & Mertens, 1985) in that he or she may be expected to share information about the child with other members of the educational system, to actively assist the child in the learning process, and to adhere to the school regulations and guidelines, including using certain modes of communication that may not be the most effective for a specific child.

In response to this difference in interpreting roles, Scheibe and Hoza (1986) have devised a code of ethics for educational interpreters. Figure 5.3 presents a much abbreviated rendition of the original. While it is easy to see the logic that supports the guidelines in Figure 5.3, some of the suggestions are not practical, nor will they work in real life school situations. For example, one aspect of the interpreter's role that has not been discussed is the age of the students. Zawolkow and DeFiore (1986) have stated that "younger children—kindergarten through second grade—often look to the interpreter as a parent figure" (p. 26). With this in mind, it is critical to re-examine the sixth guideline, which states that the educational interpreter is not responsible for discipline. If a young child blatantly misbehaves with the interpreter sitting next to her, she will expect the interpreter to react. If the interpreter

Figure 5.3: Guidelines for educational interpreters

The interpreter should discuss the student only with members of the educational team.

The interpreter may either attend IEP meetings or interpret them, not both.

It is appropriate to clarify information that a deaf or hard of hearing student will not understand due to language or culture.

If the educational interpreter works with the student as a tutor, they may discuss information regarding the student's performance during the tutoring session.

Since some schools use specific English signing systems, the interpreter must consider his or her skills in that system before accepting an assignment.

The interpreter is not responsible for the discipline of the student.

The interpreter should consider the following factors before accepting an assignment: age of the students, content of classes, the students' English skills, and special situations that may arise (field trips, assemblies).

ignores the behavior, the child has been given the idea that the interpreter is not a person who needs to be respected. Such lack of typical adult behavior by the interpreter sends signals to the child that could have unwanted results.

From the perspective of how interpreters are actually hired by school systems and for what purposes, the seventh guideline is not always possible. Many times, an educational interpreter has no idea before arriving at the school about what classes he or she will be assigned to. In addition, no person can be truly competent in all the courses that are offered at any given school, and such an expectation is quite unreasonable. If the school asks the interpreter to go into a class where information is foreign to the interpreter, the interpreter's refusal may leave the deaf or hard of hearing student without any assistance for the class. Clearly, both the student and the school system feel abandoned when this happens.

In an effort to bridge the gap between educational demands and interpreters' abilities, several school districts have outlined roles and responsibilities for educational interpreters. One set of guidelines, adopted by the Orange County, California, Board of Education, has been explained by Zawolkow and DeFiore (1986). These guidelines include additional duties that educational interpreters may perform when they are not performing their regular interpreting activities. Among these duties are tutoring students in class, acting as classroom aides, and interpreting for before- or after-school tutoring sessions between students and teachers. Furthermore, the educational interpreter may remind the teacher when a notetaker is needed, inform members of the educational team of the student's progress, and inform the teacher of a belief that the student is having problems with contents of the course.

ADJUSTING TO INDIVIDUAL LEARNERS

One of the most challenging facets of educational interpreting is the process of adjusting to individual learners. Earlier in the chapter the concept of lag time was introduced. Another facet of signing that is important to students is the rate of signing. Depending on the age and the skills of the student, the interpreter will want to vary the rate of sign presentation so that the student will have optimal understanding. This may mean slowing the rate of signing for younger students so that they can follow what is being said.

Sometimes it is important for the interpreter to be able to use additional strategies to fully communicate with a given consumer. One such instance is interpreting for deaf-blind students. Petronio (1988) interviewed 10 deaf-blind college students to try to find out what they expected from sign language interpreters. She learned that some deaf-blind students with tunnel vision preferred that interpreters reduce the range of their signs to a smaller space, perhaps about 10 inches. In addition, the interpreters would need to modify signs that are executed near the waist to conform to the same confined signing area within 10 inches from the face.

Some deaf-blind students need to use tactual interpreting, in which the student's hands are placed on top of the interpreter's hands. In this type of interpreting the interpreter must remember that the main sense for information transmission is tactual not visual. It should be noted that many interpreters feel quite uncomfortable signing when someone is holding onto their hands. This uneasiness will, of course, diminish over time with practice of tactual interpreting.

Petronio (1988) points out that some deaf-blind students need very slow, enunciated fingerspelling for tactual perception. When possible, it is better to avoid fingerspelling and use signs.

Although blindness is an extreme case necessitating adjustment to individual learners, we have already mentioned less dramatic parameters of the situation that an educational interpreter must take into consideration, such as the age of the student. Other necessary adjustments can be inferred from the role of the educational interpreter as a "tutor," including matching interpreting presentations to the students' informational needs, general intelligence level, or subject-matter familiarity.

INTERPRETING IN THE CLASSROOM

Several facets of the process of interpreting in the classroom are of concern to us, including the physical positioning of the child in the classroom and the working relationship between the teacher and the interpreter.

Rittenhouse, Rahn, and Morreau (1989) looked at the differences between interpreting service providers and consumers. The respondents were 24 teachers of the deaf, 18 college age deaf individuals, and 27 interpreters. All agreed that manual dexterity, hand coordination, general intelligence, knowledge of lighting, elevation, and other positioning variables, as well as a knowledge of the content and general interpreting skills, were important. Differences among the groups tended to be generally unrelated to perceptual ease. Severe methodological problems, particularly the way the results were analyzed, make this study suspect, but it is clear that there is agreement as to what makes for successful interpreting—the pacing of interpreting, the general intelligence of the interpreter, interpreting skills (sign selection, reverse interpreting, situation-specific interpreting), physical skills (manual dexterity, hand coordination), and etiquette of interpreting (placement, lighting, background).

Moores, Kluwin, and Mertens (1985) provide some information on what actually occurs in classrooms between interpreters and deaf or hard of hearing students. In a survey of high school programs for the deaf in three large city systems, they report that there are three basic ways that a deaf student and an interpreter can be placed in the classroom: line-of-sight, sidelined, or in some special situation. Line-of-sight placement means that the interpreter is positioned in a direct line between the deaf student and the teacher so that the deaf student only has to shift eye gaze to see the teacher, the board, or the overhead display. Sidelined means that the teacher occupies the central portion of the classroom, and the interpreter and student are off to one side. In this configuration the deaf student would have to look away from the interpreter to see either the teacher or the board. Finally, some situations were idiosyncratic to the subject matter, such as auto mechanics.

The importance of positioning in the classroom was made by Saur and her associates (Saur, Popp, & Isaacs, 1984) in a study of the "action zone" in classrooms where deaf college students were mainstreamed. In situations where action zones, or areas of intense classroom activity, could be identified, the deaf student was generally located outside the zones.

There are three activities that can be used to gauge the nature of the relationship between the classroom interpreter and the teacher of the mainstreamed class: the provision of class notes to the interpreter, the discussion of content and vocabulary prior to the lesson, and the perception of the tutorial role of the interpreter. Moores, Kluwin, and Mertens (1985) reported a high degree of variability among the three sites they surveyed, but it is possible to draw some general conclusions from their report.

Fewer than half of the teachers provided class notes to the interpreters. This ranged from one-third of the respondents to two-thirds, depending on the site. Class note procedures can also vary according to subject matter and school policy. For example, because of the highly structured nature of mathematics, teachers will often prepare class notes; science or social studies teachers, in contrast, will frequently generate lists of terms for students to memorize. While school or departmental policy can also affect this practice, the benchmark should be the ratio of teachers who regularly provide notes to students and the number that provide them to interpreters in advance of the class. A relatively easy change, such as previewing class notes, can make a huge difference for an interpreter in a novel discipline.

In Moores, Kluwin, and Mertens's (1985) study about half of the teachers reported that they would discuss content and vocabulary with the interpreter prior to the lesson. Again, subject-matter differences and school policy can condition the availability of this information in general, while personalities and time constraints can condition its actual transmission.

The expectation that the interpreter would tutor students varied greatly from site to site and was not consistent within the schools, according to Moores, Kluwin, and Mertens (1985). In some situations the interpreter was specifically not expected to

tutor, while in others attitudes ranged from an expectation of tutoring to a tolerance for it. This particular role of the interpreter
needs clearer definition within school programs as well as across
the profession. Moores, Kluwin, and Mertens (1985) report that
across the three sites they surveyed, the classroom functioning of
the interpreter was quite diverse and ill defined.

CONCLUSION

From the discussion in this chapter, it may be seen that many aspects of educational interpreting are vague and lacking in research
data. This is certainly the existing state of the field. Clearly, what
is needed now is a comprehensive approach to gathering data regarding educational interpreters. While survey information can
form a framework for future research, the current level of knowledge is inadequate to meet the demands being placed on the profession of educational interpreting. Data regarding technical aspects of educational interpreting as well as the most efficient
training methods for interpreters need to be gathered before the
field can progress into the next century.

RECOMMENDATIONS

Although positive research results are few and far between, from
the few studies that have been conducted as well as from a consideration of the current policy conflicts in this area, some recommendations are possible.

It is important to consider, theoretically, the best way to train
educational interpreters. What is proposed here is a two-tier
method of training. The first part would require the student to
complete a series of courses, including educational interpreting,
tutoring, and educational methods used in schools, in addition to
signing classes. The sign system would be PSE. Upon completion of
the training program, the student would be required to do intern-
ships, working with professional educational interpreters at
schools using the more specific English-based signing systems.
The student would be considered qualified in a given system only
after finishing an internship at a school that uses that system. An
interpreter training program structured as suggested here would
give students the opportunity to learn concepts about sign lan-

guage and interpreting that would enable them to acquire the necessary skills for working in the public schools.

It is necessary to stress, however, that to train interpreters in the manner described, the interpreter program must be located in a large metropolitan area (or be able to send students to such an area) because of the relative scarcity of deaf children. Since there are rarely more than 2 deaf children per 1,000 children in the general population (Schein & Delk, 1974), the training of educational interpreters, as well as their employment, will be easier to accomplish in areas with larger populations. Programming for educational interpreters is most effective in larger metropolitan areas where there is a greater possibility of matching specific skills with a specific job. It is important to have access to several educational programs that serve deaf or hard of hearing students to be able to provide educational interpreters with a broad base of training.

It is also important for educational interpreters to be able to experience both elementary and secondary students, because interpreters must be able to adjust to the age of the students (Zawolkow & DeFiore, 1986). Often, interpreter training programs concentrate on interpreting for adults, sometimes exclusively college students. While exposure to this group is critical, it does not prepare an aspiring interpreter to deal with a kindergarten student who may wet his pants during class and ask the interpreter to help him without telling the teacher.

A final recommendation deals with the reactions of the deaf students themselves. There is currently no research on the emotional, social, and educational needs of deaf students who use educational interpreters. For example, we are currently unaware of the average fifth-grade deaf student's expectations for classroom interpreting services provided by an educational interpreter. Does the student feel self-conscious with an interpreter sitting next to him or her? Does the interpreter impede interactions with other class members because the deaf student is afraid to talk about certain subjects when the interpreter is near? What can an educational interpreter do to make the deaf student's school experience better? Our field needs to focus on a myriad of aspects concerning the personal nature of educational interpreting from the viewpoint of the student. It is ironic that we continue to deliver services to a group that has had relatively little input into the services it receives. There are now deaf college students who have been using educational interpreters in classrooms since their early grades. These individuals could be used to form a framework of ideas regarding the delivery of educational interpreting.

REFERENCES

Anthony, D. A. (1971). *Seeing essential English*. Anaheim, CA: Educational Services Division, Anaheim Union High School District.

Bornstein, H. (1973). A description of some current sign systems designed to represent English. *American Annals of the Deaf, 118*(6), 454–463.

Bornstein, H., Hamilton, L., & Saulnier, K. (1983). *The comprehensive signed English dictionary.* Washington DC: Gallaudet University Press.

Cokely, D. (1986). The effects of lag time on interpreter errors. *Sign Language Studies, 53*, 341–375.

Dahl, C., & Wilcox, S. (1990). Preparing the educational interpreter: A survey of sign language interpreter training programs. *American Annals of the Deaf, 135*(4), 275–279.

Frishberg, N. (1986). *Interpreting: An introduction.* Silver Spring, MD: RID Publications.

Getzals, J. W., & Guba, E. G. (1957). School behavior and the administrative process. *The School Review, 65*(4), 423–441.

Gustason, G. (1985). Interpreters entering public school employment. *American Annals of the Deaf, 130*(4), 265–266.

Gustason, G., Pfetzing, D., & Zawolkow, E. (1972). *Signing exact English.* Silver Spring, MD: National Association of the Deaf.

Jordan, I. K., Gustason, G, & Rosen, R. (1976). Current communication trends at programs for the deaf. *American Annals of the Deaf, 121*(7), 627–632.

Jordan, I. K., Gustason, G., & Rosen, R. (1979). An update on communication trends at programs for the deaf. *American Annals of the Deaf, 124*(2), 250–257.

Kluwin, T. N. (1981). The grammaticality of manual representations of English. *American Annals of the Deaf, 126*(4), 417–421.

Kluwin, T. N., Moores, D. F. (1985). The effects of integration on the mathematics achievement of hearing impaired adolescents. *Exceptional Children, 52*(2), 153–160.

Moores, D., Kluwin, T., & Mertens, D. (1985). *High school program for deaf students in metropolitan areas.* (Monograph No. 3). Washington, DC: Gallaudet College, Gallaudet Research Institute.

Petronio, K. (1988). Interpreting for deaf-blind students: Factors to consider. *American Annals of the Deaf, 133*(3), 226–228.

Rittenhouse, R. K., Rahn, C. H., & Moreau, L. E. (1989). Educational interpreter services for hearing impaired students: Provider and consumer disagreements. *Journal of the American Deafness and Rehabilitation Association, 22*(3), 57–62.

Rowe, M. B. (1974). Wait-time and rewards as instructional variables, their influence on language, logic and rate control: Part one—Wait-time. *Journal of Research in Science Teaching, 11*, 81–94.

Saur, R., Popp, M., & Isaacs, M. (1984). Action zone theory and the hearing-impaired student in the mainstreamed classroom. *Journal of Classroom Interaction, 19*(2), 21–25.

Scheibe, K., & Hoza, J. (1986). Throw it out the window (the code of ethics) we don't use that here: Guidelines for educational interpreters. In M. McIntire (Ed.), *Interpreting: The art of cross-cultural mediation. Proceedings of the Ninth National Convention of the Registry of Interpreters of the Deaf* (pp. 173–182). Silver Spring, MD: RID Publications.

Schein, J., & Delk, M. (1974). *The deaf population of the United States.* Silver Spring, MD: National Association of the Deaf.

Schildroth, A. N., Karchmer, M. A. (Eds.). (1986). *Deaf children in America.* San Diego: College-Hill Press.

Zawolkow, E. G., & DeFiore, S. (1986). Educational interpreting for elementary- and secondary-level hearing impaired students. *American Annals of the Deaf, 131*(4), 350–357.

Understanding the Context of Local Public Education

MARTHA GONTER GAUSTAD

The first part of this book has mixed history, curriculum development, models of family processes, and interpreting standards in an attempt to describe the context of programs for the deaf in which individual deaf children find themselves. As Moores points out in Chapter 1, the public education of the deaf child is a relatively new phenomenon and consequently new understandings need to be developed.

This part of the book is intended to give the reader a framework for understanding the second part, where issues such as the efficacy of mainstreaming are considered. As a framework it can be as simple as the perspective offered by a window or as complex as the models or movements it presents. To organize what has been presented here, let us for a moment think of the individual within a family within a community within a nation in a series of expanding frames of reference.

The five chapters in this section each approach the topic of public school instruction of deaf students from a different perspective, examining the origins, issues, and problems associated with the local public school education of these children. Through these chapters we are broadened by viewing the deaf community both from within and without.

Kluwin and Gaustad, in Chapter 4, give us a perspective on the individual deaf child within the family and lead us toward the community as represented by the school. Janesick and Moores, in Chapter 3, raise the question of how a community exists and functions while building a bridge to the school. In Chapter 2, Kluwin focuses more specifically on the school itself and on its context and how it has been shaped. Moores's chapter is appropriately first because it contains the overarching concerns of the school within the nation, specifically how school programs have changed in response to changes in national priorities.

The context for the education of the deaf child in local public schools is large and complex. However, as Moores points out, deaf education has really never been totally independent of the forces that shape our national educational agenda. We see that special education, just as general education, is conditioned by the moral, fiscal, social, and political society it serves. Specific events or trends in education are tied to concurrent views of economics, politics, and religious tolerance. Thus, circumstances and concerns of present-day programs can be understood in the context of larger recurring cycles or patterns in the history of the nation and of public school education.

The national agenda has repeatedly altered the direction of deaf education. Even from the beginning the values that set the process of deaf education into place came from the self-confidence of a new nation to shoulder its responsibilities. Chapter 1 reiterates three forces that have consistently influenced the education of deaf children in this country. For example, the shift from the early benevolent role of the American School at the start of the nineteenth century to the segregation of the "asylums" at its close reflects two forces, the shift away from the confidence of the later years of the "enlightenment" and the rise of institutionalized racism under the guise of scientific "eugenics."

Of particular significance in the shifting picture Moores paints is the description of the swiftness with which the status of deaf education has changed over the last 15 years. Recently, we have witnessed the profound effects of mandated change. In an extremely short time, the instruction of deaf students has shifted from predominantly segregated residential schooling to the placement of a majority of deaf students in local public school programs.

Before we can examine influences on the operation of these local school programs, we must first understand the parameters of the system that has developed. Kluwin provides a straightforward definition of terms that highlights the diversity found among local public school programs for the deaf. Of the four parameters of program size, organizational structure, level of service, and communication mode, the most influential variable seems to be program size, which affects the degree of breadth possible in all other variables. Larger programs afford varied instructional options ranging from individual itinerant support to single-site programs with support staff, and are able to offer a range of communication modes. The chapter presents some preliminary data that suggest that between 125 to 150 students is the minimum enrollment necessary to support an adequate staff—audiologist, psychologist, social worker, and so on.

As Kluwin points out, the movement toward desegregation has not been without its pitfalls. In the field of deaf education where there is a history of controversy, the movement toward local public school placements has produced a bewildering variety of options. Variation is so extensive that simple categorization is not possible. While most deaf students appear to be served by programs large enough to provide a range of services, a large number are not in situations that would permit the adequate provision of services or sufficient numbers of peers to allow for meaningful interaction.

Janesick and Moores have explored one outcome of the continuing movement toward public school education of deaf children in Chapter 3, delineating the complexity of the question of the deaf as a separate linguistic minority and, within the deaf population, the existence of other "minorities." Borrowing from Reagan's (1985) review, Janesick and Moores have shown that the deaf qualify for consideration as a specific ethnic group, a fact recently recognized by the United States Department of Education. Further, within the general deaf community, there exist at least two identifiable minority groups: black deaf and Hispanic deaf. Historically, black deaf have been treated differently from white deaf and have had a different relationship with their respective hearing communities. The issue of Hispanic deaf is an important one in itself, but it also illustrates a general problem that public school programs for the deaf have been facing for the past decade: changes in the makeup of the national population that have an impact on programs for the deaf.

The authors further define the deaf community, for the most part the white deaf community, as being composed of three specific groups: the culturally deaf, persons who are audiologically deaf, and the children of deaf parents. Six characteristics are then used to provide an understanding of the culture of the deaf community, including language use, group identification, marriage patterns, history, social behavior, and the network of social clubs.

The issue of ethnic groups, such as the Hispanic deaf, raises substantial problems. Specifically, how does one educate a deaf child of non-English speaking parents, particularly when severe cultural differences may be present? The response to this complex problem could take any of three directions. Separate curricula could be established for each "ethnic" group within the deaf community; special components could be added to the general curriculum; or the appropriate topics could be infused throughout the general curriculum as "appropriate." Add to this the fact that we could be talking about either the general education curriculum incorporating awareness of deafness, or the deaf education curriculum incorporating deaf awareness or minority awareness, and the permutations become staggering.

Chapter 4, by Kluwin and Gaustad, also highlights interpersonal relations, those within the family unit and those operating between the family and the school. The authors have chosen to focus on school achievement as the basis for examining variables of family functioning that affect schooling. Issues related to study habits, feedback, discipline, and parental expectations must be mediated through the social and communication structure of the family with a deaf child. The authors describe the adverse impact of school feedback on the parents' expectations for the child's success as a result of a severe hearing loss. The important role of school personnel in providing information and feedback to parents in this regard is specifically addressed. The authors place great value on the establishment and pursuit of positive general expectations for the educational achievement of deaf children.

Stedt's chapter on interpreting (Chapter 5) harks back to the first three chapters, which in one way or another touch on school programming. The cornerstone of a public school program that hopes to mainstream deaf students in regular classrooms is the quality of the interpreting services the school district can provide. Stedt makes the point that while many interpreters specialize in educational interpreting, there is at the moment little research, training, or even standards of conduct for this large and growing field of educational specialists. Clearly, if the public school movement is to continue, much less expand further, there is a need for immediate attention to this critical area.

Taking Moores's three trends—changes in the national population, the contemporary national ethos, and theories of deafness and the education of the deaf—and using them as a point of departure, let us project into the future. The American population is currently changing in at least two ways. White or European families are becoming smaller, while at the same time "minority" birth rates are up and more immigrants are coming into the United States. Social values are undergoing steady changes as well. As the more affluent have smaller families and as better educated women delay having children, there is a growing tendency to expect more from each child and to demand more of the social support system for that child. For example, the recent rash of malpractice suits, with the concomitant rise in insurance costs, reflects parents' willingness to blame others for "less than perfect" offspring. Finally, I. King Jordan and "Big Bird" have become the emblems of a new awareness and general acceptance of deafness. Jordan's slogan, "Deaf People Can Do Anything But Hear," and Big Bird's attempts to sign or use an interpreter in order to communicate with Linda, the deaf librarian on *Sesame Street,* reflect a growing demand among the deaf to be recognized as human beings and a growing willingness among the general population to tolerate manual communication as a legitimate form of communication.

Together, these three changes suggest that the local public school education of deaf children is likely to persist into the near future. If history is any measure, the increase in minorities and immigrants will mean greater pressure to educate these children closer to their homes, which coincidentally are urban. This urban concentration of population suggests that "magnet" programs, perhaps modeled on the Philadelphia public schools, may become more rather than less popular. The changes in suburbia will also reinforce the trend toward local public education, because women who have delayed childbirth or have restricted the size of their families tend to want to keep their children at home. Finally, the changing attitudes toward deafness and the capabilities of deaf individuals will support more active involvement by deaf adults in the educational process of deaf children.

This part of the book makes the point that, in discussing the efficacy of public school education for the deaf child, the starting point cannot be the individual child, but must focus on information about the context in which the child is found. The individual deaf child cannot be shoehorned into a public school program as the basis for being shoehorned into society. The existence of the individual deaf child within a family within a community within a nation, each of which can present structural barriers to that child's development as a human being, must be taken into consideration when discussing the future and the value of local public school education.

PART II

The Process and Outcomes of Schooling

CHAPTER 6

Patterns of Communication Among Deaf and Hearing Adolescents

MARTHA GONTER GAUSTAD
THOMAS N. KLUWIN

Children who do not develop early the skills to interact with others will have problems participating in a range of social situations later on (Corsaro, 1981; Hatch, 1987) because the development of peer relationships is dependent on the development of interaction skills during communication among peers (Hatch, 1987). Therefore, social interaction is an important step toward the goal of social integration of deaf children in public school programs. Consequently, an understanding of the process and occurrence of peer interaction is an essential prerequisite to an understanding of the effects of public school programs on the social integration of deaf students.

A MODEL OF PEER INTERACTION

In this chapter we are, for the most part, concerned with peer communication in adolescents; but as Gottman and Mettetal (1986) point out, while there is a distinct stage of adolescent peer interaction, success in one stage hinges on skills developed in previous stages.

Consequently, to adequately discuss peer interaction in secondary school programs, we will require a two-stage model. The first stage of the model is the formation of the necessary skills for social interaction prior to adolescence. The second stage is the formation of adolescent friendships within a school setting during adolescence. Figure 6.1 shows the elements of stage one.

Figure 6.1.   Stage one: Development of social interaction skills

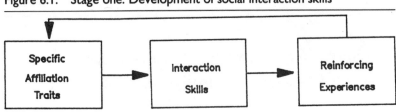

THE DEVELOPMENT OF SOCIAL INTERACTION SKILLS

The child becomes socially competent by first having specific traits that are valued by a peer group, such as popularity (Garnica, 1981; Gottman, Gonso, & Rasmussen, 1975; Kirsh, 1983), mutual interests (Corsaro, 1979, 1981), or shared backgrounds (Epstein, 1983b). Initially, interaction skills appear to be innate, but differences in their execution rapidly appear, with the final part of the sequence being the reinforcement of the interaction skills by specific experiences.

Affiliation Traits

Social ranking occurs quite early and is a basis for forming friendships (Garnica, 1981). Less popular children do not engage other children as often as more popular children do, and when conversation occurs, the number of topics is more limited (Garnica, 1981; Kirsh, 1983; Putallaz & Gottman, 1981). Other bases for affiliation, including gender (Kirsh, 1983), social background (Epstein, 1983b; Gottman, Gonso, & Rasmussen, 1975), and mutual interests (Cosaro, 1979, 1981), have also been described. Adolescents in particular associate or disassociate on the basis of race, neighborhood, physical appearance, dress, musical preference, value orientation, common social experiences, and degree of general social alienation (Hansell & Karweit, 1983; Ingersoll, 1989; Sebald, 1989; Tedesco & Gaier, 1988; Wilks, 1986). Farrugia and Austin (1980), in their study of the social integration of deaf students in public schools, make the point that "perceived similarity" is a factor in making friendships.

Interaction Skills

To establish a relationship in a peer group interaction, the entering child must behave in a way that is consistent with the peer group's frame of reference for that particular activity, and the child must be agreeable in his or her interaction style (Hatch, 1987; Putallaz & Heflin, 1986). The second requirement for peer group entry is that the child must be able to determine what the group norms are and speak about things that are relevant to those norms (Hatch, 1987; Putallaz & Heflin, 1986). To accomplish these ends, the child needs several interaction skills, including communication clarity and connectedness, information exchange, conflict resolution skills, and knowledge of appropriate play activities (Parker, 1986).

Knowledge of the necessary skills for interaction varies among children. Corsaro (1979) gives some substance to this observation by reporting that even among kindergarten children, there are as many as 15 different "access rituals" that can be employed to begin an interaction. Gottman, Gonso, and Rasmussen (1975) found that popular and unpopular children differed in their knowledge of how to make friends and in their communication styles. Putallaz and Gottman (1981) replicated the usual popularity results about frequency and quality of interaction, but they also reported that a difference between children considered popular by their peers and children considered unpopular was the ability to enter into an interaction. The less popular students were usually more negative and less skilled in their approaches to entering an activity. Specifically, less popular students would call attention to themselves, state their own feelings, ask informational questions, and focus on expressions of needs or hints to elicit desired results (Parker, 1986).

Reinforcing Experiences

Because popular children will be reinforced for participation in interactions while unpopular children will not (Garnica, 1981; Kirsh, 1983; Putallaz & Gottman, 1981), one component of a model to understand an individual's ability to socially interact as an adolescent must be a feedback loop from the experience the child had during peer interaction back to the child's interaction skills. Several studies have reported the reinforcing properties of success. Gottman, Gonso, and Rasmussen (1975) reported that popular children in the classroom distributed and received more positive reinforcement than unpopular children. Kirsh (1983), in a study of preschoolers, reported that directives were used differently by popular and unpopular children. The best-liked children spoke most and were spoken to most often; the least liked children spoke or heard the lowest amount of speech. Differences in the content of the conversations between children who are accepted into a peer group and those who are not have been noted repeatedly for younger children (Parker, 1986). For the child who is successful, the repertoire of interaction skills will expand; but the child who is unsuccessful may not receive feedback appropriate for future interactions.

The cumulative effect of the younger child's verbal experiences in social settings is to reinforce either positive and appropriate verbal routines for peer communication or to develop a set of verbal routines that serve to isolate the child further or categorize the child within a less socially desirable subtype. On entering high school, the adolescent, whether hearing or deaf, has a history of experience and verbal skill that will either promote peer communication or further limit it.

THE ADOLESCENT COMMUNICATION EXPERIENCE

The second stage of our model of adolescent peer interaction involves defining a ground on which the students are able to interact (Karweit & Hansell, 1983). This is accomplished through a definition of school characteristics and adolescent characteristics, including those described above. As can be seen in Figure 6.2, the fundamental structure of the model is a triangle defined by school activity structures, adolescent trait visibility, and adolescent value systems. These three points delineate the ground on which peer interaction takes place.

School Activity Structures

School activity structures is a generic concept that includes all the things that schools do to create opportunities for peers to interact, including task structures within the classroom (Bossert, 1979), the use of curricular tracking (Karweit & Hansell, 1983), and the timing of the decision to mainstream a student (Moores, Kluwin, & Mertens, 1985).

Hansell and Karweit (1983) reported in a study of 20 high

Figure 6.2. Stage two: Adolescent friendship formation

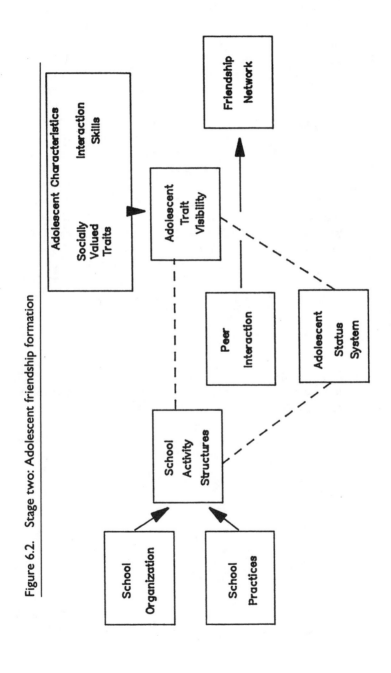

schools, 20,347 students, and 1,029 teachers, that students in college curricular tracks had more extensive friendship networks than students in noncollege tracks. The size of friendship networks was influenced more by student socioeconomic status, intellectual abilities, and extracurricular participation than by tracking, but curricular tracking still influenced students' friendship networks.

Epstein (1983) reported, in a longitudinal study of 4,163 students who entered a new school in grades 5, 6, 8, and 11, that in schools that encourage frequent student contact, more students are selected as friends and fewer are neglected by their peers; more peer friendships are reciprocated; and the circle of friends chosen is drawn from a wider pool. Epstein (l983a) identified four general environmental conditions that were found to encourage student contact: the physical arrangement of the school, instructional activities that are conducive to regrouping of students, teachers who emphasize tolerance and acceptance of others, and the demographic characteristics of the school population. In summary, educational structures, at either the school or classroom level, not only influence students' access to each other but condition the terms on which contact takes place.

Adolescent Trait Visibility

Adolescent trait visibility refers to the degree to which a certain activity highlights the characteristics of the student (Karweit & Hansell, 1983). High visibility activities are things such as sports and academic classes where specific student abilities come to the fore. Low visibility activities take place in the hallways or the lunchroom, where a trait will be less observable.

Adolescent Value Systems

The third point of the triangle that defines the ground on which peer interaction can take place is the adolescent status system (Hansell & Karweit, 1983; Ingersoll, 1989; Sebald, 1989; Williams, 1975, in Garnica, 1981). Parents generally influence topics such as college selection, in which they have some direct control over the choice; but peers set the tone for values concerning clothing, dating, drinking, social events, and club membership (Sebald, 1989).

Peer Interaction in Adolescence

The primary content of adolescent communication is attempts to understand the self in relation to others (Gottman & Mettetal, 1986). The salient verbal processes are gossip, self-disclosure, problem solving, and an abiding concern with honesty (Gottman & Mettetal, 1986). While the main goal of adolescent conversation is understanding the self, the tools for the construction of this process are honesty among friends, the vulnerability of the self-disclosure, the reciprocation of the risk involved in the other's self-exploration, and the ability and willingness to solve problems, usually personal problems or problems cast in terms of the speaker's personality. Adolescents engage in this process of talking about themselves in order to forge an understanding of their own emotions and how these emotions function in relation to other people. Into this phenomenon of language during adolescent interactions as a journey of self-discovery, we must now fit the deaf adolescent in the public school.

THE DEAF STUDENT WITHIN THE PARAMETERS OF THE MODEL

Libbey and Pronovost (1980) reported that the majority of the deaf students in public school programs did not frequently start conversations with hearing people, ask questions in class, or voluntarily answer questions. More than one-quarter of the students listed making friends and communicating with hearing people as their biggest problem in school, but most felt that hearing people did want to communicate with deaf people. Raimondo and Maxwell (1987), in a small study, reported that in large group situations in mainstream classes, hearing impaired students were not seen to communicate with each other at all. Antia (1982), in a limited study of younger students, reported that peer interaction was virtually nonexistent between deaf and hearing students.

Given a repeated picture of minimal to nonexistent peer interaction between deaf and hearing adolescents (Saur, Popp-Stone, & Hurley-Lawrence, 1987), we need to modify our model to account for the general failure of deaf students in public school programs to establish close relationships with their hearing peers (Antia, 1982; Farrugia & Austin, 1980; Libbey & Pronovost, 1980; Saur, Popp-Stone, & Hurley-Lawrence, 1987).

School Activity Structures

This construct must be redefined when discussing peer interaction for deaf students in a public school system. The pertinent issues in this context appear to be the timing and degree of integration, the opportunity for contact, and the child's access to extracurricular activities.

Timing can be expressed either as the age of the child being integrated or the time of the school year. Regarding the age of the child, it appears that older deaf children are more likely to be integrated than younger deaf children (Wolk, Karchmer, & Schildroth, 1982), which may be a negative factor because interaction skills are developed and reinforced at an early age. Concerning timing, educational practices such as the placement of deaf students in mainstream classes after the assignment of hearing students (Moores, Kluwin, & Mertens, 1985) also have a negative impact on peer interaction since they tend to stigmatize the deaf child as not being a "real part" of the school program.

Degree of contact between deaf and hearing students is highly variable within public school programs (Allen & Osborn, 1984; Moores, Kluwin, & Mertens, 1985; Wolk, Karchmer, & Schildroth, 1982). It appears that there are intact groups of deaf children who experience mainstreaming only in unsupported, nonacademic settings or not at all (Moores, Kluwin, & Mertens, 1985; Wolk, Karchmer, & Schildroth, 1984). At the other extreme, there are numbers of deaf children who have no deaf peers within the school building (Schildroth, 1988). From the literature we reviewed earlier, it would appear that formal and supportive school activity structures are required for promoting peer interaction of a positive nature. However, it is apparent from the available literature that deaf children in public schools can and do experience a number of structural barriers to successful interaction, including the degree and quality of their access to hearing peers.

Stewart and Stinson (Chapter 7) address the importance of as well as the problems faced in promoting extracurricular involvement for deaf students.

Adolescent Trait Visibility

The most obvious trait of the deaf student during peer interaction within the context of the public high school may not be the deaf child's hearing loss. Stewart and Stinson (Chapter 7) report

on instances where deaf students with outstanding personal characteristics, such as exceptional athletic ability, are able to overcome the communication barrier imposed between them and their
hearing peers and develop friendships. However, there is a strong
indication that for the average deaf student, social participation is
generally a function of the student's mode of communication.

For example, Libbey and Pronovost (1980) reported that with
hearing friends, deaf students in public schools primarily used
hearing and lipreading. With deaf friends, they less frequently
used their hearing aid or lipread. The situation was reversed in
regard to questions about sign language use. The primary mode of
communication with deaf friends was signing and fingerspelling
by both participants. Signing was used less than one-sixth of the
time by either deaf or hearing friends with each other. In about
one-quarter of the instances, writing notes back and forth was a
mode of communication between deaf and hearing students.
Speech was the nearly universal mode used by deaf students with
hearing friends, but was used only three-fourths of the time with
deaf friends.

Raimondo and Maxwell (1987) intensively studied 20 deaf students interacting with both hearing and deaf peers. They reported
that speech was the primary mode of communication used by both
participants; pantomime and gesture were the only other forms of
communication used with any frequency. In group settings the use
of speech was even more pronounced. With hearing impaired
peers, one-third of the time both participants used speech; one-
quarter of the time both participants used signs. In large group
situations in mainstream classes, the hearing impaired students
were not seen to communicate with each other at all. A limitation
of the Raimondo and Maxwell (1987) study is that their operational definitions of "pantomime/gestures" includes what many
would accept as "signing" behavior (Klima & Bellugi, 1979), thus
raising a question about the degree of signing that might actually
have occurred.

What is clear from both studies is the heavy emphasis placed
on deaf students' speech and speech reading ability. Consequently,
deaf students who are not comfortable with those modes of communication are at a serious disadvantage if other systems or
modes of communication are not available to both deaf and hearing students.

Additional adolescent traits that might influence peer interaction include gender, race, and common background. While Far-

rugia and Austin (1980) have mentioned common interest as the basis for peer interaction, and Stewart and Stinson (Chapter 7) have detailed one instance of a shared interest, little attention has been devoted to this critical factor in the study of interaction between deaf and hearing peers. Some research has shown that gender and race differences are factors in the degree of mainstreaming a deaf child experiences (Moores & Kluwin, 1987; Wolk, Karchmer, & Schildroth, 1982), but such differences have yet to be linked to peer interaction patterns between deaf and hearing students.

Any number of studies (Allen & Osborn, 1984; Kluwin & Moores, 1985, 1989; Wolk, Karchmer, & Schildroth, 1984) have shown that a deaf child's degree of contact with hearing students is a function of his or her academic ability. Generally, only the most academically able deaf students have regular contact with hearing students. Such a practice should, in theory, increase the chances of interaction on the basis of similar abilities, but it appears to be overwhelmed by the difficulties of communication.

Adolescent Value Systems

Among hearing children, awareness of deafness as a handicap starts at an early age; but there is a general ignorance of the implications of communicating with deaf peers (Budoff & Conant, 1981). Studies of hearing children's attitudes toward the deaf have been mixed, ranging from the positive (Kennedy & Bruiniks, 1974; Murphy, 1979) to the negative (Blood & Blood, 1983; Dengerik & Porter, 1984). However, simple categorizations of positive or negative attitudes may not reflect the nature of hearing adolescents' value systems. Sebald (1989) has demonstrated changes in these value systems over decades and by source (peers or parents). It is probably not possible to typify the position of the deaf adolescent in a peer status system without investigating simultaneously some of the other factors mentioned before, particularly the impact of school activities on providing information on deafness.

If we overlay what we know about the situation of the deaf student in the public high school with what we know about adolescent interaction in general, a picture of complex proportions begins to form. By focusing on all the negative components of the modified model, we would almost expect no interaction to take place between deaf and hearing peers, an observation supported by the available research (Antia, 1982; Farrugia & Austin, 1980; Libbey & Pronovost, 1980, Saur, Popp-Stone, & Hurley-Lawrence,

1987). If we adopt a "pollyanna-esque" stance toward the information we have compiled, we could paint a picture consisting of numerous individual instances of friendship formation. The consideration of an available data set may add some balance to this shifting vision.

PEER COMMUNICATION IN TWELVE AMERICAN HIGH SCHOOLS

The authors collected data on 260 deaf adolescents in 12 public school programs across the United States. Instrumentation included basic demographic information, a questionnaire on the placement history of the children prior to high school, the collection of annual reports of the students' grades and type of educational placement, information on school level indices of socioeconomic background, and a questionnaire designed to assess communication patterns and skills. The questionnaire on deaf students' communication patterns examined the students' communication with various interlocutors using different modes of communication—speech, sign, fingerspelling, writing, and gesture. Identified interlocutors were family members and school personnel, including both students (hearing and deaf) and teachers. A second section of the questionnaire asked the students to rate their skill levels for speech (receptive and expressive) signing, reading, and writing.

Results

In response to an integrated social setting, a deaf or hard of hearing student has four options. First, the student can avoid or reject any contact with hearing peers and choose to interact only with deaf peers. As an alternative, the student can choose to interact with both sets of peers but to use only a single mode of communication with both groups, that is, the student either speaks to hearing as well as deaf or hard of hearing peers, or signs to both. Finally, the student can select the mode of communication most appropriate to the characteristics of his or her interlocutor. In general, this would mean a preference for the use of speech with hearing peers and the use of manual communication with deaf peers. Figure 6.3 presents the distribution of these four types of peer interaction situations within our sample of 260 students.

It was not possible to categorize 6.5% of the students due to

Figure 6.3.   Distribution of communication modes within the total sample

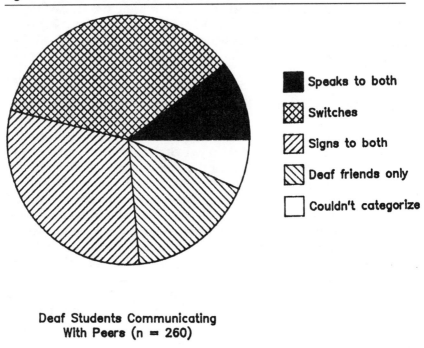

Speaks to both

Switches

Signs to both

Deaf friends only

Couldn't categorize

**Deaf Students Communicating
With Peers (n = 260)**

missing information on the questionnaire. Of the remaining students in this survey, 10.4% reported that they spoke to both deaf and hearing subjects; 35.8% reported that they changed modes or switched for their interlocutor; 30.4% reported that they signed to both deaf and hearing peers in school; and 16.9% stated that they had only deaf friends to whom they signed.

Possible School Structure Effects

The nature of the data collected in this study, that is, primarily subject level information, and the generally small number of subjects per program (averaging approximately 22) do not readily permit comparisons on a program level. However, as an approximation of possible program level differences that might be reflected in school activity structures and thus in friendship patterns, Figure 6.4 presents the data from Figure 6.3 broken down by program, excluding the 6.5% uncategorizable respondents.

Figure 6.4 was organized to reflect an apparent trend in the data on the program level. Programs E1, SE2, MW1, and NE1 are apparently unique in their distribution of peer communication types. Programs TX1, MW2, TX2, NE3, and CA2 form a relatively similar group in that fewer than 10% of the students report speech use in all situations, and between 10% and 20% report having only deaf friends. This group could be typified as the "average" programs in that their distributions reflect the general trend of the overall sample. The remaining three programs, NE2, TX3, and CA1 had no students reporting the use of speech only.

Three trends are apparent from the data, which can be tested empirically given the limits of the data.

1. Students served in an administrative unit who are placed singly or in small groups in a number of schools reported more use of speech than other students (see E1).
2. Students attending programs that have the resources to provide active sign language instruction and encourage the use of sign language by hearing students reported greater sign language use (see NE2 and CA2).
3. Students attending programs that tend to separate deaf and hearing students either physically or administratively report more sign language usage and less communication with hearing peers (See TX3 and NE1).

We cannot use program level factors from our data set to analyze peer communication patterns in more detail. However, it appears that when deaf students are scattered among a large number of different locations, spoken English becomes a preferred mode; but if the students are centrally located in a homogeneous group, with an emphasis on sign language use for the hearing students, more use of an audience-appropriate mode seems to occur.

Adolescent Trait and Trait Visibility Effects

Based on the students' own assessments of their language and communication skills on the communication questionnaire and from the demographic data available to us, we defined several individual level variables that might affect deaf students' facility in interacting with hearing peers.

Figure 6.4.   Distribution of communication modes by school program

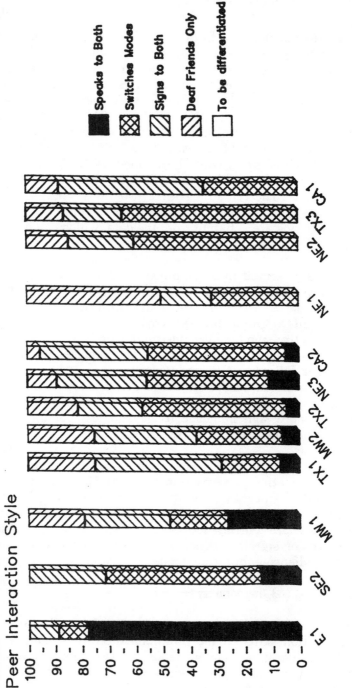

• Degree of hearing loss was defined as moderate or the un-aided, better ear average hearing loss as from 55 db to 69 db, severe or 70 db to 89 db loss, and profound or greater than 90 db loss.

• Speaking skill was defined as skilled or self-rated as good or very good on the questions regarding speech skills, and unskilled or self-rated as low on the questions pertaining to speech production and comprehension.

• Signing skill was defined as not skilled or self-rated as lacking facility in both ASL and manually coded English; English signer or self-rated as skilled in some form of manually coded English (but not ASL); ASL user or self-rated as a skilled user of ASL (but not manual English), skilled at both or self-rated as skilled in both ASL and a manual code of English.

• The students' previous school experience was defined as mainstreamed contact with hearing students or a consistent history of exposure to hearing peers in a school setting; transient or the student moved back and forth between special and main-streamed placements; and consistently in special classes.

• A communication history variable was also derived, which included the student's past experience with communication modes in schools attended from the primary through junior high grades: all oral, which included situations where students moved from cued speech to oral programs; all total communication; movement from oral to total communication programs in junior high school; and mixed history or the student changed communication philosophies more than once.

• Current placement described the students' placement with regard to mainstreaming: self-contained or no scheduled classes with hearing students; nonacademic or some class hours with hearing students but not for academic subjects; and main-streamed or one or more academic classes with hearing students.

A discriminant analysis was computed to determine what differentiated the four peer communication groups described earlier in this chapter. Current placement, placement history, signing ability, speaking ability, sign systems used, consistency of the child's educational history, and degree of the child's hearing loss were used to discriminate among the four groups. Figure 6.5 shows the differentiation of the groups.

Three canonical discriminant functions were required to differentiate among the three groups ($p = .006$). The first canonical

Figure 6.5. Differentiation of communication types through a discriminant analysis

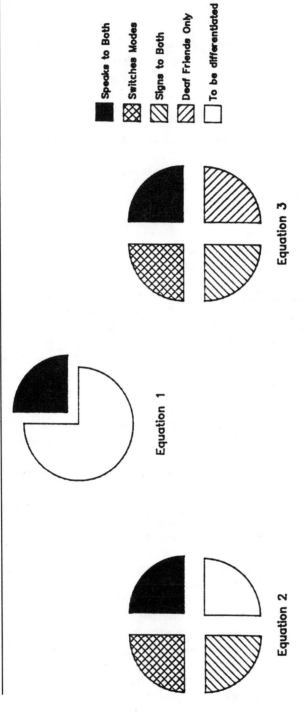

Speaks to Both
Switches Modes
Signs to Both
Deaf Friends Only
To be differentiated

Equation 1
Equation 2
Equation 3

Equation 1: Poor Signer vs. Good Signer
Equation 2: Mainstream vs. Special Class
           and English vs. ASL Signer
Equation 3: Diverse Early Modes

function, which accounted for 74% of the variance, consisted of the rated signing skill and the placement history of the student. Since the correlation was positive and this factor was scored as 0 for unskilled and 1 for skilled, the largest differentiating factor in this analysis was the perception by the student that he or she was a good signer. The second factor was the student's placement history, which was coded so that the lower the score, the more special class time the student had experienced. This factor had a negative correlation, which meant that special class placement was a stronger basis than placement in a mainstream class for differentiating among the groups.

The second canonical function consisted of the student's current placement and signing system. This function accounted for 15% of the variance. Current placement situation was coded in the same direction as the placement history, so the positive correlation for this factor meant that less restrictive current placement contributed to differentiating the groups. The positive correlation for type of signing system used, given the coding of this variable, meant that the use of ASL or of ASL and English as a signing system contributed more to differentiating among the groups.

The third function accounted for only 11% of the variance and consisted of the students' speech skills, consistency in communication training, and degree of hearing loss. For this function, greater perceived speech skill contributed most to differentiating the groups. A variety of communication philosophies and a less severe hearing loss also contributed slightly to differentiating among the groups.

From this analysis, we can observe several things. First, if a deaf student is a good speaker but a poor signer, then he or she is most likely to speak to both hearing and deaf peers. Second, if the deaf student is a good speaker and a good signer, he or she is most likely to tailor communication to the audience by changing modes; this appears to be the result of experiencing a varied communication history. Third, a more exclusively total communication background distinguishes students who choose to sign to both deaf and hearing peers. Fourth, students who communicate only with hearing impaired peers are distinguished from the other groups primarily by current placement in self-contained classes and having experienced several different communication philosophies in their early school years.

A complete analysis would, of course, include better ways of typifying the structural features of programs that contribute to the choice of these different patterns of communication, although such variables as previous communication history and placement history straddle the line between institutional and individual level variables. In addition, a complete analysis should include ways of measuring the hearing students' attitudes toward accepting deaf students into the peer system.

Clearly, greater congruence in mode use between deaf and hearing peers will facilitate communication. However, this study did support a model that includes school activity structures, such as placement and communication philosophy factors, and trait visibility factors, such as perceived communication skills, as influences on the nature of peer interaction between deaf students and their peers in public schools.

RECOMMENDATIONS

Consistent with our earlier discussions, we can make some recommendations that would conform to the general outline of our model.

Adolescent trait visibility can be viewed positively or negatively. In special education, the negative emphasis is most often used, that is, attempts are made to reduce the negative stigma of a handicap by accentuating positive contact. In deaf education, a positive approach is possible using three strategies: earlier integration, mutual skill training, and alternative modes of communication.

Earlier integration means that deaf and hearing children must be exposed to each other sooner than high school. Adolescence—with its preoccupation with self-definition in the face of others (Gottman & Mettetal, 1986)—is not the time to expect children to not only establish relationships but to develop the skills to develop friendships. The middle school or middle elementary years, when many children exhibit a willingness to explore the world (Gottman & Mettetal, 1986; Ingersol, 1989)—and before the onset of shyness in the face of new situations which often characterizes adolescence—would seem to be the best time to begin the process of developing communication skills.

Mutual skill training involves teaching deaf children the skills to interact with hearing children and teaching hearing children how to accommodate the deaf child into the group. First, deafness must be accepted as "normal" by hearing children. From this perspective, we can say that hearing children need to know what deaf children can do. At the same time, deaf children need to become aware of what hearing children expect and are interested in. Second, in order to be integrated into the school culture, a person has to sign or at least fingerspell. Hearing children can be taught to fingerspell as a minimal activity, particularly in the middle grades when they become independent readers and begin to explore the metacognitive skills of literacy through the invention of secret codes and languages. However, a later emphasis on teaching signs to hearing students will be needed to permit the breadth and depth of interaction typical of adolescents.

Alternative modes of communication means that hearing children do not need to be restricted to speaking English; nor do deaf children always have to sign. The recent appearance of large numbers of personal computers in schools makes it possible to provide local area networks as well as wider systems of communication for both deaf and hearing children. Electronic mail can be an opportunity for deaf and hearing children to form friendships. Recent work with written dialogue journals exchanged between deaf and hearing peers showed that for a quarter of the pairs real friendships developed, and for another half of the participants "acquaintanceships" or shared experiences were common (Kluwin & Kelly, 1990).

Altering the adolescent status system is within the range of school influence, particularly through deaf awareness education, establishing ASL as a foreign language option, and providing rewards for contact with deaf students. Gaustad is currently working on one solution by introducing deaf awareness topics to hearing students throughout the general curriculum. The complexity of this particular solution is discussed in Chapter 3.

Some, but not all, hearing students are rewarded by the formal institutional recognition associated with club membership (including listing it on college applications), recognition at awards days, and so on, as well as by the opportunity for structured social contact that such activities provide. Formal groups such as signing choirs or service groups such as peer interpreters are ways to encourage hearing students to interact with deaf students. Higgins (1990) offers several other suggestions for developing a greater degree of interpersonal contact in public school programs for the deaf.

School activity structures can be altered through reverse mainstreaming, interpreter and transportation support for deaf students' participation in extracurricular activities, and less "unsupported" integrated school time for deaf students. Much of this is discussed by Stewart and Stinson in Chapter 7. However, in those periods of the school day when deaf children are around hearing children outside of academic instruction—for example, time on the school bus, lunchroom time, or large group classes such as physical education where an interpreter is not provided—interpreters or signing aides might be provided. This would allow this time to be used for communication games, which would teach alternative ways for the students to communicate with each other.

This chapter has outlined a model and presented some descriptive data that tend to support the model. Out of this, two points need to be stressed. First, some of the factors that influence peer interaction during adolescence are set in place prior to adolescence. Second, there are specific school interventions that can improve the amount of contact between deaf and hearing students. Our suggested list of interventions might easily be improved upon, but nonetheless specific actions by school personnel will be necessary to ensure appropriate peer contact.

REFERENCES

Allen, T., & Osborn, T. (1984). Academic integration of hearing impaired students. *American Annals of the Deaf, 129* (2), 100–113.

Antia, S. D. (1982). Social interaction of partially mainstreamed hearing impaired children. *American Annals of the Deaf, 127* (1), 18–25.

Blood, I. M., & Blood, G. W. (1983). School-age children's reactions to deaf and hearing-impaired children. *Perceptual and Motor Skills, 57,* 373–374.

Bossert, S. T. (1979). *Tasks and social relationships in classrooms: A study of instructional organization and its consequences.* New York: Cambridge University Press.

Budoff, I. M., & Conant, S. (1981). Preschoolers' conception of deafness. *Volta Review, 83* (3), 156–161.

Corsaro, W. A. (1979). "We're friends, right?": Children's use of access rituals in a nursery school. *Language in Society, 8,* 351–363.

Corsaro, W. A. (1981). Entering the child's world: Research strategies for field entry in a preschool setting. In J. L. Green & C. Wallat (Eds.), *Ethnography and language in educational settings* (pp. 213–237). Norwood, NJ: Ablex.

Dengerik, J. E., & Porter, J. B. (1984). Children's attitudes toward peers wearing hearing aids. *Language, Speech, and Hearing Services in Schools, 15* (3), 205–209.

Epstein, J. L. (1983a). The influence of friends on achievement and affective outcomes. In J. L. Epstein & N. Karweit (Eds.), *Friends in school: Patterns of selection and influence in secondary schools* (pp. 177–200). New York: Academic Press.

Epstein, J. L. (1983b). Selection of friends in differently organized schools and classrooms. In J. L. Epstein & N. Karweit (Eds.), *Friends in school: Patterns of selection and influence in secondary schools* (pp. 73–92). New York: Academic Press.

Farrugia, D., & Austin, G. F. (1980). A study of the social-emotional adjustment patterns of hearing impaired students in different educational settings. *American Annals of the Deaf, 25* (5), 535–541.

Garnica, O. K. (1981). Social dominance and conversational interaction: The omega child in the classroom. In J. L. Green & C. Wallat (Eds.), *Ethnography and language in educational settings* (pp. 148–172). Norwood, NJ: Ablex.

Gottman, J., Gonso, J., & Rasmussen, B. (1975). Social interaction, social competence, and friendship in children. *Child Development, 46,* 709–718.

Gottman, J., & Mettetal, G. (1986). Speculations about social and affective development: Friendship and acquaintanceship through adolescence. In J. M. Gottman & J. G. Parker, *Conversations of friends: Speculations on affective development* (pp. 203–227). Cambridge, MA: Cambridge University Press.

Hansell, S., & Karweit, N. (1983). Curricular placement, friendship networks, and status attainment. In J. L. Epstein & N. Karweit (Eds.), *Friends in school: Patterns of selection and influence in secondary schools* (pp. 141–162). New York: Academic Press.

Hatch, J. A. (1987). Peer interaction and the development of social competence. *Child Study Journal, 17* (3), 169–183.

Higgins, P. C. (1990). *The challenge of educating deaf and hearing youth together.* Springfield, IL: Charles C. Thomas.

Ingersoll, G. M. (1989). *Adolescents.* Englewood Cliffs, NJ: Prentice-Hall.

Karweit, N., & Hansell, S. (1983). School organization and friendship selection. In J. L. Epstein & N. Karweit (Eds.), *Friends in school* (pp. 29–38). New York: Academic Press.

Kennedy, P., & Bruiniks, R. (1974). Social status of hearing impaired children in regular classrooms. *Exceptional Children, 40,* 336–342.

Kirsh, B. (1983). The use of directives as indication of status among preschool children. In J. Fine & R. O. Freedle (Eds.), *Developmental issues in discourse* (pp. 269–293). Norwood, NJ: Ablex.

Klima, E. S., & Bellugi, U. (1979). *The signs of language.* Cambridge, MA: Harvard University Press.

Kluwin, T. N., & Kelly, A. B. (1990). *Application of a process oriented writing program for hearing impaired students in public schools* (Final Report). Washington, DC: Gallaudet University. (OSERS Grant #G008730147).

Kluwin, T. & Moores, D. (1985). The effect of integration on the achievement of hearing impaired adolescents. *Exceptional Children 52,* (2), 153–160.

Kluwin, T. & Moores, D. (1989). Mathematics achievement of hearing impaired adolescents in different placements. *Exceptional Children. 55*, (4), 327–335.

Libbey, S. S., & Pronovost, W. (1980). Communication practices of main-streamed hearing-impaired adolescents. *Volta Review, 82* (4), 197–220.

Moores, D. & Kluwin, T. (1987). Issues in school placement. In A. Schildroth & M. Karchmer (Eds.), *Deaf Children in America* (pp. 105–124). San Diego: College-Hill Press.

Moores, D., Kluwin, T., & Mertens, D. (1985). *High school programs for deaf students in metropolitan areas.* (Monograph No. 3). Washington, DC: Gallaudet University, Gallaudet Research Institute.

Murphy, H. J. (1979). Psycho-social aspects of integration at California State University, Northridge. *Volta review, 81* (1), 50–53.

Parker, J. G. (1986). Becoming friends: Conversational skills for friendship formation in young children. In J. M. Gottman & J. G. Parker, *Conversations of friends: Speculations on affective development* (pp. 137–162). Cambridge, MA: Cambridge University Press.

Putallaz, M., & Gottman, J. M. (1981). An interactional model of children's entry into peer groups. *Child Development, 55* (2), 986–994.

Putallaz, M., & Heflin, A. H. (1986). Toward a model of peer acceptance. In J. M. Gottman & J. G. Parker, *Conversations of friends: Speculations on affective development* (pp. 205–234). Cambridge, MA: Cambridge University Press.

Raimondo, D., & Maxwell, M. (1987). The modes of communication used in junior and senior high school classrooms by hearing-impaired students and their teachers and peers. *Volta Review, 89* (6), 263–275.

Saur, R., Popp-Stone, M., & Hurley-Lawrence, E. (1987). The classroom participation of mainstreamed hearing-impaired college students. *Volta Review, 89* (6), 277–287.

Schildroth, A. (1988). Recent changes in the educational placement of deaf students. *American Annals of the Deaf, 133* (2), 61–67.

Sebald, H. (1989). Adolescents' peer orientation: Changes in the support system during the past three decades. *Adolescence, 24* (6), 937–946.

Tedesco, L. A., & Gaier, E. L. (1988). Friendship bonds in adolescence. *Adolescence, 23* (1), 127–136.

Wilks, J. (1986). The relative importance of parents and friends in adolescent decision making. *Journal of Youth and Adolescence, 15*, 323–334.

Wolk, S., Karchmer, M., & Schildroth, A. (1982). *Patterns of academic and non-academic integration among hearing impaired students in special education.* (Series R, No. 9), Washington, DC: Gallaudet University, Gallaudet Research Institute.

CHAPTER 7

The Role of Sport and Extracurricular Activities in Shaping Socialization Patterns

DAVID A. STEWART
MICHAEL S. STINSON

As schools strive to implement the spirit of the Education for All Handicapped Children Act (PL 94–142), academics and support services have been the primary if not the sole focus. This has made language development, selection of communication modes, and other classroom-oriented instructional activities the dominant themes in discussions of the educational performance of deaf students. Programs in public schools include integration with hearing peers as one of their primary aims in the education of deaf students, and efforts to achieve this aim are usually guided by in-class behavioral objectives.

Yet, concern for the education of deaf children must go beyond the confines of the classroom and academics. Within the larger sphere of educating an individual to be a productive adult, sport and extracurricular activities can make a valuable contribution toward the overall development of the deaf child. While Public Law 94–142, does not deal specifically with after-school activities, its emphasis on physical education is indicative of the potential significance of possessing skills that will help individuals get more out of recreation and sports throughout their lifespan. The Act states that physical education includes the development of "skills in aquatics, dance, and individual and group games and sports (including intramural and lifetime sports)" (Federal Register, August 23, 1977, p. 42480).

Extracurricular activities can also influence socialization skills because they involve interaction with other students. Relevant questions relating to these effects include the following:

1. Does participation in extracurriculars affect student-teacher and student-student relationships?
2. Does involvement with classmates in extracurriculars lead to greater self-esteem?
3. Do extracurriculars foster a support system for deaf students that goes beyond the playing field?

At present, there is no empirical evidence to provide answers to any of these questions. However, we can draw from our knowledge of socialization processes and of how deafness and communication skills affect interactions between a deaf person and others, to build a framework for discussing these and other questions relating to involvement in extracurriculars.

The purpose of this chapter is to examine the role of sports and other extracurricular activities in shaping the socialization patterns of deaf and hard of hearing students in public schools and to suggest how schools might support this process. There will be a review of relevant literature on socialization and deafness and an examination of the relationship between involvement in activities and socialization patterns. This will lead to a presentation of a model depicting the dynamics of involvement in extracurriculars. Based on this model, actions that schools can take to encourage involvement will be discussed. Initially, a brief discussion of the roles that sports and extracurricular activities have had during different historical periods is given. Formal physical education as a subject in the school curriculum is included in this discussion because it has often served as a means of introducing youngsters to sports and in stimulating their interest in extracurricular activities.

A BRIEF HISTORY OF PHYSICAL EDUCATION, SPORTS, AND EXTRACURRICULARS

Throughout ancient and modern history, physical activity in games and sports has often been associated with the interests and values of a state or nation. The Sumerian and Assyrian civilizations (3000–600 B.C.) favored games and sports that prepared individuals for military activities (Howell & Howell, 1979). In ancient Greece, excellence was highly valued, and performance in athletics demonstrated this quality. The Greeks expanded on the benefits of sports by also perceiving sports and athletics as a means of promoting social order. The Greeks reasoned that for athletes and spectators, sports provided a way to vent hostility and form new social networks. A case in point is given by Solon, a lawgiver in sixth-century B.C. Greece, who regarded athletics as a means of bringing harmony to the city of Athens (Thompson, 1988).

More recently, in the United States, members of Turnverein Societies were responsible for convincing legislators to mandate physical education as a part of the school curriculum during the nineteenth century. Turverein societies were responsible for introducing German gymnastics into the United States. By the time of the Civil War, there were 150 societies and 10,000 Turners throughout the country (Bucher & Wuest, 1987). Consequently, *Turnen*, a German system of exercising that emphasized gymnastics, became an integral part of many American public school curricula, peaking in popularity during the latter part of the nineteenth century. These early efforts to teach gymnastics in American schools gave way to a broader perspective of physical education during the first quarter of the twentieth century.

In addition to physical education classes, students were also being exposed to sports during after-school hours. In Chicago, for example, the beginnings of after-school sports in public schools can be traced to the end of the nineteenth century when extracurriculars consisted of activities initiated and managed by students (Gutowski, 1988). Indeed, it has been noted that the first clubs, teams, and interscholastic leagues at the high school level were all created by students (Powell, Farrar, & Cohen, 1985). During these early years, a major reason extracurriculars were initiated was because the appeal of fraternities and sororities as a status symbol had been eroded by school administrators who feared they were losing control of their student body (Gutowski, 1988). As fraternities and sororities were driven underground and as it became increasingly more difficult to form and maintain a secret society, students turned to legitimate extracurricular activities as a way to mimic the activities of colleges and to gain special status within a school.

Although sports have always been identified as the most prominent extracurricular activity, there were other activities that appealed to the interests of students. During the latter part of the nineteenth century, these activities included school newspaper clubs, bands, debating societies, literary societies, biology clubs, and glee clubs (Gutowski, 1988). At that time, extracurriculars were endorsed by the faculty and administration because they countered the secrecy and power of fraternities and sororities.

During the beginning of the twentieth century, faculty began taking control of extracurriculars, in part because they could then assist in the administrative responsibilities. Without faculty support, students were victims of untrained coaches who were often students themselves, broken game schedules, unruliness among players, and other factors that worked against participation in extracurriculars (Gutowski, 1988). The assumption of power by the faculty established adult control of student affairs and hence of school activities. Because the very nature of extracurricular activities encourages social interactions among students, the assumption of control of these activities allowed adults to influence socialization processes.

Today, although the purpose of physical education and extracurriculars in schools remains, the availability of each may be changing. For example, the priority of physical education within a school's overall education plan has deteriorated in many schools, while the magnitude of interscholastic sports has increased (Zeigler, 1979). Interestingly, sports were initially introduced to schools through physical education. It is in physical education that many students are first exposed to the fun and skills involved in playing various sports. Hence, the decline of the role of physical education in the school curriculum has decreased the number of students who are exposed to the benefits of exercise and sports.

With respect to the education of deaf children, the origin of physical education and extracurricular activities has not been well documented, although the work of Gannon (1981) provides some insights. For example, it is known that the Ohio School for the Deaf became the first school for the deaf to play organized baseball during the 1870s and several of its graduates went on to play professional baseball. In 1881, Gallaudet College added a gymnasium and the first indoor swimming pool in the eastern United States. At this time, physical education became a compulsory college requirement. Perhaps following Gallaudet College's example, schools for the deaf "soon began adding physical education to their programs and opening gymnasiums in attics, empty shop rooms, and wherever they could find space" (Gannon, 1981, p. 70).

Extracurricular activities were especially important in residential schools for deaf students. Students had much to gain from an after-school support system for sport, recreation, and other activities, including the fact that these activities helped keep students busy while on campus. In addition, they gave special status to participating students, and they equipped students with sport and recreation skills that they might find useful as adults. Initially, schools for the deaf competed mainly with local and state public schools, and a number of them enjoyed much success. For example, the Arkansas School for the Deaf won 13 consecutive state wrestling championships from 1929 to 1941 (Gannon, 1981). Eventually, as transportation improved, schools for the deaf were able to compete with one another for regional championships.

More recently, we have witnessed a major movement to integrate deaf students in public schools. Over the past 20 years, this movement has resulted in students traveling long distances to school and thus being prevented from remaining for an after-school activity. Nevertheless, the effects of integrating deaf students in public schools have already been revealed in the characteristics of deaf athletes competing in international games. When Canada first started sending a Deaf team to the World Games for the Deaf in 1965, before the push for integration had taken hold, 91% of its athletes were students or graduates of schools for the deaf. At the 1989 World Games for the Deaf, 54.5% of the Canadian Deaf Team were associated with a school for the deaf (Stewart, Robinson, & McCarthy, 1991). Declining enrollment at schools for the deaf and increasing numbers of students in public schools have contributed to the changing demography of the Canadian Deaf Team as well as Deaf sport clubs all over North America (Stewart, 1991).

Although brief, the foregoing historical perspective illustrates that sports, physical education, and extracurriculars have had a long association with schools. Indeed, it might be argued that the importance of physical fitness and an increasingly leisure-oriented society dictate that schools prepare students for a lifetime of involvement in activities that accentuate fitness, sport, recreation, or leisure activities.

FACTORS ASSOCIATED WITH PARTICIPATION IN EXTRACURRICULAR ACTIVITIES

Karweit (1983) identified three main benefits of extracurricular activities that sets them apart from conventional education. These benefits are voluntary participation, the fact that such activities "make a wider range of student aptitudes, skills, and interests visible" than are visible in academic classrooms, and that extracurriculars can lead to an increase in status among other students (Karweit, 1983, p. 131). But can we expect deaf and hard of hearing students to share in these benefits? The first step in addressing this question is to examine some of the factors affecting the socialization patterns of these students.

In a study of 84 deaf and hard of hearing students, Stinson and Whitmire (1990a, 1990b) discovered a number of factors that appear to influence socialization patterns and that have implications for involvement in extracurricular activities. The students studied used oral or signing modes of communication and were enrolled in either a secondary or postsecondary school program in England. They were queried on the number of different kinds of activities they had engaged in during the past year and their communication preferences. Other data collected included students' perceived social competence, hearing and deaf composition of activity groups, and amount of integration in school. The activities that students indicated were then categorized as being structured or unstructured, and in-school (e.g., school-sponsored extracurricular activities) or out-of-school activities (e.g., drama club, church group).

Briefly, Stinson and Whitmire's analysis of the above data identified five critical factors relating to socialization patterns of deaf and hard of hearing students. These factors are participation in structured social activities, hearing status of other participants in structured social activities, communication preference, characteristics of the education program, and self-perceived social competence. A review of each of these factors provides insights into how extracurricular activities might be planned so as to account for the socialization needs of each deaf or hard of hearing student.

Participation in Structured Social Activities

Deaf or hard of hearing students who are involved in *structured* social activities out of school also tend to participate in *unstructured* activities in and out of school (Stinson & Whitmire, 1990a, 1990b). For example, adolescents who reported being members of community-based drama groups or sport clubs (structured) were also likely to report relatively frequent participation in social activities such as visiting friends at their homes or dating (unstructured). This finding was significant for social activities involving deaf, hard of hearing, and hearing peers. On the other hand, involvement in structured activities in school was not significantly related to participation in unstructured activities. This lack of relationship is surprising and may reflect a small emphasis on extracurricular activities in most secondary schools in England.

It appears that involvement in structured activities out of school results in positive social experiences. Students with this kind of experience were more likely to be involved in informal social relationships with their peers. Therefore, structured social activities may be a means by which deaf, hard of hearing, and hearing students develop closer relationships.

Hearing Status of Other Participants in Structured Activities

Participants in structured activities in which a deaf or hard of hearing student engages may be all hearing, such as when a single deaf student joins an all-hearing baseball team; all deaf, such as when the student attends a club for deaf people; or integrated. Positive social experiences for a deaf or hard of hearing individual with any of these groups will likely lead to further socialization between the individual and the group. In Stinson and Whitmire's (1990a, 1990b) study students who were most involved in structured activities out of school showed a strong tendency to participate in unstructured social activities with hearing peers in and out of school. Likewise, participation in structured social activities open to both deaf and hearing peers was associated with development of ongoing relationships with both peer groups, as measured by participation in unstructured social activities.

Communication Preference

One of the strongest identifying characteristics of the deaf community is the use of sign language. It is only natural that people will seek to socialize with those with whom they can readily communicate. Deaf students who rely on signing will be attracted to activities involving other deaf signers (Stewart, 1991). In addition, research by Gaustad and Kluwin (1990) has shown that deaf and hard of hearing students who perceived themselves as proficient in speech tended to use it readily in interaction with hearing schoolmates. Hence, perceived competence in communication, in whatever modality, may be a critical factor in determining involvement in extracurriculars. Support for this proposition is found in a report by Mertens (1989), which revealed that students who had negative social experiences in hearing schools indicated that communication considerations hindered their attempts to participate in extracurricular activities.

Further support is found in the study by Stinson and Whitmire (1990a, 1990b), who assessed communication preference by asking students what method of communication they preferred to use most often with deaf friends: speech and lipreading, speech with sign support (i.e., speech and sign together), or sign language. Students who preferred sign language frequently reported that they went to a Deaf club, whereas those using speech and lipreading tended not to visit one. Furthermore, students who preferred sign language tended to use an interpreter to facilitate participation in after-school activities, whereas students who used oral communication did not (Stinson & Whitmire, 1990b).

Students' communication preference was related to their friendship patterns as well. Students who preferred sign language frequently participated in unstructured social activities with deaf, as opposed to hearing, peers and reported having many deaf friends out of school. However, communication preference was not related to having deaf friends in school. Given that all the students in the study attended regular schools and were mainstreamed all or part of the time, this result indicates the importance of out-of-school friendships with deaf peers for students who prefer signing. Hence, deaf community-related activities might serve as a "bridge" or "connector" that helps those deaf students who use sign language to meet others like themselves and to develop friendships. For such mainstreamed students, these organizations play an important role in promoting friendship and social development.

Characteristics of the Education Program

For regular secondary schools in England, three program characteristics were associated with participation in structured activities: the extent to which the child was integrated with hearing peers, the availability of an interpreter for extracurricular activities, and the opportunity for the student to stay after school. The degree of integration with hearing peers was found to be positively correlated with participation in structured activities in school (Stinson & Whitmire, 1990b). There are two explanations for this finding. First, students who spend most of their time in special classes might not have the oral skills necessary for effective participation with hearing peers. Also, special classes are not available at every school; therefore, some students may be transported a considerable distance to their classes, which restricts their opportunity to participate in extracurricular activities.

However, participation in extracurricular activities at school was positively correlated with provision of an interpreter; that is, degree of integration was no longer a significant factor influencing participation when interpreters were available. Signing interpreters facilitated participation in extracurriculars by making communication with hearing peers, coaches, and sponsors more accessible. It was also found that the option of staying after school was associated with students' engaging in unstructured social activities with hearing peers and having many hearing friends at school.

Self-Perceived Social Competence

Involvement in structured, organized activities can provide a basis for self-appraisals that one is socially competent. As used here, perceived social competence refers to the extent to which people evaluate their social selves favorably (Asher, Parkhurst, Hymel, & Williams, 1990; Stinson & Whitmire, Chapter 8). Students with high perceived social competence tended to report enjoying comfortable relationships with their peers and engaging in a relatively large number of social activities with them. This was the case, for example, with deaf and hard of hearing students who perceived themselves as being socially competent. These students reported participating actively in both in-school and out-of-school unstructured social activities (Stinson & Whitmire, Chapter 8). In this study of deaf students in English schools, relatively frequent participation in structured activities was associated with high perceived social competence (Stinson & Whitmire, 1990a).

Based on the work of Stinson and Whitmire, there appear to be several factors associated with social interactions and participation in extracurricular activities among deaf and hard of hearing students. Exposure to structured activities outside of school may be one way of stimulating more social interactions in school during structured or unstructured activities. An environment conducive to effective communication, defined by students' ability to communicate with others directly or indirectly through the use of an interpreter, must be available. Students must be provided with an option for remaining after school in order to participate in extracurriculars. Efforts should be made to ensure that the social interactions of deaf and hard of hearing students are successful. Finally, success in social interactions should lead to students perceiving themselves as being socially competent, which could mean more involvement in social activities.

RATIONALE FOR EXTRACURRICULAR INVOLVEMENT

The work of Stinson and Whitmire shows various relationships between involvement in activities and socialization patterns. There is other corroborating evidence to suggest that extracurricular activities, and sports in particular, influence the social development of school age students. An overview of the literature by Sage (1986) reveals that social interaction with peers serves to introduce individuals into sports; spontaneous play and informal games are crucial in the social development of young children; physical fitness contributes toward positive self-concepts; participation in high school sports heightens educational goals; and cooperation in physical activities and games leads to more cooperative social behavior in general. In addition, studies with hearing children have shown a positive relationship between participation in extracurricular activities, such as high school sports, and students' self-esteem (Holland & Andre, 1987). Holland and Andre (1987) suggest that students receive publicity and recognition for their participation, especially in sports, which boosts self-esteem. They also note that favorable relationships with peers during extracurricular activities may enhance perceived social competence.

Extracurricular activities may shape socialization patterns of deaf students by emphasizing the development of skills and personal attributes that are common to all students participating in these activities. This benefit was suggested in the work of Griffin (1988). Some of the skills and attributes that might be developed are:

1. Physical fitness,
2. Athletic skills,
3. Effective cooperation skills,
4. Greater self-esteem,
5. Positive self-concept,
6. Leadership skills,

7. Personal recognition for those who do not find it in the classroom,
8. Ability to use leisure time,
9. Improved student and teacher relationships, and
10. Tolerance for differences in others.

Stewart, McCarthy, and Robinson (1988) investigated various socialization aspects of sports among deaf individuals. They found that deaf teachers, coaches, and friends were the primary social forces that introduced deaf sports directors to sports during their school years. However, many of these sports directors had attended a school for the deaf. A later study that included a larger sampling of deaf students who had attended a hearing school showed that hearing coaches played a key role in socializing them into sports activities, followed by deaf friends and deaf sports directors (Stewart, Robinson, & McCarthy, 1991).

The social benefits of extracurricular activities other than sports have received scant attention. However, there are indications that participation in extracurriculars is beneficial to students. For example, Griffin (1988) surveyed teachers at an elementary and a junior high school to determine learning outcomes of student activities. Cooperation was rated the highest outcome. Other identified learning outcomes were:

1. The development of self-esteem,
2. Leadership skills,
3. Greater recognition for work accomplished during extracurricular activities than in the classroom,
4. Ability to better use leisure time, and
5. Healthier student and teacher relationships.

In addition to these findings, the stress of sociocultural and linguistic demands on the socialization patterns of deaf individuals calls for a reconceptualization of the role of extracurriculars in the education of deaf students. For example, studies have documented various perceptions of social experiences of deaf students in different educational settings. Dale (1984) found that elementary school age deaf students integrated in a hearing class exhibited faster rates of social maturation than deaf students in a self-contained classroom. The students in the integrated setting benefited from a concerted effort on the part of parents, teachers, and other support persons to promote interactions with hearing peers. Farrugia and

Austin (1980) explored the social-emotional patterns of deaf students in residential schools and self-contained classes. Students from the residential schools demonstrated a higher level of self-concept.

Mertens (1989) investigated factors contributing to positive and negative social experiences. Based on the responses of 49 students attending Gallaudet University, students who had attended a residential school described more positive social experiences than those who had been educated in a hearing school. Factors contributing to the positive experiences of residential students included teachers' ability to sign, opportunities to interact with deaf friends, and opportunities to participate in extracurricular activities. Extracurricular involvement was also noted among those who indicated having positive social experiences in their interactions in hearing schools.

Caution is needed when interpreting these results and those of other social-emotional studies of school age students. As Mertens (1989) stated, "Research to date has not answered the question concerning the effect of a sheltered environment on self-concept and social maturity when the student leaves the residential setting" (p. 18). Indeed, in the absence of research, it is not unreasonable to suggest that for some deaf students negative social experiences in public schools may, for example, translate into greater determination to succeed during their adult years, a stronger character that is not easily intimidated in the presence of hearing people, or a greater sensitivity to the social inequity prevalent in our society.

In sum, an overall aim of sports and other extracurricular activities is to provide a platform for deaf students to develop a host of skills and personal characteristics that will allow them to capitalize on social, sport, and recreational opportunities found in deaf and hearing communities. Initially, extracurricular activities provide a framework for participation. Once a student becomes involved, socialization will occur through natural channels that are influenced by the social idiosyncrasies of the deaf participant and others. In addition, extracurriculars provide deaf students with opportunities to enjoy themselves, to experience school in a more relaxed environment divorced from the threat of grades (although participation in some activities may require that students maintain at least a minimum grade in all subjects), and to interact with others on a common ground and in some instances in a more equitable fashion.

Figure 7.1. Critical components of involvement in extracurricular activities

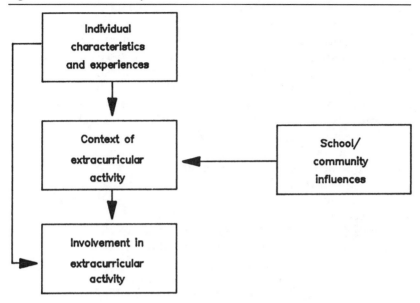

THE DYNAMICS OF INVOLVEMENT IN
EXTRACURRICULAR ACTIVITIES

Based on the foregoing discussion, a model can be presented that illustrates the key components relating to the involvement of deaf and hard of hearing students in extracurricular activities in public schools. Figure 7.1 depicts the major components of this model. The first component revolves around those factors relating to a deaf individual, including demographic and experiential factors. Some relevant demographic factors are degree of hearing loss, communication preference, interest in sport and other extracurricular activities, and self-perceived social competence. Critical experiential factors are involvement in out-of-school structured activities, positive social interactions with different peer groups (i.e., deaf, hard of hearing, and hearing), and past involvement in extracurricular activities.

Prior to becoming involved in extracurricular activities, students weigh their individual characteristics within the context of an extracurricular activity in which they may have an interest. The three major factors of this component are the nature of the activity itself (e.g., is it an activity that the student wishes to participate in?), the hearing status of other participants, and the relationship of the student to other participants. The presence of other deaf or hard of hearing participants may inspire a student to sign up for a particular activity. In addition, participation may be stimulated by the knowledge that one's friends or classmates are involved in an extracurricular activity. For example, although he had no interest in competitive running, Stinson joined his high school track and field team because a friend was on the team.

The context of an extracurricular activity is influenced by two external agents. First, there are school and community influences that need to be considered. School influences pertain mainly to the extent of integration of deaf, hard of hearing, and hearing peers in a classroom setting. Community influences reflect the involvement that a student has with community activities. For instance, a deaf student who aspires to play basketball at the World Games for the Deaf may seek to join a school basketball team but may have little regard for the socialization implications of playing with a group of hearing peers. Also, a student who swims competitively for a community swim club will be likely to join a school swim team.

The other external agent influencing the social context of an extracurricular activity is the extent to which the activity is accessible to a deaf or hard of hearing student. In this regard, communication and transportation are two major considerations. The ability to communicate with peers and with coaches or sponsors of an activity is important. Students who rely on oral communication but do not think that they can communicate with other participants in an activity might be reluctant to join. They might perceive the activity as being communicatively inaccessible. Likewise, for students who rely on signing, the availability of an interpreter may be a condition for participation in an activity. In lieu of an interpreter, a necessary condition might be that at least one other participant have basic signing skills. Transportation affects accessibility when students have to travel long distances to attend school. This is often the case with deaf students who are brought by bus to a school that has a program for the deaf. If no other arrangements are made for transportation, some of these students might not be able to participate in an extracurricular activity, regardless of their desire to do so. Accessibility can be improved if coaches and sponsors are aware of the social implications of deafness and take measures to enhance the participation of a deaf or hard of hearing student.

The final component of the model is the actual involvement in an extracurricular activity. The positive and negative experiences of this involvement will be likely to affect future participation in extracurricular activities. With this model it is possible to examine some of the ways in which schools can enhance opportunities for a deaf or hard of hearing person to be involved in various extracurricular sports and clubs.

ENHANCING THE ACCESSIBILITY OF SPORTS AND EXTRACURRICULARS FOR DEAF STUDENTS

Schools must expand the goals of extracurriculars to accommodate the specific needs of deaf and hard of hearing students. This suggestion finds support in the 1988 report of the Commission on Education of the Deaf, which stated that "a child who is deaf should be placed where his or her needs can be met by meaningful participation in after-school or extracurricular activities. This is typically more significant for older children of secondary age who need to learn mature social relationships and behavior" (p. 22). In the following discussion, the role of extracurriculars centers around efforts to make these activities purposeful by attending to the context of being deaf and preparations to interact in both deaf and hearing communities.

The role of extracurriculars can be conceptualized from a lifelong educational and social perspective. This entails, for example, knowledge of what learning outcomes in the social domain can be expected to develop through involvement in extracurriculars. If a student is a signing-dependent communicator, it is obvious that some difficulties will arise in communicating with hearing people who cannot sign. Hence, one concern about students placed among their hearing peers in public schools is the lack of meaningful social interactions because of the incompatibility of preferred communication modes. One possible response is to encourage participation only in activities that expose deaf students to others who can sign. Alternatively, an interpreter could be used to facilitate communication. Although these approaches may initially seem plausible, however, they may not serve the interest of preparing deaf students for contact with hearing persons. Therefore, another approach might be to ask what activities facilitate social experimentation with hearing peers and lead to effective social interaction behaviors over a lifetime of experiences?

Conversely, deaf and hard of hearing students not only come in contact with hearing individuals but can expect much contact with other deaf and hard of hearing people throughout their life. For many deaf individuals, the adult Deaf community becomes their primary source of social interactions. Therefore, schools should consider incorporating into their extracurricular activities opportunities to promote greater awareness of social options available in the Deaf community. This can occur in a number of ways.

• Emphasize opportunities for participating in Deaf sports. Deaf sports are perhaps the best organized social institution in the Deaf community. Various sports are sponsored by Deaf associations at the local, regional, national, and international levels. For example, a deaf volleyball player could play for the Greater Vancouver Association of the Deaf, participate in a tournament sponsored by the British Columbia Deaf Sports Federation, compete in the Canada Deaf Summer Games, and ultimately represent Canada in the World Games for the Deaf. Knowledge of these opportunities could be a strong motivational force for deaf youngsters to compete in high school sports.

This kind of motivation may even be sufficient to override concerns about communication difficulties. That is, in the above example, future participation in Deaf sports becomes the principal rationale for a deaf athlete's involvement in high school sports. Once committed to a sport, the athlete is then placed in a situation that provides a range of opportunities for interacting with other deaf peers, hearing peers, or both. When this happens deaf youngsters are given a chance to learn about different kinds of values—communication, striving to be the best one can be in a sport, social identities—and the roles that each assumes in their lives.

• Relate adult Deaf activities to extracurricular activities. School clubs such as drama, photography, yearbook, and computer all offer a chance to hone skills that could be useful in the Deaf community or elsewhere. Drama is a popular event in talent shows; a good photographer can contribute photos to newsletters, magazines, or books about deaf people; yearbook experience can be used in the layout of newsletters and magazines; and computer skills can help a person balance the books as the treasurer of a Deaf association, keep statistics at sport events, or correspond through electronic mail. As in sports, a rationale for involvement in an extracurricular activity that highlights future social possibilities may be the deciding factor in convincing a deaf or hard of hearing student to participate.

• Extracurriculars designed specifically for Deaf students. Just as many schools sponsor choirs and bands, those with sufficient numbers of deaf students should consider having clubs that are either primarily for deaf students or for both hearing and deaf students. In one instance, a school might endorse a Deaf Club that will allow students to dictate their own line of activities. Deaf awareness week, Deaf culture explorations, or camping trips are examples of some of the activities that students might pursue.

Schools might also endorse a club that mainstreams hearing students into the communication world of deaf students. A sign language club would be an excellent opportunity for deaf students to assume responsibility for planning and teaching signs. In this situation, their rank among hearing peers is elevated because their language (e.g., American Sign Language) and their mode of communication become the status quo. Teaching peers to sign is a good means for expanding the social group with whom deaf students may communicate. As a result, more meaningful social interactions are likely to ensue throughout the school day.

In each of the above suggestions, deaf students are given a reason for participating in extracurriculars that relate to being deaf. The focus of their participation is more on the activity itself and less on the socialization aspect. A deaf student joins the photography club not necessarily because he or she wishes to socialize with hearing peers but because of the skills that will be learned. Consequently, initially the reward for learning new skills and parlaying them into productive participation in deaf community activities at a later time may be seen to outweigh the perceived difficulties of communicating with hearing peers.

Hard of hearing students, on the other hand, present a different set of social concerns. Their primary mode of communication is more likely to be speech and therefore they are more likely to associate with hearing social groups. Still, extracurricular sponsors need to be cognizant of communication techniques that can facilitate their interactions with hard of hearing students and to help them maximize the benefits of participation in extracurriculars. In addition, there are many hard of hearing individuals in the deaf community. Thus, although at the school level hard of hearing students should be able to benefit from the range of extracurricular activities offered, their options for participating in different sociocultural groups need to be recognized.

This approach to extracurriculars summons a shift in the current thinking of those school administrators and teachers who maintain that the fundamental purpose of involvement is to integrate deaf and hard of hearing students with their hearing peers. Relegating socialization to a lesser role may remove some of the stress associated with extracurriculars. A less threatening environment may thus be conducive to better socialization skills. Eventually, positive experiences affiliated with extracurricular involvement may begin to feed other interests, and a student may become more intrinsically motivated to socialize with hearing peers.

CONCLUSION

Tanner and Tanner's (1975) note that evidence showing that "extra-class activities can exert significant influences on cognitive as well as affective learning" (p. 22) demands that the curriculum encompass more than just formal courses of study. Over the past 20 years, curriculum design in general education has come to include a wide range of school learning experiences beyond traditional coursework confined to the classroom. Impetus for this movement stemmed from a general feeling that activities occurring outside the classroom can positively influence the personal and academic performance of students.

It is possible that prudent use of extracurricular activities could lead to making each educational placement better equipped to meet the educational and social needs of deaf and hard of hearing students. What is right for hearing students is not necessarily appropriate for deaf or hard of hearing students and vice versa. Still, the range of extracurriculars in schools provides all students with a common ground for developing socialization skills as well as skills in sports, drama, and other areas of interest.

In planning extracurricular activities thought must be given to the transportation concerns of deaf and hard of hearing students who may travel long distances to school, to interpreting requirements, and to staff requirements. One means of addressing transportation concerns would be for school districts to establish alternative transportation for students desiring to participate in extracurricular activities. This option may involve an added financial consideration for the districts. Alternatively, parents could make their own arrangements for bringing their children home following extracurricular activities. Interpreting and staffing requirements might also involve an additional expense for schools.

At times, the fundamental goal for participation by deaf and hard of hearing students may differ from that for their hearing peers. However, involvement need not assume a standard set of outcomes for all participants. Deaf students are unique in their sociocultural and linguistic needs. This uniqueness exists across the deaf population as well as among deaf individuals. On the other hand, hard of hearing students have social needs that reflect their dependence on speech for social interaction purposes. Schools must develop educational and social programs that are based on prior assessment of the needs of each student. In this respect, extracurricular activities can provide a strong support base for implementing socialization strategies.

REFERENCES

Asher, S., Parkhurst, J., Hymel, S., & Williams, G. (1990). Peer rejection and loneliness in childhood. In S. Asher & J. Coie (Eds.), *Peer rejection in childhood* (pp. 253–273). New York: Cambridge University Press.

Bucher, C. A., & Wuest, D. A. (1987). *Foundations of physical education and sport.* St. Louis: Times Mirror/Mosby College.

Commission on Education of the Deaf (1988). *Toward equality: Education of the deaf.* Washington, DC: U. S. Government Printing Office.

Dale, D. (1984). *Individualized integration: Studies of deaf and partially hearing children and students in ordinary schools and colleges.* Springfield, IL: Charles C. Thomas.

Farrugia, D., & Austin, G. F. (1980). A study of the social-emotional adjustment patterns of hearing impaired students in different educational settings. *American Annals of the Deaf, 125* (5), 535–541.

Gannon, J. (1981). *Deaf heritage: A narrative history of Deaf America.* Silver Spring, MD: National Association of the Deaf.

Gaustad, M., & Kluwin, T. (1990, April). *Contribution of communication mode to the social integration of hearing impaired adolescents.* Paper presented at the annual meeting of the American Educational Research Association, Boston.

Griffin, S. (1988). Student activities in the middle school: What do they contribute? *NASSP Bulletin, 72,* 87–92.

Gutowski, T. W. (1988). Student initiative and the origins of the high school extracurriculum: Chicago, 1880–1915. *History of Education Quarterly, 28,* 49–72.

Holland, A., & Andre, T. (1987). Participation in extracurricular activities in secondary school: What is known, what needs to be known. *Review of Educational Research, 57,* 437–466.

Howell, M., & Howell, R. (1979). Physical activities and sport in early societies. In E. Zeigler (Ed.), *History of physical education and sport* (pp. 1–56). Englewood Cliffs, NJ: Prentice-Hall.

Karweit, N. (1983). Extracurricular activities and friendship selection. In J. L. Epstein & N. Karweit (Eds.) *Friends in school: Patterns of selection and influence in secondary schools* (pp. 131–139). New York: Academic Press.

Mertens, D. (1989). Social experiences of hearing-impaired high school youth. *American Annals of the Deaf, 134* (2), 15–19.

Powell, A., Farrar, E., & Cohen, D. (1985). *The shopping mall high school: Winners and losers in the educational marketplace.* Boston: Houghton-Mifflin.

Public Law 94-142. (November 29, 1975). Education for all Handicapped Children Act. U.S. Congress.

Sage, G. (1986). Social development. In V. Seefeldt (Ed.), *Physical activity & well-being* (pp. 342–371). Reston, VA: American Alliance for Health, Physical Education, Recreation, and Dance.

Stewart, D. (1991). *Deaf sport: The impact of sports in the Deaf community.* Washington, DC: Gallaudet University Press.

Stewart, D., McCarthy, D., & Robinson, J. (1988). Participation in Deaf sport: Characteristics of Deaf sport directors. *Adapted Physical Activity Quarterly, 5,* 233–244.

Stewart, D., Robinson, J., & McCarthy, D. (1991). Participation in Deaf sport: Characteristics of elite deaf athletes. *Adapted Physical Activity Quarterly, 8* (2), 136–145.

Stinson, M. S., & Whitmire, K. (1990a, July-August). *Self-perceptions of social relationships among hearing-impaired adolescents in England.* Paper presented at the International Congress on Education of the Deaf, Rochester, NY.

Stinson, M. S., & Whitmire, K. (1990b). *Factors influencing self-perceptions of social relationships among hearing-impaired adolescents in England.* Unpublished data, National Technical Institute for the Deaf, Rochester, NY.

Tanner, D., & Tanner, L. (1975). *Curriculum development.* New York: Collier Macmillan.

Thompson, J. G. (1988). Political and athletic interaction in Athens during the Sixth and Fifth Centuries B.C. *Research Quarterly for Exercise and Sport, 59,* 183–190.

Zeigler, E. (1979). Physical education and sport in a historical perspective. In E. Zeigler (Ed.), *History of physical education and sport* (pp. 228–286). Englewood Cliffs, NJ: Prentice-Hall.

CHAPTER 8

Students' Views of Their Social Relationships

MICHAEL S. STINSON
KATHLEEN WHITMIRE

Peer relationships contribute to the development of social skills that reduce the likelihood of social isolation; to the acquisition of attitudes, values, and information for mature functioning in society; and to the promotion of future psychological health (Johnson, 1980). However, for peer relationships to be constructive, they must create feelings of belonging and acceptance rather than rejection and alienation. When children are accepted they feel better about themselves, are more positive and realistic about their relationships with others, and are more likely to enjoy successful future relationships (Johnson, 1980; Johnson & Johnson, 1980).

There has been variation in hearing impaired children's and adolescents' social experiences. While these students often experience social difficulties, in a few studies interaction has been positive (e.g., Ladd, Munson, & Miller, 1984). With regard to social difficulties, Foster (1988) reported that mainstreamed students' descriptions of their social experiences included many references to loneliness, rejection, and social isolation. Mertens (1989) found that students who had attended a residential school reported more positive social experiences than those who had been mainstreamed. Greenberg and Kusche (1989) summarized several descriptive studies of peer interactions between hearing and hearing impaired children in integrated settings where only oral communication was used. Hearing impaired children appeared to have difficulty relating to hearing peers, which was reflected by their more frequent interaction with their teachers and hearing impaired peers than with hearing peers.

In contrast to these findings, Ladd, Munson, and Miller (1984) found that when special efforts were made to establish a climate that supported positive interaction between hearing impaired and hearing peers, positive interaction occurred and friendships developed. Furthermore, Kluwin, Wismann-Horther, and Kelly (1989) found that hearing and hearing impaired students who participated in a journal writing program developed positive relationships with each other. Additionally, when Mertens (1986) used the Meadow-Kendall Social Emotional Inventory, she did not find consistent differences between the social development of students who were mainstreamed for at least some of their classes and those who were always in self-contained classes. The results indicating social difficulties (preceding paragraph) and those indicating positive social experiences (this paragraph) illustrate the variation in social relationships experienced by mainstreamed hearing impaired students. This variation needs to be examined further to specify the individual characteristics and situational factors that account for it. This information may then be used to help alleviate the social difficulties of mainstreamed students.

The social experiences of mainstreamed students are further complicated by the development of their own self-identity. It is important for adolescents to find answers to the questions "Who am I?" and "How do I fit into the deaf and hearing world?" Glickman (1986), writing about his counseling experiences with hearing impaired youngsters, has suggested that the establishment of identity with hearing impaired and hearing social groups is often a complex task for hearing impaired adolescents, especially those who have been mainstreamed. On the one hand, contacts in the family, neighborhood, and school are predominantly with hearing individuals. On the other hand, it is generally easier for hearing impaired individuals to communicate and establish friendships with each other. Orally trained students from mainstream programs who have had little experience with deaf culture may undergo internal conflict as they discover sign language and the deaf community. They may struggle in their efforts to clarify their affiliation with the deaf and hearing worlds (Glickman, 1986).

A MODEL OF SOCIAL RELATIONSHIPS

One way of thinking about social development is in terms of how people see themselves functioning in various aspects of their social lives. The remainder of this chapter focuses on hearing impaired adolescents' self-perceptions of their social relationships, including consideration of interrelations among these perceptions and other causal factors. We will present a model of self-perceptions followed by a discussion of the educational implications of research findings pertinent to the model.

Self-perceptions are one way of assessing the quality of social relationships (Parker & Asher, 1987). Since the general literature about hearing children's social relations indicates that their self-perceptions are related to the extent of actual peer rejection (Asher, Parkhurst, Hymel, & Williams, 1990), the study of the self-perceptions of hearing impaired children may help identify particular educational settings where such students are less likely or more likely to enjoy peer acceptance. Such a study may also identify individual differences in peer acceptance among students. Furthermore, these self-perceptions may be viewed as indicators of students' confidence, and such confidence is itself important (Covington & Beery, 1976; Johnson, 1980; Jones, 1977).

The model in Figure 8.1 is used to organize sets of perceptions, or dimensions, regarding social relationships; interrelationships between these dimensions, including intervening variables; and individual characteristics and program factors that influence these self-perceptions. As shown in the figure, the individual characteristics that the hearing impaired student brings to the public high school setting and the program factors of the school program itself are hypothesized to directly influence the social relationship outcomes, which include the need for closer relationships, emotional security, and perceived social competence. In addition, the individual characteristics and program factors influence the sense of participation variables, which are closely attached to the relevant situation (e.g., classroom setting). In turn, the sense of participation variables influence the social relationship outcomes, which are viewed as more generalized perceptions. In this way, sense of participation functions as an intervening variable. In addition, effects of the social relationship outcomes are assumed to feed back to the sense of participation variables; that is, reciprocal causation is assumed between these two sets of variables.

This model is restricted to educational programming factors existing in the public school setting and to personal characteristics the individual brings to the setting. Less direct influences, notably family background, are not included. Variables were in-

Figure 8.1. Proposed model of self-perceptions of social relationships and hypothesized influencing factors

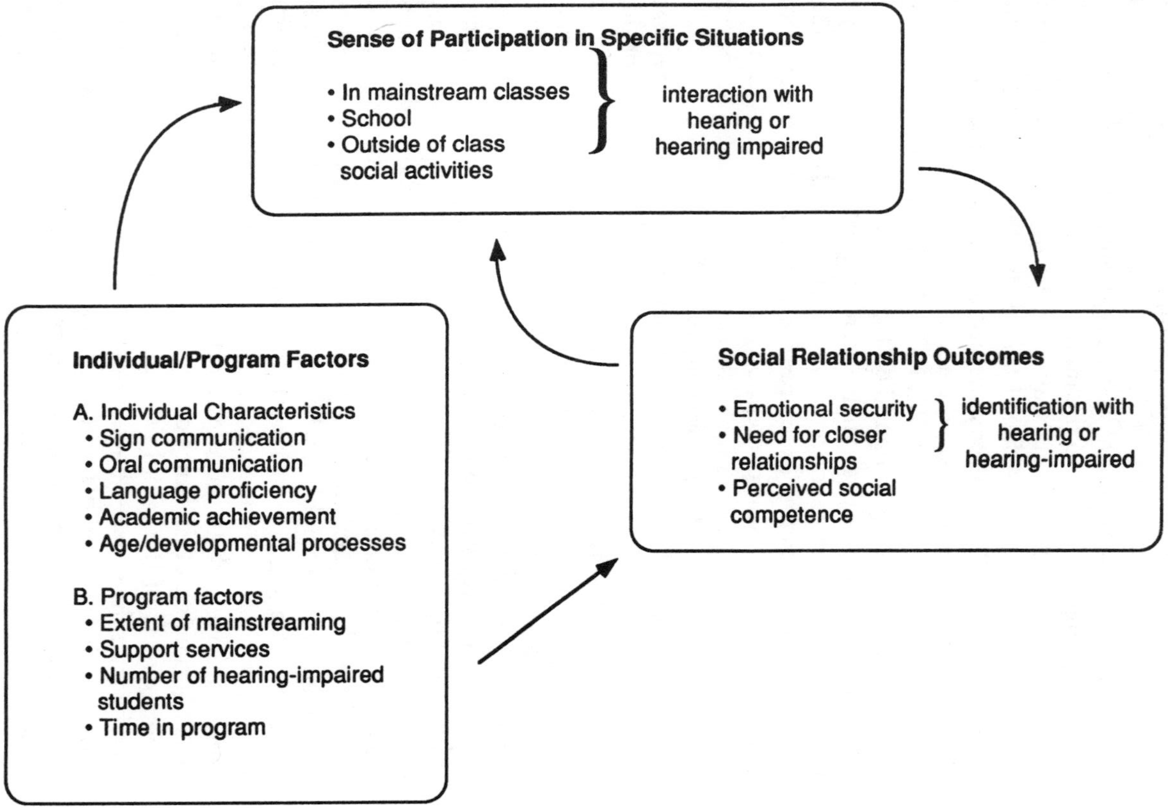

Sense of Participation in Specific Situations

- In mainstream classes
- School
- Outside of class social activities

} interaction with hearing or hearing impaired

Social Relationship Outcomes

- Emotional security
- Need for closer relationships
- Perceived social competence

} identification with hearing or hearing-impaired

Individual/Program Factors

A. Individual Characteristics
- Sign communication
- Oral communication
- Language proficiency
- Academic achievement
- Age/developmental processes

B. Program factors
- Extent of mainstreaming
- Support services
- Number of hearing-impaired students
- Time in program

cluded in the model on the basis of previous research, our own work on self-perceptions of social relationships, and theoretical relevance.

Self-Perceptions of Social Relationships: Dimensions

Three sets of perceptions, or dimensions, regarding social relationships are included in our model:

1. Participation,
2. Relatedness, and
3. Perceived social competence.

Participation. In previous research, hearing impaired students have stated that limited participation is a major concern in the mainstream setting (Foster, 1988; Saur, Lane, Hurley, & Opton, 1986). As used in our model, participation refers to self-reports of the level of involvement in three areas: class (e.g., helping other students); school (e.g., eating lunch with friends); and outside-of-school activities (e.g., visiting a friend's house). In addition, a distinction is made between interaction with hearing impaired peers and interaction with hearing peers.

A student's perception of participation may be influenced by factors such as the extent of contact, situational difficulties, support of others, and personal capabilities. For example, students who are frequently placed in classes with hearing peers may report more participation with hearing peers than is reported by those always in self-contained classes, regardless of actual interaction. Also, for many mainstreamed students a major situational difficulty is the inability to adequately understand the teacher and classroom discussion (Foster, 1988; Saur, Lane, Hurley, & Opton, 1986). Perceptions regarding participation may also reflect the extent to which students think that peers and adults are supportive and cooperative. For example, hearing impaired students may attribute their lack of participation in social activities to the unwillingness of hearing schoolmates to maintain conversations beyond superficialities, to extend invitations to parties, and so on (Foster, 1988). Finally, the extent of participation may depend on personal qualities of the student, such as preparation for class, willingness to contribute to class discussion, friendliness, and outgoingness.

Relatedness. In our model, the first two social relationship outcome variables are emotional security and need for closer relationships. Following a motivational framework proposed by Connell (1990), these two variables contribute to a sense of relatedness. Relatedness refers to self-appraisals of the security of one's relationships with significant others. The need for closer relationships is an attitude expressed in statements such as, "I wish I had more friends who were hearing (or hearing impaired)." Emotional security is a perceptions of the stability of those relationships in statements such as, "When I'm with hearing (or hearing impaired) students my age, I feel nervous." As with participation, feelings of relatedness with hearing impaired peers and hearing peers are assessed separately.

In Connell's motivational model (1990), relatedness is regarded as a fundamental psychological need "to feel securely connected to the social surrounding" (p. 4). Relatedness may be closely associated with the extent to which individuals identify with particular social groups and feel relational bonds with individuals within them. Ainsworth (1989) has characterized such bonds as reflecting relationships that are close, enduring, and affectionate. There are feelings of cooperation, reciprocity, and trust that permit friends to reveal their feelings to each other and feel that there is mutual understanding.

Perceived social competence. The third social relationship outcome variable is perceived social competence. This pertains to appraisals of the skills and personal characteristics needed to establish good peer relationships (e.g., being willing to talk or sign in groups) and the extent to which one has successfully established peer relationships (e.g., having a lot of friends). Individuals who assign positive evaluations to items tapping these domains are assumed to evaluate their social selves favorably. As used here, perceived social competence is a general self-appraisal, and items designed to tap it do not refer specifically to either hearing or hearing impaired peers.

The types of items used to assess perceived social competence (Stinson, Chase, & Kluwin, 1990) are in some respects similar to those in the loneliness questionnaire for children developed by Asher, Hymel, and Renshaw (1984). Both instruments include questions concerning prerequisite characteristics for establishing relationships. Also, the two measures contain items about current peer relationships as well as the extent to which relationship needs are being met (e.g., "I have friends I can talk with."). Asher and his colleagues (Asher, Hymel, & Renshaw, 1984; Asher, Parkhurst, Hymel, & Williams, 1990) have provided much empirical support for the connection between dissatisfaction with peer relationships and loneliness. Their research indicates that children who are poorly accepted tend to express greater feelings of loneliness than do children who are well accepted.

Interrelations of Self-Perceptions and Reference Group Orientation

The model of self-perceptions and related factors suggests that students who report greater participation, that is, who engage in many activities, will also report higher levels of relatedness and greater perceived social competence. This association is consistent with previous research with hearing adolescents that has demonstrated links between participation and self-esteem (Holland & Andre, 1987).

A related issue here is whether the perceptions of hearing impaired peers parallel those of hearing peers. For example, participation in activities with hearing classmates might be associated with relatedness for hearing peers but not for hearing impaired peers. When examined from a social or ethnic perspective (Stewart, 1984; Wright, 1987), these relationships may provide information regarding the nature of the cultural identity or social orientation of hearing impaired students. Positive identification with both hearing and hearing impaired students would suggest that individual differences can be described in terms of a dual reference group or bicultural orientation to the two groups (Glickman, 1986; Rotheram & Phinney, 1987). However, negative responses to one group or the other would suggest polarization in reference group orientation; either students view relationships with hearing impaired peers favorably and those with hearing ones unfavorably, or the reverse. Finally, if the pattern of responses about one peer group was unrelated to that about the other peer group, this would suggest that the two orientations are independent of one another.

Differences in Relationships with Hearing and Hearing Impaired Peers

Hearing impaired adolescents may feel more comfortable in relationships with each other than in relationships with hearing peers. The assignment of more favorable ratings of relatedness to items referring to hearing impaired peers than to those referring to hearing peers would suggest that relational bonds and identification with the former group are stronger. Even so, the reason students might indicate that they do not participate in activities with hearing impaired peers more frequently may relate to availability. For example, hearing impaired students attending public school generally live some distance from each other; therefore, opportunities to engage in social activities with each other outside of school may be limited. On the other hand, there are often opportunities to participate in activities with hearing students in these neighborhoods.

One consideration here is the possible discrepancy between the peer groups many hearing impaired youngsters feel most comfortable with and those with whom they most frequently interact. In local neighborhoods, relationships with hearing peers may be relatively superficial rather than close friendships. Such superficial relationships may occur especially often among students who rely more on sign language and who have difficulty communicating with hearing peers. Yet, for healthy social development to occur, it is important that children and adolescents feel comfortable and accepted in their relationships (Johnson, 1980).

Individual Characteristics and Program Factors Influencing Self-Perceptions

Individual characteristics. A variety of individual characteristics may affect the quality of social adjustment in the mainstream setting. Students with proficient oral communication skills may have more positive social experiences with hearing classmates than do those with weak skills (Davis, 1986). Murphy and Newlon (1987) have provided some evidence for this proposition in a study of loneliness in hearing impaired students in mainstream programs at eight colleges. Among hearing impaired students who identified themselves as hard of hearing, those who were more comfortable with using their speech reported fewer feelings of loneliness than did those who were less comfortable with speech use.

Furthermore, students proficient in sign language may enjoy better relationships with hearing impaired peers than do those with limited skills. In support of this idea, Murphy and Newlon (1987) found that among students who identified themselves as deaf, those who were relatively comfortable with communicating in sign language had fewer feelings of loneliness than those who were uncomfortable with sign language. Individuals who are comfortable with sign language may feel a closer bond to hearing impaired people as a social group because shared ways of communicating are basic to the formation of social relationships and to access to social networks, and because the development of sign skills demonstrates personal commitment to the group (Heller, 1987). One question here relates to the quality of relationships between students proficient in sign language and their hearing peers. Such relationships may depend on whether the student is also proficient in speech, as it seems reasonable for individuals skilled in both to enjoy successful relationships with both groups.

Language proficiency, in speech, sign, or both, is also important for the development of positive social relationships. The vocabulary necessary for self-analysis of internal events includes cognitive words such as "thinking," "knowing," and "guessing," and also feeling words such as "sad," "happy," "excited," and "frustrated" (Meadow, 1980). This vocabulary is a key component of a sensitive self-analysis of personal thoughts and feelings in the social situation, for sharing thoughts and feelings with others, and for accurately interpreting the actions and comments of others (Greenberg & Kusche, 1989). In addition, language is not merely a series of utterances or signs, but a communication system that requires knowledge of referents, cultural symbols, and socially shared meanings of contexts, and such knowledge is intricately connected to the ability to relate to others. For these reasons, students with greater language proficiency may learn more and interact more appropriately in social situations (Antia, 1985; Vaughn, Hogan, Kouzekanani, & Shapiro, 1990). In support of this reasoning, Brackett and Henniges (1976) found that social skills of hearing impaired children were directly related to proficiency on several linguistic measures. Other research findings consistent with the language-social skills connection are those that have found academic skills correlated with social adjustment in the mainstream setting (Davis, 1986; Moores & Kluwin, 1986; Saur & Stinson, 1986). In making this connection, it is assumed that language proficiency is closely associated with academic skills.

Program factors. There are also multiple program factors that influence social adjustment. With respect to self-perceptions, one issue is whether variation in the extent of mainstreaming exerts differential effects on participation, relatedness, and perceived social competence. With increased mainstreaming, participation of hearing impaired students in activities with hearing peers might increase because the physical placement generates more contact and opportunities. Furthermore, even if there is some interaction between hearing and hearing impaired students in the main-

stream setting, such placement might not imply greater relatedness or bonding with hearing schoolmates. Success in the mainstream setting may also depend on the extent of support services.
Research by Reich, Hambleton, and Houldin (1977) and by Peterson (1972) indicates that students who are fully integrated without
any support services or itinerant teachers are more likely to experience social difficulties. Additional work by Foster (1989) suggests
that the presence of other hearing impaired students at the same
school and enrollment in the school for a relatively long period
promote social adjustment.

RESEARCH FINDINGS

Interrelations of Self-Perceptions

Correlates with perceived social competence.   The first relationship in
the model for which data will be presented is the correlation between perceptions of participation and social relationship outcomes. Findings support the hypothesis that perceived social competence correlates with other components of social experiences.
This is consistent with previous research with hearing adolescents
(Holland & Andre, 1987). Data in support of this hypothesis were
gathered as part of the Public School Program Study (Stinson,
Chase, & Kluwin, 1990), which included 16 programs for hearing
impaired students throughout the United States and Canada. Subjects were 257 hearing impaired high school students.
    The perceived social competence scale, in which items did not
specifically refer to hearing or hearing impaired groups, correlated significantly with scales pertaining to both hearing and hearing impaired peers. High ratings of perceived social competence
were associated with greater participation in class, in school, and
in social activities, and also with greater emotional security with
hearing peers. In addition, perceived social competence was associated with greater participation in social activities with hearing
impaired friends and with higher emotional security with that
group. These results indicate that students who engage in many
activities and who are emotionally secure in their relationships
are also likely to feel confident about their social skills and relationships.
    These findings also suggest that it is desirable for students to
actively participate in school and outside-of-class activities in or-

der to foster feelings of emotional security and perceived social competence. As used here, active participation in social activities means such things as talking to other students, helping each other, eating lunch together, and so forth, since these events can lead to friendship. Another reason for the connection between participation and acceptance is that students may be more likely to participate in activities with others whom they regard as their friends (Antia, 1985).

Furthermore, it is interesting that participation and emotional security with either hearing or hearing impaired reference groups are independently associated with social competence. Thus, even though there are potential communication difficulties and negative attitudes toward deafness (Meadow, 1980) that may make establishment of rewarding relationships with hearing peers difficult, those hearing impaired students who feel they can establish such relationships appear to also enjoy a sense of social competence. Taking an ethnicity perspective, these findings are consistent with Cross's (1987) conclusions based on a review of research on black and white reference group identification and the self-esteem of black persons. He found that identification with either white or black reference groups could provide a basis for positive self-esteem.

Reference group orientation. Results from the Public School Program Study indicated that self-perceptions were interrelated with social orientation toward hearing or hearing impaired reference groups. That is, students who participated at a relatively high level in their classes with other hearing impaired students also tended to engage in activities with their hearing impaired peers in school as well as socially. Furthermore, these students indicated greater emotional security with hearing impaired peers as well as a greater expressed need for closer relationships with other hearing impaired teens. The same pattern of consistent orientation in participation and relatedness is evident toward hearing peers.

In addition, students' social orientations toward hearing and hearing impaired peers appeared to be independent of each other. Hearing versions of subscales, with two exceptions, did not correlate significantly with any of the hearing impaired versions. Thus, hearing impaired students who are favorably oriented toward hearing impaired peers may be favorably or unfavorably oriented toward hearing ones. These results are consistent with previous research on ethnic group orientation, such as Jewish-American identity, which has found majority and minority group orientation unrelated (Kerlinger, 1984; Zak, 1973). The findings are also consistent with Glickman's (1986) theoretical scheme that recognizes the duality of hearing/hearing impaired social orientation.

Differences in Participation and Relatedness with Hearing and Hearing Impaired Peers

Participation. In the Public School Program Study (Stinson, Chase, & Kluwin, 1990), students in general rated themselves as interacting more frequently with other hearing impaired students than with hearing peers in mainstreamed classes and at school. For both class and school, mean ratings of participation with hearing impaired classmates were significantly higher than those with hearing ones. This is not surprising within the school setting, since for the most part subjects were enrolled in relatively large special programs attached to local public high schools and thus had numerous opportunities to interact with other hearing impaired peers. The tendency of hearing impaired students to prefer interaction with each other, and to form separate social networks when there are many hearing impaired peers, was also observed by Foster and Brown (1989) in their study of mainstreamed postsecondary students. Much of the basis for this separation is, of course, the communication barrier. The difficulty of crossing this barrier for most students means that the quality of social interaction with hearing schoolmates is likely to be strained and unpleasant, often resulting in the interactants having distorted perceptions of each other (Gaustad & Kluwin, 1990). Given these difficulties, positive interaction between hearing and hearing impaired students rarely occurs, especially in the "unwritten curriculum" of riding on school buses, in hallways, in the cafeteria, and in extracurricular activities such as sports (Farrugia & Austin, 1980).

The finding of preference for interaction with hearing impaired peers is more striking for hearing impaired students in mainstream classes, who were literally surrounded by hearing classmates and therefore had considerable opportunity to interact with hearing peers. Such a preference for interaction with hearing impaired classmates when in mainstream classes was also noted by Foster and Brown (1989). Again, the communication barrier is probably an important reason for this preference. In addition, hearing impaired students tend to sit together, at the front of the class, so that they can clearly see the interpreter (if there is one), instructor, and blackboard (Foster & Brown, 1989). Sitting together may reflect social preference as well.

Outside the school setting, there were no overall differences for social interactions with hearing and hearing impaired friends. One plausible explanation is that hearing impaired adolescents rarely live in the same neighborhood.

Relatedness. Overall, students indicated that they were more emotionally secure in relationships with other hearing impaired peers than with hearing peers. This preference for hearing impaired classmates is consistent with findings for school and class participation, and is congruent with Foster's (1989) conclusions that these youths regularly turn to others like themselves to meet such needs as to have "real" conversations, develop close friendships, and feel a sense of belonging. Furthermore, they turn to each other because of communication ease, because they think hearing peers often "look down" on them, and because they have experienced rejection and isolation from hearing peers. In addition, these students may see themselves as belonging to the deaf social world, while hearing students have a different world, and the two groups have little need to do much with each other (Foster & Brown, 1989; Gaustad & Kluwin, 1990).

Individual Characteristics

Oral and sign communication. Findings on relations between communication preference and self-perceptions come from a second study of 64 hearing impaired students, 15–19 years of age, who were participants in *Explore Your Future,* a "summer camp" program held each July at the National Technical Institute for the Deaf. In this study, students were asked on a questionnaire to state whether their preferred mode was oral, American Sign Language (ASL), or simultaneous communication. Relationships between these preferences and self-perceptions concerning participation, relatedness, and perceived social competence were then examined. Analyses of data for the scales that tapped participation in out-of-school social activities yielded a statistically significant interaction between communication preference and reference of the scale to hearing or hearing impaired peers. Users of oral communication reported more frequent social interaction with hearing than with hearing impaired individuals; whereas users of ASL and simultaneous communication reported more frequent interaction with hearing impaired peers, with this preference being more pronounced for the ASL group.

There was also a significant interaction between communication preference and reference group orientation for scales that tapped need for closer relationships with hearing or hearing impaired peers. Users of oral communication assigned higher ratings of need for closer relationships with hearing than with hearing impaired peers, in line with the finding for participation. Users of ASL and simultaneous communication assigned higher ratings to the scale pertaining to hearing impaired peers (Stinson, Chase, & Bondi-Wolcott, 1988).

Those proficient in both speech and signing may have the greatest flexibility in establishing relationships with both hearing and hearing impaired peers, since they can switch to the most appropriate mode depending on with whom they are communicating (Gaustad & Kluwin, 1990). In the *Explore Your Future* study (Stinson, Chase, & Bondi-Wolcott, 1988), students who used simultaneous communication reported more interaction with hearing peers than those using ASL, which would be expected, given the greater likelihood of those using simultaneous communication to use oral communication with hearing peers.

Age/Development. Findings from the Public School Program Study (Stinson, Chase, & Kluwin, 1990) include data showing changes in relatedness with age. Students were divided into three cohort groups that were roughly equivalent to grade levels 10, 11, and 12. Results for the scales assessing need for closer relationships included a significant interaction between grade level and reference group. Mean ratings of need for closer relationships with hearing peers decreased from grades 10 to grades 11 and 12, while those regarding hearing impaired peers increased from grades 10 and 11 to grade 12. As students become older they may have increased acceptance of their deafness and want closer relationships with each other. Such changes in commitment or identity are congruent with work that proposes that adolescence is a time of change in ethnic or social group identity (Phinney & Alipuria, 1987).

Program Factors—Extent of Mainstreaming

Participation and reference group. The only program factor for which we can currently cite results is extent of mainstreaming.

Extent of mainstreaming did influence perceptions regarding participation in classroom and school activities. In the Public School Program Study (Stinson, Chase, & Kluwin, 1990) an index of mainstreaming was created on the basis of responses to a questionnaire item that asked for the number of mainstream classes students had attended at each grade level during high school. The index had four categories: mainstreamed for zero to two classes in past 2 years; for three to four classes; for five to nine classes; and for 10 to 23 classes.

The changes in mean ratings were similar for the pairs of scales tapping participation in class and in school. For each pair, there was a statistically significant interaction between extent of mainstreaming and hearing or hearing impaired reference group. Figure 8.2 presents a plot of the relevant means for the interaction pertaining to participation in class. Although there were slight differences in which post hoc comparisons of means were statistically significant, the general pattern was as follows: Students who were least often mainstreamed (zero to two classes) rated interaction with hearing impaired peers as significantly higher than that with hearing peers. With increased mainstreaming, interaction with hearing peers increased, and was significantly higher for those who were most often mainstreamed (10 to 23 classes) than for those who were least often mainstreamed (zero to two classes). In contrast, ratings of interaction with hearing impaired peers dropped markedly for those mainstreamed for 10 to 23 classes relative to those mainstreamed for fewer classes.

These changes in rated participation may reflect changes in the opportunity for interaction, since those who experience more mainstreaming spend less time with hearing impaired classmates; changes in rated participation may also reflect differences in characteristics of students, since those who are frequently mainstreamed may have better oral skills, academic ability, and so forth (Davis, 1986).

Relatedness and reference group. Given these changes in ratings of participation, might not similar changes occur in ratings of relatedness as a function of mainstreaming? Results do show changes in emotional security with increases in mainstreaming, but they are clearly different from those for participation. These results provide no evidence that increased mainstreaming promoted identification and relational bonds with hearing classmates. Figure 8.3 shows the somewhat surprising pattern of means for the

Figure 8.2.   Mean rating on in-class participation with hearing impaired and hearing students as a function of extent of mainstreaming

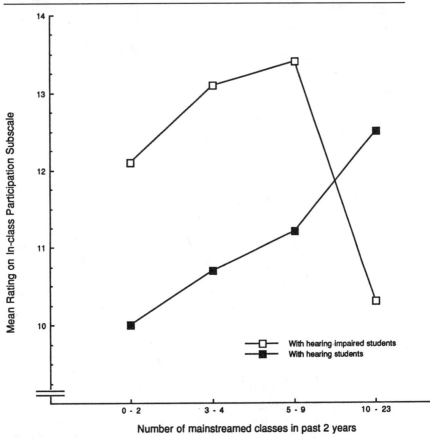

interaction between mainstreaming and reference group. Mean ratings of emotional security with *hearing impaired* peers were higher for students who were mainstreamed less (zero to two, three to four classes). The ratings of security with hearing impaired peers by students who were mainstreamed more frequently were also significantly higher than their ratings of security with hearing peers. On the other hand, ratings of emotional security with hearing peers were relatively constant across the four levels of mainstreaming. While there is no readily apparent explanation of these results, perhaps those who were most frequently main-

Figure 8.3. Mean rating on emotional security with hearing impaired and hearing peers as a function of extent of mainstreaming

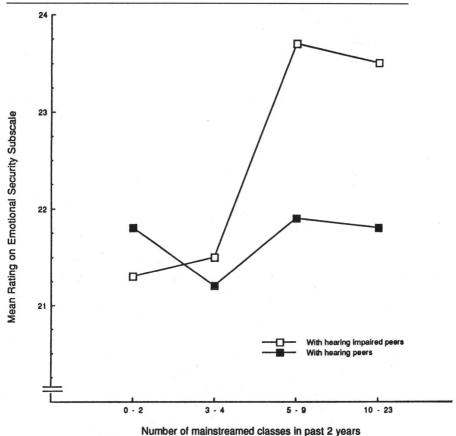

Number of mainstreamed classes in past 2 years

streamed were also most acutely aware of the differences in ease of communication and in establishing relationships with the two groups.

For students who were most frequently mainstreamed, there was a discrepancy between ratings of participation and emotional security. While participation in class and in school was more frequent with hearing than with hearing impaired peers, emotional security was greater with hearing impaired peers. The implication of this pattern is that some of these students may have unmet needs for more social contact with hearing impaired classmates.

This discrepancy between participation and emotional security can be viewed as a reflection of differences in the depth, quality, and endurance between relationships with hearing impaired students and those with hearing students. Hearing impaired students have characterized their relationships with hearing peers as frequently being "acquaintanceships" rather than deep friendships, casual in nature, and relatively short-term (Foster & Brown, 1989). Greater mainstreaming does appear to increase such acquaintanceships with hearing peers. On the other hand, emotional security reflects trust, affection, and long-lasting friendship, and hearing impaired students more often turn to each other for such relationships. This is just as true of frequently mainstreamed students as of those less frequently mainstreamed. We consider the discrepancy between participation and emotional security of frequently mainstreamed students an important finding that merits further attention, since satisfying peer relations play a critical role in healthy social development (Johnson, 1980).

Overall participation and relatedness. The Public School Program Study also found that extent of mainstreaming was related to overall ratings of need for closer relationships and of participation; that is, there were differences in these ratings, regardless of whether the scale referred to hearing or hearing impaired schoolmates. Mean ratings of need for closer relationships were highest for students who were least often mainstreamed (i.e., almost always in special classes) and dropped steadily as a function of mainstreaming. The expression of a greater need for friendship by these least mainstreamed students can be interpreted as a feeling of being "left out" socially. Another finding that may have reflected such feelings in this group was that ratings of participation in school were lower for it than for the three groups that were mainstreamed more frequently.

For hearing impaired students, lack of contact with hearing students in a public high school that includes a special program may engender feelings of having no part in the hearing community and of being "rejected" by that group. In addition there may be feelings of detachment from other hearing impaired students who are mainstreamed at least some of the time. In a study of effects of mainstreaming relative to self-contained placement for educable mentally retarded students, Strange, Smith, and Rogers (1978) found that students who were partly mainstreamed had better feelings about themselves than those always in self-contained classes. The authors suggest that students may have viewed mainstreaming as an indicator of progress and academic success. Furthermore, by participating in some self-contained classes at the same time, students had fellow handicapped students available as a reference group, and consequently they could selectively compare themselves with either handicapped or nonhandicapped peers. This combination of circumstances appeared to boost self-esteem.

Returning to the present study, hearing impaired students who were partly mainstreamed may have viewed the experience as an indicator that they "belonged" to the school and may have experienced boosted self-esteem, as manifested by higher self-reported participation in school and lower need for closer relationships.

SUMMARY OF RESEARCH FINDINGS

To facilitate applying this research to education practice, the findings discussed above may be compiled and summarized in two ways: first, to confirm the model proposed in the early part of this chapter; and second, to create a profile of students with certain individual and school placement characteristics.

Figure 8.4 presents the model emerging from these findings. Our results indicate that three individual characteristics—sign communication, oral communication, and age—and one program factor—extent of mainstreaming—are associated with both levels of participation and social relationships. Also, social relations outcomes and level of participation are interrelated.

The relationships suggested by this model can be further delineated by representative profiles of students with specific characteristics. These profiles are given in Figure 8.5, which details the ratings on outcome variables that are associated with particular program factors and student characteristics. The reader should note that findings have been presented for only some of the variables included in the model of social relationships and influencing factors. Further research will be carried out to determine whether other factors listed in the model are also relevant. For example, data on the roles of academic achievement and on the number of other hearing impaired students in the school need to be analyzed.

Figure 8.4. Self-perceptions of social relationships and influencing factors supported by reasearch findings

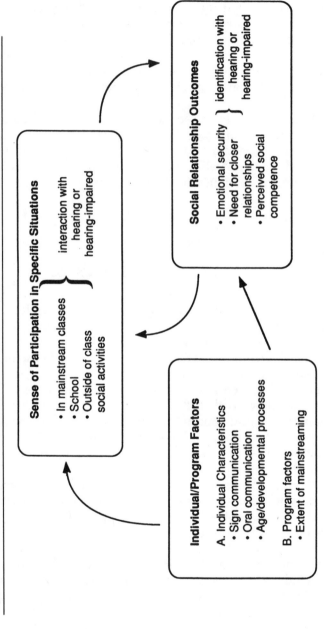

Sense of Participation in Specific Situations

- In mainstream classes
- School
- Outside of class social activities

} interaction with hearing or hearing-impaired

Social Relationship Outcomes

- Emotional security
- Need for closer relationships
- Perceived social competence

} identification with hearing or hearing-impaired

Individual/Program Factors

A. Individual Characteristics
- Sign communication
- Oral communication
- Age/developmental processes

B. Program factors
- Extent of mainstreaming

Figure 8.5. Summary of selected individual characteristics
and program factors

Program Factor	Ratings on Related Outcomes
Lowest extent of mainstreaming	High participation in class with hearing of impaired students High participation in school with hearing impaired students Low overall participation in school High overall need for closer relationships
Highest extent of mainstreaming	High participation in class with hearing students High participation in school with hearing students High emotional security with hearing impaired peers
Individual Characteristics	
Prefer oral communication	High social participation with hearing peers High need for closer relationships with hearing peers
Prefer ASL or simultaneous communication	High social participation with hearing impaired peers High need for closer relationships with hearing impaired peers
Older students	Low need for closer relationships with hearing peers High need for closer relationships with hearing impaired peers

IMPLICATIONS FOR EDUCATIONAL PROGRAMMING

It is important for school programs to include in their educational plans opportunities for social growth and development and to monitor this development in an ongoing fashion (Davis, 1986). On the basis of our research findings, the following suggestions are offered in regard to educational programming.

First, it is desirable to provide hearing impaired adolescents numerous opportunities to enjoy social relationships with each other. Students are generally more secure in relationships with hearing impaired classmates and may be more likely to have positive social experiences, which are important in the development of social skills and mental health, with them (Johnson & Johnson, 1980). All adolescents struggle to find appropriate social roles and identities, and it is helpful if they have choices in social relationships and opportunities to explore these options and experiences (Damon, 1984). Findings suggest that the appropriate social context for such exploration is one that includes many hearing impaired schoolmates. Centralized, or "regional," public school programs provide such a context.

Second, in public school programs, students who are always in self-contained classes and students who are extensively mainstreamed, for perhaps half or more of their classes, may require special consideration in regard to their social needs. Students who are always in self-contained classes may feel isolated from the social context of the school. Perhaps ways can be found to increase feelings of "belonging," such as mainstreaming for a nonacademic class, greater participation in school-wide activities, and so forth. A different problem occurs for students who are mainstreamed extensively; these students may feel deprived of desired opportunities to interact with hearing impaired classmates. It does not seem psychologically healthy to provide minimal opportunity for interaction and relationship with those with whom students are most comfortable. For these mainstreamed students, it is desirable to provide additional opportunities such as mainstreaming two or more hearing impaired students into a class, scheduling hearing impaired students into the same lunch period, and so on.

Third, it is desirable for teachers and counselors to be sensitive to individual differences in hearing impaired students' orientations toward hearing and hearing impaired social groups in planning students' educational programs. While research showed general preference for relationships with hearing impaired schoolmates, findings also indicated that some students found friendships with hearing peers rewarding, and thus they probably benefit from programming that includes opportunities for such relationships.

Fourth, it may be helpful for counselors and teachers, when planning educational placements and conducting programs, leading discussions, and so on, to promote social development, to consider developmental changes in identification with and commitment to the hearing impaired social group. As they become older, high school students seem to show greater commitment to hearing impaired peers. Thus, with age, hearing impaired adolescents may have stronger needs for contact with each other and for opportunities to learn about deaf culture.

Fifth, one way to increase students' feelings of social confidence and acceptance may be to increase participation in class and school activities. Greater participation in activities with hearing peers may increase feelings of being accepted by that group; greater participation with hearing impaired peers may increase feelings of acceptance by them. More participation in activities with either group may enhance hearing impaired students' general sense of social competence. Possible ways of increasing participation include greater involvement in extracurricular school activities and reduction of communication barriers for greater participation with hearing peers (Saur, Lane, Hurley, & Opton, 1986).

Sixth, scales that tap students' self-perceptions, such as those described in this chapter, might be used as measures to help decide what level of mainstreaming is appropriate for individual students. For example, if a student expresses clear dissatisfaction with social relationships on these scales, and there is additional evidence such as impressions from teachers and parents, counseling or a change in educational placement, or both, may be needed.

REFERENCES

Ainsworth, M. (1989). Attachments beyond infancy. *American Psychologist, 44*, 709–716.

Antia, S. (1985). Social integration of hearing impaired children: Fact or fiction. *Volta Review, 87*, 279–289.

Asher, S., Hymel, S., & Renshaw, P. (1984). Loneliness in children. *Child Development, 55*, 1456–1464.

Asher, S., Parkhurst, J., Hymel, S., & Williams, G. (1990). Peer rejection and loneliness in childhood. In S. Asher & J. Coie (Eds.), *Peer rejection in childhood* (pp. 253–273). New York: Cambridge University Press.

Brackett, D., & Henniges, M. (1976). Communicative interaction of preschool hearing impaired children in an integrated setting. *Volta Review, 78*, 276–285.

Connell, J. (1990). Context, self and action: A motivational analysis of self-system processes across the life-span. In D. Cicchetti (Ed.), *The self in transition: Infancy to childhood* (pp. 173–195). Chicago: University of Chicago Press.

Covington, M., & Beery, R. (1976). *Self-worth and school learning.* New York: Holt, Rinehart and Winston.

Cross, W. (1987). A two-factor theory of black identity: Implications for the study of identity development in minority children. In J. Phinney & M. Rotheram (Eds.), *Children's ethnic socialization: Pluralism and development* (pp. 117–133). Newbury Park, CA: Sage.

Damon, W. (1984). *Social and personality development*. New York: W. W. Norton.

Davis, J. (1986). Academic placement in perspective. In D. Luterman (Ed.), *Deafness in perspective* (pp. 205–224). San Diego, CA: College-Hill Press.

Farrugia, D., & Austin, G. F. (1980). A study of the social-emotional adjustment patterns of hearing impaired students in different educational settings. *American Annals of the Deaf, 125* (5), 535–541.

Foster, S. (1988). Life in the mainstream: Reflections of deaf college freshmen on their experiences in the mainstreamed high school. *Journal of Rehabilitation of the Deaf, 22,* 37–56.

Foster, S. (1989). Social alienation and peer identification: A study of the social construction of deafness. *Human Organization, 48,* 226–235.

Foster, S., & Brown, P. (1989). Factors influencing the academic and social integration of hearing impaired college students. *Journal of Postsecondary Education and Disability, 7,* 78–96.

Gaustad, M., & Kluwin, T. (1990, April). *Contribution of communication mode to the social integration of hearing impaired adolescents*. Paper presented at the annual meeting of the American Educational Research Association, Boston.

Glickman, N. (1986). Cultural identity, deafness and mental health. *Journal of Rehabilitation of the Deaf, 20,* 1–10.

Greenberg, M., & Kusche, C. (1989). Cognitive, personal and social development of deaf children and adolescents. In M. Wang, M. Reynolds, & H. Walberg (Eds.), *Handbook of special education: Research and practice* (pp. 95–132). New York: Pergamon Press.

Heller, M. (1987). The role of language in the formation of ethnic identity. In J. Phinney & M. Rotheram (Eds.), *Children's ethnic socialization: Pluralism and development* (pp. 180–200). Newbury Park, CA: Sage.

Holland, A., & Andre, T. (1987). Participation in extracurricular activities in secondary school: What is known, what needs to be known. *Review of Educational Research, 57,* 437–466.

Johnson, D. (1980). Group processes: Influences of student-student interaction on school outcomes. In J. McMillan (Ed.), *The social psychology of school learning* (pp. 123–168). New York: Academic Press.

Johnson, R., & Johnson, D. (1980). Integrating handicapped students into the mainstream. *Exceptional Children, 47,* 90–98.

Jones, R. (1977). *Self-fulfilling prophecies*. Hillsdale, NJ: Lawrence Earlbaum.

Kerlinger, F. (1984). *Liberalism and conservatism: The nature and structure of social attitudes*. Hillsdale, NJ: Lawrence Earlbaum.

Kluwin, T., Wismann-Horther, L., & Kelly, A. (1989, April). *The development of relationships between hearing impaired and hearing writers sharing journals*. Paper presented at the annual meeting of the American Educational Research Association, San Francisco.

Ladd, G., Munson, H., & Miller, J. (1984). Social integration of deaf adolescents in secondary-level mainstreaming programs. *Exceptional Children, 50*, 420–428.

Meadow, K. P. (1980). *Deafness and child development*. Berkeley: University of California Press.

Mertens, D. (1986). *Social development for hearing impaired high school youth*. Paper presented at the annual meeting of the American Educational Research Association, San Francisco.

Mertens, D. (1989). Social experiences of hearing-impaired high school youth. *American Annals of the Deaf, 134* (2), 15–19.

Moores, D. F., & Kluwin, T. N. (1986). Issues in school placement. In A. Schildroth & M. Karchmer (Eds.), *Deaf children in America*. (pp. 105–123). San Diego, CA: College-Hill Press.

Murphy, J., & Newlon, B. (1987). Loneliness and the mainstreamed hearing impaired college student. *American Annals of the Deaf, 132* (2), 21–25.

Parker, J., & Asher, S. (1987). Peer relations and later personal adjustment: Are low-accepted children at risk? *Psychological Bulletin, 102*, 357–389.

Peterson, J. (1972). *Achievement of hard of hearing student in regular public schools*. Unpublished doctoral dissertation, Wayne State University, Detroit.

Phinney, J., & Alipuria, L. (1987, April). *Ethnic identity older adolescents from four ethnic groups*. Paper presented at the biennial meeting of the Society for Research in Child Development, Baltimore, MD.

Reich, C., Hambleton, D., & Houldin, B. (1977). The integration of hearing impaired children in regular classrooms. *American Annals of the Deaf, 122* (7), 534–539.

Rotheram, M., & Phinney, J. (1987). Introduction: Definitions and perspectives in the study of children's ethnic socialization. In J. Phinney & M. Rotheram (Eds.), *Children's ethnic socialization: Pluralism and development* (pp. 10–31). Newbury Park, CA: Sage.

Saur, R., Lane, C., Hurley, B., & Opton, K. (1986). Dimensions of mainstreaming. *American Annals of the Deaf, 131* (2), 325–330.

Saur, R., & Stinson, M. (1986). Characteristics of successful mainstreamed hearing impaired students: A review of selected research. *Journal of Rehabilitation of the Deaf, 20*, 15–21.

Stewart, D. (1984). Mainstreaming deaf children: A different perspective. ACEHI/ACEDA, *10*, 23–29.

Stinson, M., Chase, K., & Bondi-Wolcott, J. (1988). *Use of social activity scale as part of personal/social development activities during "Explore Your Future."* Working paper, National Technical Institute for the Deaf, Rochester, NY.

Stinson, M., Chase, K., & Kluwin, T. (1990, April). *Self-perceptions of social relationships in hearing impaired adolescents*. Paper presented at the annual meeting of the American Educational Research Association, Boston.

Strange, L., Smith, M., & Rogers, C. (1978). Social comparison, multiple reference groups, and the self-concepts of academically handicapped children before and after mainstreaming. *Journal of Educational Psychology, 70,* 487–497.

Vaughn, S., Hogan, A., Kouzekanani, K., & Shapiro, S. (1990). Peer acceptance, self-perceptions and social skills of learning disabled students prior to identification. *Journal of Educational Psychology, 82,* 101–106.

Wright, L. J. (1987). *A study of deaf cultural identity through a comparison of young deaf adults of hearing parents and young deaf adults of deaf parents.* Paper presented at the Student Research Colloquium, University of Pittsburgh.

Zak, I. (1973). Dimensions of Jewish-American identity. *Psychological Reports, 33,* 891–900.

CHAPTER 9

Considering the Efficacy of Mainstreaming from the Classroom Perspective

THOMAS N. KLUWIN

Walk into a mainstream classroom where a deaf student is sitting, most likely studying mathematics if it is an academic class, and look around. Then, head down the hall to where the special or separate classes for the deaf are located. Even a casual consideration of these two situations will uncover differences between the two settings, including class size, availability of support staff, training and experience of the instructor, and the general instructional focus of the teacher (e.g., the difference between large and small groups or remediation vs. new content instruction). Class size in regular classrooms can range from 20 to 35 students while class size in special classes for the deaf can range from 1 to 12 (Evertson, Emmer, & Brophy, 1980; Kluwin & Moores, 1989). Mainstream classes hew to the district curriculum, which is designed with the assumption that new material is to be taught, while special classes are often seen as sites for the remediation of missing skills (Evertson, Emmer, & Sanders, 1980; Kluwin & Moores, 1989). Unfortunately, these observations have sometimes been lost on those who have done research on the efficacy of mainstreaming for deaf or other special education populations. Global statements have been made about the efficacy of mainstreaming, without any consideration of the fundamental structural and procedural differences between regular and special classes (Bogdan, 1983).

Before beginning to consider these differences, it would be useful to have, as a starting point, a theoretical framework that would predict outcomes of the differences between classrooms. One possible organizing device is Walberg's (1984) model of educational productivity. The result of a review of thousands of research studies of classroom learning, it was developed to consistently differentiate effective learning situations from ineffective ones. Walberg's model consists of three primary components:

1. Aptitude,
2. Instruction, and
3. Environment.

Each of these three primary components is further divided into three subcomponents, which in turn predict learning outcomes. The complete Walberg model includes interactions among the three primary components as well as feedback loops from learning back to the primary components. We won't require that degree of detail for our discussion, but by using parts of Walberg's model of effective schooling—specifically, the aptitude and instruction constructs—as an outline to organize the available research, we can consider the differences between mainstream and special classes for the deaf and draw some conclusions about the effects of those differences. In addition we can examine in detail how those differences might be related to teacher performance differences that predict achievement. Finally, we will make some recommendations as to what can be done to make instruction more effective.

EDUCATIONALLY SIGNIFICANT DIFFERENCES
BETWEEN PLACEMENTS

Student Aptitude

In Walberg's model, student aptitude consists of ability or prior achievement (generally what is measured on standardized tests), maturation or development, and motivation, which is an umbrella construct that covers self-concept as well as perseverance.

Ability. Deaf students in mainstream placements differ from deaf students in special classes on several educationally significant variables, including ability (Schildroth, 1988; Wolk, Karchmer, & Schildroth, 1982). For example, Allen and Osborn (1984), utilizing demographic and achievement data on 1,465 hearing impaired children sampled from a national database, reported statistically significant effects for type of educational placement and for student ability as one of many of the demographic covariates used to control between group differences. From this, they concluded that a positive effect for integration was established but, more important, ability and other demographic factors were the major contributing factors in the outcome differences found.

Kluwin and Moores (1985), using a matched-groups design in a study of three metropolitan high school programs to assess the effect of educational placement on achievement, emulated the selection process used in the schools, in order to identify a group of special class students who were similar to mainstreamed students but who had not been integrated. In this study, placement did have a statistically significant effect on achievement, but demographic factors, including prior mathematics achievement, also contributed substantially to the differences between the groups.

Both studies accounted for about 40% of the variance using placement, demographic information, and the interaction between the demographic characteristics of the students and their placement. Placement alone accounted for only 1% of the variance, while ability and other demographic factors accounted for about 12% of the variance.

Subsequently, Kluwin and Moores (1989) conducted a process-product study of over 70 classrooms around the United States to determine which placement type is more effective for deaf students. The measures of achievement were regressed scores on the mathematics computation and mathematics concepts subtests of the Hearing Impaired version of the Stanford Achievement Test, which had been adjusted for sex, race, prior ability, and length of time between test administrations. For both measures, demographic factors accounted for about 15% of the variance. Placement, that is, whether or not the child was in a mainstreamed setting, accounted for less than 1% of the variance in computation achievement, and it was not even entered into the equation for mathematics concepts achievement. Again, differences between groups, primarily initial ability, were a larger factor in determining achievement differences than were placement differences.

As a result of placement decisions made for the benefit of deaf children, there are profound population differences between mainstream classes and special classes for the deaf. Consequently, the achievement differences between the groups are to a large extent describable more by reference to ability differences than by differences in placement types.

Development. Walberg (1984) includes two areas of developmental differences in his model: chronological and maturational. Wolk, Karchmer, and Schildroth (1982) noted age differences between special class populations and mainstream populations. Specifically, they point out that as a child becomes older, he or she is more likely to be mainstreamed. However, it is not possible to infer simply that special class students are less mature because they tend to be younger chronologically. A separate consideration of the maturity levels of these students needs to be made prior to asserting this as a substantive difference.

In the Kluwin and Moores (1985) study referred to earlier, one of the matching criteria used was social development as measured by the Meadow-Kendall Social Emotional Inventory. Kluwin and Moores (1985) report that the "possibly integrated" students had a higher average score than did the actually integrated students, which suggests that teachers perceived the students in the special classes as more mature.

Motivation or self-concept. One way to ask how motivated students are or how likely they are to persevere is to ask them about what causes success or failure for them in school. Individuals who attribute success to themselves are more likely to be motivated, while those who attribute success to external forces are less likely to initiate activities that will result in success in school since they have no sense of control over their own situations. Using this line of reasoning, Wolk (1985) asked 422 deaf college students to read a short paragraph representing a summary of the academic experiences of a hypothetical college freshman during the first semester of the year. After reading the paragraph, the students were asked to rate each of four casual factors along a nine-point scale.

Wolk (1985) reported a significant interaction between the attribution of success or failure and the hearing status of the teacher described in the paragraph. In the classroom of a hearing teacher, student ability and effort were seen as relatively more important keys to success. When the teacher was deaf, success was attributed to the teacher or to luck. In the alternative setting, that is, in failure scenarios, with a hearing teacher failure was attributed to the teacher and to luck. However, failure with a deaf teacher was thought to be just bad luck.

What Wolk's (1985) study suggests about the motivational structures of hearing impaired students is that mainstreamed students may differ considerably in their motivation from students in special classes. Since it is not possible to equate Wolk's experimental conditions with specific placements, we cannot predict the direction of the attribution; however, it would appear that motivational structures are different in different placements since deaf students encounter only hearing teachers in mainstream classes, but may have a more deaf-oriented environment in a special class.

Studies of the self-concept of deaf students in public schools have generally been done irrespective of placement type within the school. The available comparisons are either between public school students and residential school students or between deaf public school students and hearing public school students (e.g., Craig, 1965; Farrugia & Austin, 1980).

There is no specific study we can point to that could highlight motivational differences between mainstream and special classes, but such differences are highly likely given the pattern of the study described.

Instruction

Walberg (1984) describes two important instructional parameters in his model of effective schooling: the amount of student engaged time and the quality of the instructional experience.

Amount of engaged time.   Precise descriptions of what occurs in the use of time in mainstream or special classes are not readily available; however, a study by Kluwin and Lindsay (1984) of attention patterns in various classes in a residential high school program showed that positive student attitudes were related to teacher behaviors that actually kept students on task. Kluwin and Lindsay (1984) conducted a live observation study of 20 experienced teachers of the deaf in secondary school programs in three residential schools on the east coast. The teachers whose classes had a positive perception of the instructional environment avoided excessive monitoring of the students, persisted with students who did not understand the content of the lesson, provided adequate information about how to do tasks, and preferred an overt and task-oriented reward structure. Teacher behavior that assisted in the understanding of the instructional task by the students was seen favorably, while teacher behavior that focused on the ability of specific individuals to perform or understand the task was viewed negatively.

In a more recent study by Kluwin and Moores (1989), about

30% of the total achievement variance was attributable to teaching behavior differences that enhance student engaged time. While this does not give us precise information on the distribution of time in these settings, it does point out that this factor, or collection of variables, can be an important component of the differences between the two placements.

Quality of instructional experience.   Teaching activities that result in higher achievement include:

1. Devoting time to the instructional task,
2. The use of instructional strategies such as grouping in reading or direct laboratory experiences in science classes,
3. Measures of movement through the curriculum, such as pacing and sequencing,
4. The use of evaluations of student progress to direct teaching, and
5. The students' clear perception of the nature of the task and their responsibilities within the classroom (Berliner, 1982; Evertson, Emmer, & Sanders, 1980; Walberg, 1984).

Larrivee (1982) found these same factors, including giving positive feedback, responding supportively to low ability students, and the efficient use of classroom and student transition time, to be positively predictive of the achievement of special education students in mainstream classes.

Before we discuss specific differences in the quality of the instructional experience between placements, it is necessary to mention some general characteristics of teaching behavior in classrooms for the deaf. For example, Kluwin (1985) examined the problem of reception of content during a signed lecture and reported that the students who were most able to retain the structure of the content to be presented were able to retain the largest volume of information about the topic.

This finding is buttressed by two other studies of classroom language behavior in classrooms for the deaf. In the first study, four English teachers in a residential school for the deaf were videotaped so that the devices they used to control the structure of the classroom discourse (i.e., how they marked boundaries and signaled transitions) could be observed (Kluwin, 1983). Differences existed in the classroom behavior of deaf and hearing teachers. The deaf teachers were more likely to persist with a topic until they achieved a successful conclusion and were more likely to clearly mark transition boundaries. While this study addressed primarily the difference in behavior between deaf and hearing teachers, it has implications for special versus mainstream classes. Since the acquisition of the appropriate context for the communication is critical in a signed communication, the failure of a mainstream teacher to mark topical boundaries clearly or an interpreter's "lag" could readily degrade the ability of a mainstreamed deaf student to follow the content.

In a related study, Mather (1987) pointed to the importance of eye gaze as a device in effective communication in the deaf classroom. In a study of two teachers, Mather reported that eye-gaze behavior regulates turn-taking behavior, such as the opening of an opportunity to ask a question, to interrupt, or to request a response from a group.

The point that should be taken from the Kluwin (1983, 1985) work and the Mather (1987) study is that in classrooms where manual communication is used, different forms of behavior regulate organization and participation than in classrooms using spoken English. The addition of an interpreter is not necessarily "just as good" because as the modality changes so do behavioral markers. Even if one allowed for perfect interpretation, the behavioral rules for participation alone would be one major difference between a mainstream and a special class.

Starting with the caveat that the basic control system of classroom discourse is different between signed and spoken lessons, we can find other instructional differences. Kluwin and Moores (1985) speculated on some differences between mainstream and special class placements that might explain variations in achievement, including teachers' expectations for achievement, exposure to more demanding content, differences in teacher training, and the degree of academic support provided to mainstream students. Subsequently, Kluwin and Moores (1989) defined several instructional quality variables that differentiate effective from ineffective mathematics instruction for the deaf. These variables included having a supportive teacher, the frequency and length of content review, the use of teacher praise, active engagement with the student, the frequency of unit tests, and the pace of the teacher's questions. However, Kluwin and Moores (1985) did not differentiate between mainstream and self-contained placements in their study.

An elaborate study of teacher behavior in mainstream classes was done by Saur and her associates (Saur, Popp, & Isaacs, 1984), who looked at the "action zones" or the area of most activity in six mainstream college level classes. The action zone is a "T" consisting of the front row and the center row in a classroom. In classes of all sizes the deaf students were twice as likely to be seated outside the action zone as within it; however, it was possible to clearly define the action zone in only one-third of the classrooms. In the other two-thirds, the interactions were more evenly distributed. In classes where an action zone exists, the deaf students are outside the teacher's directed attention, but in classes where there is none they are just as likely as anyone else to receive the teacher's attention.

Direct comparisons between special classes for the deaf and mainstream classes are rare, but Johnson and Griffith (1986) conducted a study of one fourth-grade hearing impaired classroom and one fourth-grade hearing classroom at the same school. The self-contained classroom had five students, while the general education classroom had 20 students, none of whom were identified as handicapped. Total data collection time for both settings was 30 minutes. The mode of communication in the self-contained classroom was total communication using a mix of signed English, some ASL vocabulary, fingerspelling, and speech. Johnson and Griffith (1986) report that interactions were very different in the two settings. Interactions in the general education class exhibited rapid conversational shifts, complex academic task structures, and complex language, while the self-contained class was marked by routinized academic tasks and simple language structures. The generalizability of this study is nil because of the selection of only two nonrepresentative sites, because the structure of the classrooms is very different—large group versus small group instruction—and because of an absence of information on the intellectual ability of the students in the two classrooms. Consequently we can only speculate on the source of the variation.

We will dispense with the other portions of Walberg's model because they are covered in more detail in other chapters in this book and because they do not bear as directly on the question of process differences in the classroom as those we have discussed.

Summary

From the available literature, some generalizations are possible. For example, students in special classes are less able and may have different motivations than students in mainstream classes. To date, it has been more difficult to make direct comparisons between settings using instructional process differences, but given the differences between special and mainstream classes that result from different populations and instructional agendas, one might expect to find several categories of potential process differences. To investigate these differences, I looked at effective teaching behavior in the two settings.

ACHIEVEMENT IN TWO DIFFERENT SETTINGS

This study involved 215 hearing impaired secondary students from 11 school districts around the United States with an average hearing loss of 88.3 dB in the better ear, with a standard deviation of 20.2 dB. Sixty-three teachers in both regular and special classes participated in the study.

Achievement data were provided by the regular school administration for the Hearing Impaired version of the Stanford Achievement Test. A teacher opinion instrument was administered to each teacher to solicit information about activities such as planning and reward systems, which would not be readily available from live observations. To get a sense of the quantity and level of work that the teachers demanded of their classes, we asked them to keep logs of their assignments and classwork. A classroom observation system provided a record of activities that occurred in the classroom, the interactions between teachers and students, and the function of the interpreter in the classroom.

The attitudinal items from the teacher survey were factor analyzed to yield five factors:

1. Degree of individualization,
2. Instructional flexibility,
3. Rule flexibility,
4. Inductive teaching, and
5. Student responsibilities.

Only the two most statistically reliable factors were used in the analysis.

The variables generated from the live observation system are presented in Figure 9.1. To test two hypotheses—first, that there were process differences between the mainstream and special classes and, second, that these differences were related to achieve-

Figure 9.1: Operational definitions of classroom process variables

Variable	Operational Definition
Teacher oral presentation	Three-fourths of class is an oral presentation by teacher.
Seatwork	Amount of time class spends doing seatwork.
Question pace	Frequency of teacher asking questions.
Positive feedback	Frequency of teacher praise or positive response to students.
Degree of individualization	Teacher questionnaire factor score.
Instructional flexibility	Teacher questionnaire factor score.
Tutorial time	Amount of class time spent teaching one student.
Whole group instruction	Amount of class time devoted to instruction where teacher presents to entire class as a group.
Content demand	Cognitive level of material covered.
Homework	Number of days per week homework is given.

ment differences—a two-by-three, repeated measures analysis of variance was computed for the 10 classroom process variables described in Table 9.1. The independent variables were type of classroom (mainstream or special) and level of achievement in the classroom (high, mixed, or low).

To create the achievement groups, individual regressed achievement scores were computed by regressing the pre-observation achievement score, as well as race, sex, and time between test administrations, against the post-observation achievement score. The achievement measures were the mathematics computation and the mathematics concepts subscale scores for the SAT–HI. Class average scores were then computed for each teacher. If a teacher had a class average regressed score on an achievement measure above the grand mean, he or she was coded as a high achieving teacher for that subtest. This process yielded three types of achievement based on the class average regressed scores: high

Table 9.1: A priori contrasts for classroom process variables (p <.01)

Variable	t Values for Contrasts	
	Mainstream vs. Special Placement	Achievement by Placement Interaction
Teacher oral presentation	3.225	−2.707
Seatwork	−3.915	4.913
Question pace	−5.906	
Positive feedback	4.518	
Degree of individualization	−10.170	
Instructional flexibility		
Tutorial time		
Whole group instruction	5.946	
Content demand	5.387	
Homework		2.776

level of achievement on both tests, contrasting levels of achievement on the two tests, and low achievement on both tests.

To identify which of the variables in the repeated measures analysis of variance would contribute to the expected difference between the two types of placements, the difference between mainstream and special classes was also tested using an a priori contrast for each of the dependent variables. Since some previous research had suggested that only high achieving classes would be readily describable (Schneider & Treiber, 1984), a nonlinear relationship was hypothesized where only teachers whose classes were high on both measures would be significantly different from the other types of teachers. This secondary hypothesis was tested using an a priori contrast between the high achieving special classrooms and the high achieving mainstream classrooms.

There was an interaction between the type of placement and the process variables (F = 14.46, df = 4,160; p < .001), but there was no other statistically significant main effect or interaction effect. However, as can be seen in Table 9.1, the specific contrasts revealed patterns of differences between the types of placements.

Mainstream classes were distinguishable from special classes on the basis of the greater frequency of oral presentations by the teacher, by a greater use of positive verbal feedback, by more time devoted to instructing the whole group, and by a higher level of content demand. Teachers in special classes used more seatwork, more frequent questions, and a greater degree of individualization than did mainstream teachers.

Teachers in high achieving mainstream classes made greater use of oral presentations, while teachers in high achieving special classes had the least amount of oral presentation time. Teachers in high achieving mainstream classes used the least amount of seatwork, while high achieving special classes exhibited the greatest amount of seatwork. Teachers in high achieving classes, both mainstream and special, assigned more homework than teachers in the other classrooms.

There is a general difference in classroom process between mainstream and special classes for the process variables that reflect group orientation, such as the amount of the teacher's oral presentation and the use of whole group instruction. There was a tendency in the special classes toward individual forms of instruction as seen in the greater amount of seatwork and the higher degree of individualization. Of the process variables that differ between the mainstream and special placements, only two showed differences for class achievement as well. What distinguishes a successful mainstream placement from an unsuccessful one is a greater degree of oral presentation and less seatwork. What describes a successful special class is less teacher to group talk and more work.

This study was able to demonstrate that there are process differences between mainstream and special placements. As would be expected, the primary finding was that teachers in mainstream classes use large group processes, while teachers in special classes use more individualized processes. Effectiveness was not found to be identical in the two situations, but specific differences were not clearly established in great detail. The failure to lay an unequivocal track of evidence from setting differences to process differences to achievement may lie in the relatively small number of classrooms examined, or, as Schneider and Treiber (1984) suggest, it may be possible to describe effective instruction because it is systematic. It may not be possible to describe ineffective instruction because it may be inherently chaotic.

DISCUSSION

Since different instructional settings have been created for specific reasons, placements will vary along several parameters, including the ability, maturational level, and motivation of the students, and the quality of the instruction within the type of setting.

Let us for a moment consider a "typical" high school mathematics classroom. There are between 20 and 30 or more students in the class. The teacher's primary concern is with covering a specific amount of content in a set period of time. In most general mathematics classes, students are in attendance by requirement and not by choice and are not highly motivated to learn the content. One of the great advantages of the large classroom is that students can avoid the teacher by simply being quiet. To engage the students' interest, move through the material, and maintain discipline, the teacher must create the impression that every child could be called on at any minute to recite (Evertson, Emmer, & Brophy, 1980).

Consider also for a moment what occurs in a special classroom for the hearing impaired within a public school building. There are from one to ten students in the room, who may be heterogeneous as to age, ability, and instructional need. The children in this classroom are here because they are not expected to be able to function in a regular classroom for intellectual, learning, or social reasons or some combination of the three. The pace is slower, the children are on their own for much of the classroom time, and there is a great deal of concern with finishing specific tasks. Preplanning by the teacher, with an emphasis on engaging rather than monitoring students, is a must.

Whether one reflects on the results of the study described in this chapter or merely reflects on a few instances of the two different types of placements, several points rapidly become clear. The students are different; the classroom structures are different; and the classroom processes are different. What we have tried to show as well is that within each placement type, it is possible to define effective versus ineffective instruction.

In summary, process differences between mainstream and special class settings for the deaf, coupled with ability differences, probably contribute to the apparent advantage of mainstreamed education for deaf students (Kluwin & Moores, 1989). While some view mainstreaming as an educational "treatment," it is more informative to view it as a process that varies along several parameters. To discuss the efficacy of mainstreaming for hearing impaired students is too simplistic because it ignores the complex interrelationship of setting, process, and achievement. Since a variety of differences exist between the populations, the real issue should be the appropriateness of the instructional environment for the individual child, not the supremacy of a method.

RECOMMENDATIONS FOR MAINSTREAMED STUDENTS

Close cooperation at the instigation of the program for the deaf. A public secondary school teacher teaches five or six classes a day and can face between 125 and 160 or more students each day depending on the school system. Research on teacher thinking in these situations has shown that the mainstream teacher focuses on issues of covering content and coping with the class as a whole. This is a philosophy alien to many in special education; therefore, the responsibility for better classroom situations for deaf children must be borne by the program for the deaf. Coordination between the mainstream teacher and the staff of the program for the deaf cannot be seen as a burden for the mainstream teacher, or resistance to accepting and working with deaf students will develop.

The solution must start minimally at the building level with a close working relationship between the program for the deaf and the principal. The principal and the department chair or lead teacher must perceive the program for the deaf as an integral part of the overall school program and, as a result, be willing to allocate teacher time and resources to working through the cooperative arrangements necessary for effective classroom instruction.

Identification of mainstream teachers who are competent instructors. Principals and department chairs or lead teachers are expected as part of their job requirements to be aware of the strengths of the teachers in the school. Their help should be sought in identifying and securing the cooperation of teachers who would be particularly effective instructors. While informal relationships are integral to the smooth functioning of any human system, the use of formal relationships reinforces the positive effects of informal relations.

Cooperation between the interpreter and the classroom teacher. The interpreter should take the initiative in asking for lists of terms, copies of syllabi, or any other written forms of the teacher's plans for the future. This will permit the interpreter to be aware of topics as they are being introduced and not be surprised by a new concept. The diligent interpreter would be expected to look up or verify specific technical signs. For example, before class the interpreter could tell the student that the teacher is going to be talking about similes and metaphors and that the interpreter will use specific signs to represent those concepts. That will relieve the child of some of the burden of learning both the concept and the sign at the same time. The conceptual associations can be made with the sign instead of requiring the child to acquire a new sign or another association for a known sign while trying to learn a concept at the same time.

Subject-matter familiarity for the interpreter whenever possible. The interpreter will be aided by developing a better knowledge of the subject matter. Because interpreting involves making rapid decisions about how to represent a concept, familiarity with the subject matter will aid in sign selection and subsequently in the clarity of representation.

Note-taking support for the mainstreamed deaf student. Since manual communication requires visual attention and the verbal environment of mainstream classrooms means that several things can be happening at the same time, it is imperative that the deaf student be able as much as possible to attend to the interpreter or teacher. Writing notes should be an option for the deaf student in that situation and not a requirement. The enlistment of other students in the class to assist in this task is one option. Early and systematic cooperation between the deaf education program and the general education program can provide other alternatives.

Interpretation access for study sessions or a subject-matter competent resource teacher. In some subject-matter situations, particularly high school mathematics, there is a tendency for teachers to move at a pace set by the majority of the students. Anyone who cannot keep up is expected to see the teacher outside of school time for tutorial sessions. If the bus schedule does not mediate against the deaf child's participation in these sessions, then interpreter time should be provided so that the deaf child has access to this help. An alternative would be a subject-matter competent resource room teacher who would work with the deaf student. However, since the process of seeking help is itself integral to some mainstream teachers' systems for monitoring class progress as well as a personally gratifying encounter for the teacher, face-to-face contact between the deaf student and the hearing teacher should be supported.

RECOMMENDATIONS FOR STUDENTS IN SEPARATE CLASSES

While there has been a major effort in special education to eliminate special classrooms, it is likely to be a very long time before all experts in the education of the deaf agree that all deaf students could function in a mainstream classroom. For one reason or another, special classrooms will be necessary in the foreseeable future. Consequently, the question of creating an effective special class is critical.

A distinction should be made between the intact class for the deaf that residential or day schools are able to organize and the often heterogeneous special classes that are found in public school programs. The following discussion is directed toward the special classes.

Until 1960, large numbers of Americans were educated in one-room schoolhouses covering eight grades. Adequate and sometimes outstanding educations were provided in these situations; consequently, it is not possible to argue de facto that heterogeneous classrooms are in themselves bad. They may not be preferable for reasons such as teacher planning demands, but they are not, by definition, substandard education. Consequently, the recommendations for more effective special class placements will follow some of the better principles of the one-room schoolhouse including:

1. High expectations,
2. Peer tutoring, and
3. Variation not reduplication.

High expectations.   Because a child may not be ready for a particular situation does not mean that he or she is not ready for a challenge. The starting point in this setting must be on what the child will do and not on what the child can't do. This is reflected in the pace of the work as well as the level of content required of a student.

Peer tutoring. Teaching time is finite. One way the teacher in the one-room schoolhouse dealt with this was to have the older and more skilled children listen to the lessons of younger children while the teacher taught another group of children. Obviously, the introduction of computers and other forms of educational technology have provided instructional substitutes for the teacher, but what is apparent from the research reported in this chapter is that seatwork without human contact can have a negative effect on achievement in special classes. Face-to-face interaction with a human being who holds one accountable is what promotes learning. There are benefits for the tutor as well, since there is a need to recall previously learned material and present it to someone else, thus forcing the tutor to "relearn" the material.

Variation not reduplication. Sometimes learners require multiple examples in order to acquire a concept; at other times they require more attributes of the situation in order to acquire the concept. For example, to acquire the multiplication tables or to expand vocabulary in a foreign language, the learner must repeat the same information again and again until the connections are made. In the case of generalizing a "simple" process to another situation, the learner must acquire a slightly different set of attributes. For instance, imagine a child who has been to MacDonald's hundreds of times is brought to a fancy French restaurant. The process is highly similar—you order, pay, and eat—but the location of information and the sequence of events—order, pay, sit, eat versus sit, order, eat, pay—is quite different. For learners in special classes, their "inability to learn" may be due to their failure to perceive the relevant attributes of a situation rather than an inability to retain specific facts. Teachers in special classes who give more worksheets of identical problems are not addressing the problem. Practice in the special classroom, because it often involves no immediate monitoring by a teacher, must be more carefully designed. Slight and successive variation must be built into each practice page or tutorial.

In this chapter, we have argued for and demonstrated that differences exist between mainstream and special class deaf students and that teachers in the two situations organize instruction differently. We have also been able to suggest some characteristics of effective instruction in the two different settings. We have done the easy part, which is to establish the validity of simple observations of the situation. The hard part, the selection of appropriate situations for children and the design of beneficial experiences, remains.

REFERENCES

Allen, T., & Osborn, T. (1984). Academic integration of hearing impaired students. *American Annals of the Deaf, 129* (2), 100–113.

Berliner, D. (1982). *The executive functions of teaching*. Paper presented at the Wingspread Conference, Racine, WI.

Bogdan, R. (1983). A closer look at mainstreaming. *The Educational Forum, 47* (4), 425–434.

Craig, H. B. (1965). A sociometric investigation of the self concept of the deaf child. *American Annals of the Deaf, 110* (4), 456–474.

Evertson, C., Emmer, E. & Brophy J. (1980). Prediction of effective teaching in junior high mathematics classes. *Journal for Research in Mathematics Education, 11*, 197–198.

Evertson, C., Emmer, E. & Sanders, C. (1980). Relationships between classroom behaviors and student outcomes in junior high mathematics and English classes. *American Educational Research Journal, 17*, 43–60.

Farrugia, D. & Austin, G. F. (1980). A study of the social-emotional adjustment patterns of hearing impaired students in different educational settings. *American Annals of the Deaf, 125* (5), 535–541.

Johnson, H., & Griffith, P. (1986). The instructional pattern of two fourth-grade spelling classes: A mainstream issue. *American Annals of the Deaf, 131*(4), 331–338.

Kluwin, T. N. (1983). Discourse in deaf classrooms: The structure of teaching episodes. *Discourse Processes, 6*, 275–293.

Kluwin, T. N. (1985). The acquisition of content from a signed lecture. *Sign Language Studies, 48*, 269–286.

Kluwin, T. N. & Lindsay, M. (1984). The effects of the teacher's behavior on deaf students' perception of the organizational environment of the classroom. *American Annals of the Deaf, 129* (5), 386–391.

Kluwin, T. N. & Moores, D. F. (1985). The effects of integration on the mathematics achievement of hearing impaired adolescents. *Exceptional Children, 52* (2), 153–160.

Kluwin, T. N. & Moores, D. F. (1989). Mathematics achievement of hearing impaired adolescents in different placements. *Exceptional Children, 55*, (4), 327–335.

Larrivee, B. (1982). *Effective teaching for successful mainstreaming*. New York: Longman.

Mather, S. (1987). Eye gaze and communication in a deaf classroom. *Sign Language Studies, 54*, 11–30.

Saur, R., Popp, M., Isaacs, M. (1984). Action zone theory and the hearing-impaired student in the mainstreamed classroom. *Journal of Classroom Interaction, 19,* (2), 21–25.

Schildroth, A. (1988). Recent changes in the educational placement of deaf students. *American Annals of the Deaf, 133* (2), 61–67.

Schneider, W., & Treiber, B. (1984). Classroom differences in the determination of achievement changes. *American Educational Research Journal, 21,* 1.

Walberg, H. (1984). Improving the productivity of American schools. *Educational Leadership, 41* (8), 19–27.

Wolk, S. (1985). The attributional beliefs of hearing impaired students concerning academic success and failure. *American Annals of the Deaf, 130* (1), 32–38.

Wolk, S., Karchmer, M., & Schildroth, A. (1982). *Patterns of academic and nonacademic integration among hearing impaired students in special education.* (Series R, No. 9). Washington, DC: Gallaudet College, Gallaudet Research Institute.

CHAPTER 10

Identifying the Contributions of School Factors to the Success of Deaf Students

Angela O'Donnell
Donald F. Moores
Thomas N. Kluwin

"The conditions of effective schools may only be temporary, and as principals, teachers, and student cohorts change, so too may the level of school effectiveness."

—Good & Brophy, 1986

Given the trend toward the increased enrollment of deaf and hard of hearing students in the public schools, it is time to go beyond comparisons of school achievement of deaf students with their hearing peers. Such comparisons, while providing information about the outcomes of schooling for two radically different populations, do not contribute to an understanding of the conditions of schooling necessary to promote the achievement of the deaf or hard of hearing child within the local public school. Likewise, comparisons between the achievement of deaf students in residential schools and public schools do not provide a great deal of assistance in developing instructional programs for deaf students in public schools. As the majority of deaf or hard of hearing students are being educated in public schools, it is necessary to begin an informed analysis of the structural conditions under which a deaf child can succeed in the public school.

The main question with respect to the identification of effective schools is whether schools make a difference. Effective schools are often thought to be those that produce high achievement on the part of their students as measured by standardized test scores. The issue of whether schools matter has been of great concern since the publication of the Coleman Report (Coleman et al., 1966), which suggested that schools in fact contribute little to achievement that is not accounted for by factors such as socioeconomic status. Research on effective schools during the decades following the publication of the Coleman Report supported its pessimistic findings (Dwyer, Lee, Rowan, & Bossert, 1982; Hauser, Sewell, & Alwin, 1976; Jencks, et al., 1972). Variables such as family background affect student achievement more than school variables do (Walberg, 1984). These kinds of findings provided a stimulus for research that resulted in alternative conceptualizations of the variables to consider in studying effective schools (Scheerens, 1990). Efforts to refute the message of the Coleman Report were made by studies with titles such as *Schools Can Make a Difference* (Brookover, Beady, Flood, Schweitzer, & Wisenbaker, 1979) and "*School Matters*" (Mortimer, Sammons, Stoll, Lewis, & Ecob, 1988).

Assuming that schools in fact do make a difference, school effects, however, are often underestimated because of the methods chosen to study effectiveness, the outcome variables measured, variability of the outcome measures, the predictor variables used, and the levels of analysis chosen.

The grouping of school effectiveness studies by methodology (Pukey & Smith, 1983) makes different limitations apparent. Three prevalent approaches include outlier studies, case studies, and program evaluations (Good & Brophy, 1986). The outlier approach, or disparate groups analysis (Good & Brophy, 1986), identifies effective and ineffective schools that are statistically different on some outcome measure such as achievement (e.g., Lezotte, Edmonds, & Ratner, 1974). Since the outcome is known to be different, it is assumed that the structural or procedural differences found are the cause of the outcome differences. Because the outlier approach uses a priori different samples, a practice that violates the randomness of sample selection condition, no further statistical tests are legitimate. The strength of the method is that small samples can be used and specific programs considered in detail. However, problems in identifying causality within the context of this specific method remain.

Case studies (which may overlap with outlier studies) are another alternative when process description, rather than outcomes, is the goal of the analysis. While case studies provide in-depth descriptions of school activities (e.g., administrative decision making), that may seriously affect achievement, the generalizability and causality of case studies are questionable. It is difficult to generalize from one case study to other situations with any degree of certainty, and in the absence of more experimentally controlled research, it is not possible to establish a cause–effect relationship from the described process to the observed outcome.

A third method used in school effectiveness research is program evaluation. Such program evaluations are often made of school improvement projects (Achilles & Lintz, 1986; Miller, Cohen, & Sayre, 1985). Program evaluations attempt to get at "real time" results by using a mix of large-scale statistical analyses of objective data and subjective data such as unstructured interviews. A number of critical limitations of such research include the use of group averages (Good & Brophy, 1986). Averages can be greatly distorted by extreme scores. Likewise, the use of an average in subsequent data analyses to identify significant contributors to school performance may result in few implications for any individual teacher, class, or school.

Most research on school effectiveness uses the school-wide average on particular tests as the outcome measure of interest, thereby masking important variance within an individual school system. For example, two schools that would be operationally similar on all predictor variables could be seen as differentially effective if one school had a small, specialized population with chronically lower achievement or had a particularly high-achieving subgroup. In other words, special populations with unique characteristics can easily distort schoolwide measures of "effectiveness." In addition, the predictors of achievement used for the general population within such a school may not be relevant to predicting the achievement of special populations within the school. Likewise, important variables for predicting the school achievement of special populations may be ignored when the analysis of effective schooling is made at the school level only. In the case of educational programs for the deaf, there is sufficient evidence to support the position that variation in gender, race, socioeconomic status, type and quantity of previous language training, or degree of hearing loss will produce educationally significant differences between populations.

In considering predictor variables in studies of school effectiveness, it may not be enough, therefore, to consider only school level factors. For example, Kluwin (Chapter 9) addresses the importance of classroom variables in promoting school achievement. School level and within-classroom social structures, school-wide and within-classroom socioemotional milieux, and instructional quality variables also account for important variations among schools and among classrooms (Brophy & Good, 1986; Good & Brophy, 1986).

Finally, there can be variation in the outcome measures used in defining effectiveness. Partially, this is a traditional philosophical problem in American schools as emphases shift from equity to quality or from cognitive skills to social skills. It is, however, a fundamental problem in deciding what an "effective" program is. For example, the entire debate over the efficacy of mainstreaming seems to center on the fact that integration appears to promote academic achievement (Kluwin & Moores, 1989), while some degree of segregation enhances deaf students' self-images (Stinson & Whitmire, Chapter 8). An important limitation of past research on school effectiveness has been the reliance on academic achievement as the sole indicator of school effectiveness. Good and Brophy (1986), in a comprehensive review of the literature on school effects, note that "student achievement on standardized test scores can hardly be equated with effectiveness per se" (p. 570). Other important aspects of schooling, such as social and emotional growth experienced by students, have not been included in the outcomes used to classify effective and ineffective schools (Good & Brophy, 1986; Scheerens, 1990). The need to consider other indices of school effectiveness, such as socioemotional growth, is particularly critical for deaf students who are at grave risk of being socially isolated in public school programs in which they constitute a minority. The difficulty experienced by deaf students in communicating with their hearing peers (and vice versa) requires a broader consideration of school effects than is typically used.

In summary, a complete picture of an effective school is likely to require information from many levels. Anything short of a complete analysis conducted at the classroom, schoolwide, and district level may obscure identification of some important variables. Almost all school effectiveness research is therefore greatly constrained, particularly by its lack of applicability to the identification of successful components of public schooling for special populations.

In response to the problems described previously, a variety of models for understanding school effectiveness have been developed (Averch, Carroll, Donaldson, Kiesling, & Pineus, 1984; Centra & Potter, 1980; Glasman & Biniaminov, 1981; Scheerens, 1990; Walberg, 1984). Models of school effectiveness differ on a number of dimensions. One important dimension of difference is whether the examined predictor variables are static or dynamic. For example, such characteristics as financial resources of the school may be considered static and relatively enduring, in comparison with time on instructional tasks, which may be considered more dynamic and unstable. Many models (e.g., Walberg, 1984) include some variables that are relatively static (e.g., aptitude) and those that are rather unstable and dynamic (e.g., instructional practices).

For a variety of reasons, data-driven models of school or district level effects have not been completely satisfactory in describing effective school programs. Consequently, we need to consider the various models of school effectiveness from a new perspective: that of the individuals responsible for operating the program.

A MODEL OF SCHOOL LEVEL EFFECTIVENESS

From the perspective of the school administrator, there are four categories or district level variables that are common across all models of school effectiveness:

1. Population traits,
2. Physical plant characteristics,
3. Personnel, and
4. Procedures.

Population traits define the community in which the school is found as well as the characteristics of special populations that may make up the total school population, such as deaf or other special education populations using the school as a central site. Physical plant characteristics include such factors as available classroom space, size of the library, specialized rooms, handicapped access systems, and similar school facilities. Personnel is a reasonably self-explanatory term, which will be taken up in detail below. Procedures describe how the overall system runs and include such events as the timing and extent of mainstreaming, the degree to which services are provided to individual students, as well as adult concerns such as the school governance system, teacher evaluation, grievance procedures, and instructional arrangements (e.g., team teaching). The effects of many of these factors are attenuated through various mediating variables or have an impact only in concert with other variables. For example, faculty governance

Figure 10.1   An administrator's view of effective programs

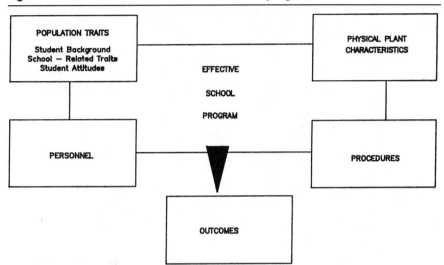

procedures do not directly affect student learning but do influence the overall climate of the school and faculty performance, which in turn affect student achievement or adjustment within the school. The "importance" of any one of these variables will be conditioned by the outcome measure that is being used, the level of aggregation of data that is employed, and the extent to which data on other relevant variables are collected. Figure 10.1 shows the components of an effective school program from the administrator's perspective.

Glasman and Biniaminov (1981) would further partition population traits into student background characteristics, school-related characteristics, and student attitudes. Student background characteristics include family size, family income or other measures of family affluence, parental education, home educational environment, student gender, kindergarten attendance, and the age of the student relative to his or her grade level. School-related student characteristics include educationally significant demographic characteristics of the student population and student attendance characteristics. Student attitudes include constructs such as self-concept and academic aspirations. Where self-concept and academic aspirations are higher, achievement is higher. These factors, however, should be considered in the context of a feedback loop of undetermined causality. School success will produce, on the average, higher self-concept and a greater desire for achievement. Higher levels of self-concept and aspiration will in turn promote achievement-oriented behavior. A conclusion that might reasonably be drawn from Glasman and Biniaminov's analysis is that higher levels of parental affluence and education are associated with higher achievement and more positive attitudes toward school.

A note of caution with respect to the entering demographic characteristics of students is warranted. The use of demographic characteristics as predictors in school effectiveness research requires some qualification or clarification. First, schools have no control over the race, intelligence, or degree of hearing loss of students. Thus, these variables are not educationally manipulable variables and may be viewed as irrelevant to the educational purposes of the school because of their unchangeable nature. Second, the aggregation of these demographic traits is what makes up the "flavor" of the school or program and creates a context in which education occurs. As such, these characteristics can be related in a definite way to what happens in schools and must be taken into account when talking about more or less effective schools. On the one hand, student demographic characteristics should be ignored because of their unchangeable nature. On the other hand, many of these characteristics are associated with variables that are related to schooling. Examples of such behaviors include student turnover, measures of school attendance, and measures of tardiness. Low absenteeism rates, low course dropout rates, and higher ratings of discipline within the school are all associated with positive achievement (Scheerens, 1990). From an administrative standpoint, therefore, the relationship of student characteristics to the process of schooling is a critical issue.

Glasman and Biniaminov (1981) do not use a "physical plant" construct per se but include in other categories some of the variables related to the physical plant. Some physical plant characteristics reviewed are library characteristics, special rooms or facilities, and expenditures. The number of books per student, the newness of the facility, and the amount of space per student are positively related to achievement outcomes. Higher per-student expenditures for materials, instruction, and extracurricular activities are also positively related to academic outcomes (Glasman & Biniaminov, 1981). It is not clear, however, whether such positive relationships are mediated by variables such as socioeconomic status. Specifically, more resources are available in schools whose population is of high socioeconomic status. Likewise, fewer resources are often characteristic of schools whose population is from lower socioeconomic strata.

Personnel traits were also reviewed by Glasman and Biniaminov (1981), including the size of the administration, the size of the support staff, teacher turnover, and teacher salaries. The size of the administration and the size of the support staff were generally negatively associated with achievement, but since larger administrative teams can be found in schools with discipline problems or large numbers of special students, this result must be considered cautiously. The relationship of staff turnover to achievement was mixed. In effective schools, teachers were characterized by subject-matter preparation, more advanced degrees, longer teaching experience, and higher levels of verbal ability. When teachers taught smaller loads and in their fields of specialization, there were higher levels of achievement among the students. Teacher job satisfaction was positively associated with school achievement, but as with student attitudinal variables, the relationship between student achievement and teacher job satisfaction clearly contains a feedback loop. In schools where there are better students who succeed academically, teachers are more likely to view their experiences positively. In addition, such teachers are likely to experience other intrinsic rewards associated with teaching.

Although Glasman & Biniaminov (1981) do not specifically include "school climate" as a variable in their model, they do include teacher attitudes. Teacher attitudes would certainly be an important component of school climate. According to Apple (1991), school climate is the product of the nature of the organizational structure and the strength of ongoing attitudes, feelings, and personalities that group members bring to and express in the organization. School climate has been shown to influence achievement in schools (Anderson, 1982; Kelly, 1980; Mortimer & Sammons, 1987; Smith, 1975). School climates are often defined along a continuum of openness (Halpin & Croft, 1963; Hoy & Clover, 1986). Measurement of school climate involves analysis of the perceptions of individuals related to the organization. Perceptions of the administration and the leadership within the school are usually included in the measurement of school climate. Educational leadership is consistently found to be related to positive achievement (Scheerens, 1990). Such leadership is characterized by the amount of time the principal spends on educational matters (as opposed to time on other administrative tasks), the number of instructional issues on the agenda of staff meetings, and discussion with teachers of students' test results. Additionally, teachers' perceptions of the educational leadership of the principal have a stronger relationship to student achievement than do self-reports by principals (van de Grift, 1990).

Procedural considerations in schooling include the use of tracking, class size, and types of classes available in the school. The administration of a school (usually embodied by the principal) may affect student learning through its influence on teachers and teaching practices (Centra & Potter, 1980). Tracking was reported by Glasman & Biniaminov (1981) to have a negative effect on achievement. More recent work (Slavin, 1987) supports this conclusion. In general, large class size was also reported to be associated with lower achievement, although findings with respect to class size are often inconsistent (Glasman & Biniaminov, 1981).

An important element of procedural considerations in schooling are the instructional practices of teachers. Good and Brophy (1986) describe teaching behaviors associated with student achievement. In their review of school effect research, Good and Brophy (1986) outline a series of instructional practices that are primary determinants of successful schools. These include the following:

1. Devoting class time to instruction,
2. A concern for students,
3. A general expectation for achievement,
4. An emphasis on the subject matter, and
5. A careful evaluation of student progress.

In summary, four aspects of schools (population traits, physical plant characteristics, personnel, and procedures) contribute in complex ways to the effectiveness of schools. Certain aspects of this complexity can be identified only by examining school functioning at the classroom level. Other contributions to effective schooling can be identified only by a school-wide analysis.

EFFECTIVE PROGRAMS FOR DEAF STUDENTS

There has been little evaluation of programs for deaf students in public schools. Furthermore, the evaluations that have been conducted do not seek to describe the elements of the educational programs that contribute to their effectiveness. Efforts to identify effective programs have been hampered by the small numbers of deaf or hard of hearing students in many programs. Evaluations of programming for deaf students have come in the form of either comparisons of the general effectiveness of residential schools versus nonresidential schools (Jensema, 1975) or comparisons within local school programs on such factors as the amount of time in the school program or in integrated classes (Moores, Kluwin, & Mertens, 1985; Reich, Hambleton, & Houldin, 1977). For the most part, emphasis in the evaluation of the programs has been on the characteristics of the child (e.g., degree of hearing loss) rather than on the quality of the programs (Jensema, 1975; Reich, Hambleton, & Houldin, 1977; Wolk, Karchmer, & Schildroth, 1982).

During the early years of the integration movement in deaf education, Brill (1978) visited several local public school programs for the deaf and documented some of their procedures. To be included in the Brill (1978) study, a program had to serve a minimum of 30 students. His study ultimately included 11 programs out of a possible pool of 14. He then conducted structured interviews in each program and produced a list of recommendations as shown in Figure 10.2. While Brill (1978) offers some useful insights into the operation of an effective program, there is nothing to support his recommendations as being more effective than others.

Of the four classes of variables described earlier, it is clear that most of the research on school effectiveness for deaf students has focused on population traits, particularly student body characteristics and school-related characteristics. This is understandable given the concern over the ability of deaf students to function in an integrated setting. The general finding of this body of research (e.g., Allen & Osborn, 1984) is that the students in different placements are different a priori, thus making school effectiveness comparisons difficult (Schildroth, 1988). Background factors such as socioeconomic status influence placement decisions (Allen & Osborn, 1984); higher socioeconomic status is associated with increased availability of resources for deaf children (Kluwin & Gaustad, Chapter 4). Kluwin (Chapter 9) offers some insight into student attitude differences, but these are not tied to school effectiveness criteria.

There is simply no information on physical plant characteristics as they are related to school level effectiveness, although concerns such as the placement of deaf students in temporary trailers outside the regular school building have repeatedly been men-

Figure 10.2. Effective mainstream programs

District enrollment should be at least 100,000 children.

Family background should be considered in designing a program.

Programs should remain at one site over time.

Central sites are preferable to itinerant locations.

Coordination is needed between the general education program
and the deaf education program.

Class size for integrated classes should be reduced.

Trained teachers of the deaf should teach special classes.

Mainstreaming will not lower costs
because appropriate services are needed.

"Pull out" programming should not be used.

Reprinted by permission of the publisher, from D. Moores and K.
Meadow-Orlans, Eds., *Educational and Developmental Aspects of Deafness*
(1990): 81. Washington, DC: Gallaudet University Press.

tioned by practitioners. Except for Brill's (1978) survey, there is no
information on the relationship of school procedures to school effectiveness for deaf students, other than the amount of time spent
by deaf children in integrated placements. Likewise, information
about the personnel who come in contact with these children is
very sparse.

SOME CHARACTERISTICS OF EFFECTIVE PROGRAMS

Sample

Data from two studies were pooled to obtain a broader picture
of public secondary school programs for deaf students. In the first
study, data from 42 public schools were collected. Schools from
each of five geographical regions (northeast, southeast, midwest,
southwest, and far west) were included (Moores, 1991). Of the 42
schools that supplied data, only 18 provided data related to each

of the components of the model previously described. This deficiency in the provision of data was compensated for in part by the addition of data from another study of 14 programs. Half of the programs in the second study were also in the first study (Kluwin, 1990). While the addition of the second study did not materially increase the number of possible candidate schools, it did provide a larger database on which to set the sample means. The final data pool consisted of seven programs.

Instrumentation

A questionnaire was sent to parents of students that solicited demographic information about the family, including parental level of education and desired educational levels for their hearing impaired child. A questionnaire was provided to school principals that was designed to collect information about the composition of the student body, the qualifications of the teaching personnel, the school's social structure, and the degree of differentiation in instruction within the school. Specific information about certified teachers of the deaf was collected through a variety of teacher questionnaires.

Two instruments were used to assess teachers' attitudes toward various aspects of school life: the *Purdue Teacher Inventory* (Bentley & Rempel, 1980) and the *Teacher Opinion Inventory* (National Study of School Evaluations, 1988). Ten subscale scores can be derived from responses to the *Purdue Teacher Inventory*, which provides a measure of teacher morale. These subscales provide teachers' assessments of:

1. Rapport with the school principal,
2. Rapport with other teachers,
3. Satisfaction with salary,
4. Teaching load,
5. Curriculum involvement,
6. Facilities of the school,
7. Community support for the school,
8. Community pressure on teachers,
9. Satisfaction with teaching, and
10. Satisfaction with the prestige associated with teaching.

The *Teacher Opinion Inventory* assesses teachers' opinions about many facets of the school.

The *Piers–Harris Self-Concept Scale* was used to assess students' self-concept. The scale provides a measure of global self-concept and also scores on six subscales. These subscales reflect how students perceive themselves in specific areas.

1. General behavior,
2. Intellectual and school status,
3. Physical appearance and attributes,
4. General anxiety,
5. Popularity, and
6. General happiness and satisfaction.

Dependent Variables

To create the first dependent variable, ninth-grade scores on the reading comprehension, mathematical concepts, and mathematical computation subtests of the SAT–HI were factor analyzed to produce a single composite achievement score. To adjust for population differences between the programs, these composite achievement scores were adjusted through a regression analysis using the student's age at testing, student gender, minority group status, and degree of hearing loss as predictor variables. Next, program-wide averages were computed for the predicted achievement score. The second dependent variable used was the program-wide average on global self-concept derived from the *Piers–Harris Self-Concept Scale.*

Predictor Variables

Population traits. Several measures of the quality of the school population—including the general community, the mainstream student body, and the deaf education student body—were computed:

1. Amount of community support for the deaf education teachers,
2. Degree of "problem" students in the general education population,
3. Academic orientation of the general education student body,
4. Percentage of minority deaf students,
5. Average hearing loss of the deaf education students,

6. Median family income of the deaf students' families, and
7. Number of years of education of the deaf students' mothers.

Community support was defined by the average of the teachers' scores on the generated subscale for the *Purdue Teacher Inventory*. Problem students were defined as a factor score consisting of the number of students who came from a different school the year before, the number of students who would transfer out of the school at the end of the current year, the number of students involved in criminal activities, the number of students who would drop out before graduation, the number of students taking remedial subjects, and the number of students in remedial summer school. Academic orientation of the student body was determined by a factor score consisting of the number of regular education students in college prep classes and the number of students who attend college after graduation. All nonwhite, that is, black, Hispanic, Asian, or Native American, students were considered as "minority" group members, although in most programs they made up a majority of the students. The median family income for a program was the modal of a categorical variable for family income ranges. Parental education level was the program-wide average of the number of years of education of the mothers of the deaf children.

Physical plant characteristics. Relatively few of these data were available and, of those that were available, most did not associate into factor scores. General school traits was a factor score consisting of the age of building since its last renovation, the size of the library collection, and the availability of areas for special facilities. School facilities for deaf education were defined by the average of the teachers' scores on the generated subscale for the *Purdue Teacher Inventory*.

Personnel. This variable included the following information about both the general education staff and the deaf education staff:

1. The professional quality and experience of the general education staff,
2. The deaf education staff's rapport with and attitude toward the supervisor of the deaf education program,
3. The deaf education staff's personal satisfaction with teaching,

4. The quality of the relationship between the deaf education staff and other teachers,
5. The deaf education staff's perceptions of their salaries,
6. The quality of the interpreters, and
7. The degree of on-site support for deaf education.

The quality of the general education instructional staff was evaluated by a factor score that included the frequency of teacher transfers, the degree of participation in school-based or district-based experimental curricula, and the percentage of the faculty having master's degrees. The deaf education staff's rapport with and attitude toward the supervisor of the deaf education program was defined by the average of the teachers' scores on the generated subscale for the *Purdue Teacher Inventory*. The deaf education staff's personal satisfaction with teaching was defined by the average of the teachers' scores on the generated subscale for the *Purdue Teacher Inventory*, as was the quality of the relationship between the deaf education staff and other teachers and the deaf education staff's perceptions of their salaries. The quality of the interpreters was defined by a factor score consisting of their years of general education, their described level of skill, and their self-reported level of training. The degree of on-site support for deaf education consisted of a count of the number of deaf education specialists other than instructors (e.g., counselors, school psychologists), divided by the total number of students in the program.

Procedures.   The types of school procedures were assessed using four measures:

1. Tracking and administrative policies in the school as a whole,
2. Class size in general education,
3. Instructional time available in all classes, and
4. Percentage of the deaf education program that was mainstreamed.

Tracking and administrative policies were a factor score consisting of the amount of in-school study time available to students, the use of grades to reward individual achievement, the use of a multiple criteria system for assigning students to classes, the use of tracking, and policies to promote slow learners socially. Class size was defined by the number of students in different types of classes and by the absence of advanced placement coursework. In other words, higher values meant larger classes and fewer advanced placement opportunities. Instructional time was a measure of the total amount of time available for instruction each year and the amount of homework time that was expected of each student. Mainstreaming was defined strictly as those deaf students in regular education mathematics, English, science, or social studies classes. Nonacademic mainstream classes, such as physical education, and noninstructional integration, such as lunch or extracurriculars, were not included.

Results

There was a serious problem with any analysis of the data we had available to us. Since we had complete data on only seven programs and several dozen possible variables that could be defined from the various data sources, we were faced with a problem of too many comparisons or too few subjects. The subjects in our analysis were seven individual school programs, which was too few to use solutions more appropriate to an analysis with a large number of variables, such as a multiple regression analysis. Consequently, we computed separate correlations and reported only results with a p value less than .02. In other words, a large number of comparisons were done with more stringent criteria for statistical significance. As a result, if a correlation is statistically significant, it accounts for half or more of the variance for that variable. The correlations are shown in Figure 10.3.

Population traits. Community support for teaching was positively associated with both achievement and self-image, but was statistically significant only for the achievement measure. This factor accounted for one-fourth of the variance for self-image, which suggests that it is a component of students' self-image and may appear as such in a larger sample study. Degree of "problem" students in the general education student population was negatively associated with achievement but positively associated with self-image, and both results were statistically significant. The negative relationship for achievement seems readily apparent, but the positive relationship for self-image is more difficult to explain. The reader might wish to consider Chapter 8, where Stinson and Whitmire speculate that sometimes when deaf students are equal to or better than their hearing peers, their self-esteem may be en-

Figure 10.3.   Correlations of achievement, self-image, and program traits

	Adjusted Achievement	Average Self - Image
POPULATION TRAITS		
Community support for teaching	+	
Degree of "problem" students in general education	-	+
Academic orientation of the student body		
Minority deaf students	-	
Degree of hearing loss	-	
Deaf students' median family income		
Deaf students' parental education level		
PHYSICAL PLANT CHARACTERISTICS		
General school traits		
School facilities for deaf education		
PERSONNEL		
Quality of the general education instructional staff		
Deaf educators' attitude toward supervisor		
Deaf educators' satisfaction with teaching	+	+
Deaf educators' relations with other teachers		
Deaf educators' feelings about salary		-
Quality of interpreting		
On-site deaf support specialists		
PROCEDURES		
Tracking and administrative policies		+
Class size		
Instructional time		
Proportion of program mainstreamed		

+ Positive correlation where p value < .02
- Negative correlation where p value < .02

hanced. In the case of these data, it would seem that the cost of more positive self-esteem is reduced achievement.

Academic orientation of the general education student body or the degree to which the general education program is college-oriented was positively associated with achievement and negatively associated with self-image. Neither result was statistically significant and both correlations accounted for less than one-fifth of the variance in either correlation. The reversal of the trend for the "problem" population relationship suggests that a problem site will enhance the self-image of deaf students, while an academically oriented site will not necessarily improve achievement.

The percentage of minority deaf students in the program was associated with lower overall adjusted achievement level but did not affect the group's self-image. Part of the effect of minority populations in a program should have been eliminated in the process of using regressed achievement scores; however, some description of the populations is in order. In the less effective programs, the students' median family incomes were lower; parental education was less; and the parents were less likely to own communications devices such as VCR's, TDD's, or TV decoders. Other educationally significant factors such as parental education and family resources are often associated with minority group membership and may in fact account for the observed differences.

Physical plant characteristics. The deaf education teachers' perceptions of the quality of the physical arrangements did not differentiate among the programs; nor did the building traits, such as the age of the building and so on, have any effect on the two outcome measures.

Personnel. There was an anomalous effect for the quality of the general education instructional staff on the self-image of the deaf education students. This may be related to the previously mentioned phenomenon of the perceived pressure by deaf students to compete in a difficult environment. The highly competitive situation posed by a more academically oriented student body and a highly qualified faculty may have a negative effect on the deaf students' self-image.

The rapport measure suggests a smoothly functioning and positive institutional environment in which education has a primary emphasis. The rapport between the deaf education staff and the deaf education supervisor did contribute to achievement and was positively associated with self-image, although the relationship was minuscule. The same effect on student achievement and self-image was noted for relationships among the deaf education staff. Positive staff relationships were related to higher achievement levels, but not to the self-image of the students.

Procedures. The use of various tracking procedures in the general education program did improve the achievement in the deaf education program, but was negatively associated with self-image. Class size in the general education program was not related to either achievement in the deaf education program or the self-image of the students. The total amount of instructional time available in the school was not related to greater achievement in the deaf education program, but was negatively (but not statistically significantly) related to self-image. Again, the issue of academic pressure and deaf students' self-image comes up. Longer school days and longer class periods are generally indicative of greater pressure for academic achievement. However, they do not necessarily reflect greater levels of achievement because total instructional time is a weak predictor of achievement. The negative self-image may be the product of a greater emphasis on achievement and the deaf students' perception of difficulty in responding to that pressure. When greater proportions of the program were mainstreamed, the results were higher achievement and lower self-image. Both correlations accounted for less than one-fifth of the variance for the two measures. With a greater proportion of the students mainstreamed, more are exposed to the demands of the general education program, and consequently self-image can be reduced. Greater exposure to mainstream instruction also means in many cases more content covered (Kluwin & Moores, 1989); consequently, higher levels of achievement are seen.

Discussion

The results of this study can be summarized in the following way. Achievement in programs for the deaf in local public high schools is related to educationally manageable variables such as staff quality and administrative effectiveness; community support and attitudes also play a contributing role. Unfortunately, from our data we cannot separate the degree to which staff quality and administrative effectiveness are independent of community support and attitudes. Deaf students' self-image as measured at the program rather than the individual level is the product of personal traits and experiences, such as the perception of the quality of the overall school environment and the degree of academic demand perceived by the deaf students. For a discussion of individual level results, see Chapter 8.

Some specific recommendations follow.

Expand community support and parent involvement. There has been a gratifying improvement in parent–child communication and in the percentage of parents signing with their deaf children in recent years. However, there are still unacceptably large numbers of parents, especially fathers, who do not sign with deaf children who use signs in their classrooms (Kluwin & Gaustad, 1991). Schools should make sign classes available, along with opportunities to communicate with deaf adults, especially to fathers.

More careful site selection for the deaf education program. Programs for the deaf should be housed in central locations with highly skilled general education staffs that have the time and resources to respond to the demands of a special population. A staff already burdened with massive social problems will have little, if any, time to develop the extra skills or information need to cope with a special population. Deafness is a special educational problem that cannot be addressed in an environment that must cope with other complex educational problems. Programs for the deaf should be located where greater emphasis can be placed on deafness and the integration of the deaf students into the general school population.

Greater attention to minority student concerns. Fewer than half of the children attending large public school programs for the deaf are white (Moores, 1991). In addition to Deaf culture and Deaf heritage, programs for the deaf in local public schools must teach about and show sensitivity to the pluralistic nature of our society (see Chapter 3).

Tracking as a mixed blessing. Tracking has had a controversial and inconsistent history in American education. Put very broadly, it seems to help the most able students by giving them access to a faster rate of content presentation, while segregating the least able into less effectively taught classes. However, it may be a boon to deaf education programs in that it may give the program administrators more specific and more focused choices for the deaf students. Effective programs for the deaf do not have to seek school sites that track their general population; however, appropriate placement of deaf students may be easier in such settings.

Press for success. Along with the quality of the staff and greater community involvement, a program for the deaf needs to be located where there is moderate pressure for academic success. There is a balance in most large school systems between schools where virtually all graduates will go on to major universities or colleges and those where it is questionable whether a majority of the student body will graduate. In environments where there is the expectation of moderate academic success, the deaf student will be able to balance the demand for achievement with the level of pressure he or she can tolerate.

Exposure to more academic content. As Kluwin (Chapter 9) points out, higher achievement is a matter of providing more information to more students. At the district and school level, this is not represented by more class periods or longer days or even longer school years but by the content of the curriculum, the requirements for graduation, and the accountability system for both teachers and students to complete the curriculum. For example, while standardized or graduation requirement testing presents a severe barrier for many deaf students, such programs at the district level represent a commitment to maintaining specific standards.

REFERENCES

Achilles, C. M., & Lintz, M. N. (1986, April). *Evaluation of an "effective schools" intervention.* Paper presented at the annual meeting of the American Educational Research Association, San Francisco.

Allen, T., & Osborn, T. (1984). Academic integration of hearing impaired students. *American Annals of the Deaf, 129*(2), 100–113.

Anderson, C. A. (1982). The search for school climate: A review of the research. *Review of Educational Research, 52,* 368–420.

Apple, W. G. (1991). A study of school achievement and the perception of school climate by teachers of the hearing-impaired in North Carolina. Manuscript in preparation.

Averch, H. A., Carroll, S. J., Donaldson, T. S., Kiesling, H. J., & Pineus, J. (1974). *How effective is schooling?* Santa Monica, CA: Rand Corporation.

Bentley, R. R., & Rempel, A. M. (1980). *Manual for the Purdue Teacher Opinionaire.* Lakeland, FL: Purdue Research Foundation.

Brill, R. G. (1978). *Mainstreaming the prelingually deaf child.* Washington, DC: Gallaudet College Press.

Brookover, W. B., Beady, C., Flood, P., Schweitzer, J., & Wisenbaker, J. (1979). *School social systems and student achievement: Schools can make a difference.* New York: Praeger.

Brophy, J., & Good, T. (1986). Teacher behavior and student achievement. In M. C. Wittrock (Ed.), *Handbook of research on teaching* (pp. 328–375). New York: Macmillan.

Centra, J. A., & Potter, D. A. (1980). School and teacher effects. *Review of Educational Research, 50,* 273–291.

Coleman, J., Campbell, E., Hobson, C., McPartland, J., Mood, A., Weinfield,

F., & York, R. (1966). *Equality of educational opportunity.* Washington, DC: U.S. Government Printing Office.

Dwyer, D. C., Lee, G. V., Rowan, B., & Bossert, S. T. (1982). *The principal's role in instructional management: Five participant observation studies of principals in action.* San Francisco: Far West Laboratory.

Glasman, N. S., & Biniaminov, I. (1982). Input–output analyses of schools. *Review of Educational Research, 51,* 509–539.

Good, T. L., & Brophy, J. E. (1986). School effects. In M. C. Wittrock (Ed.), *Handbook of research on teaching* (pp. 570–602). New York: Macmillan.

Halpin, A. W., & Croft, D. B. (1963). *The organizational climate of schools.* Chicago: University of Chicago Press.

Hauser, R. M., Sewell, W. H., & Alwin, D. F. (1976). High school effects on achievement. In W. H. Sewell, R. M. Hauser, & D. L. Featherman (Eds.), *Schooling and achievement in American society* (pp. 309–341). New York: Academic Press.

Hoy, W. K., & Clover, S. I. R. (1986). Elementary school climate: A revision of the ocdq. *Educational Administration Quarterly, 22,* 93–110.

Jencks, C. S., Smith, M., Ackland, H., Bane, M. J., Cohen, D., Gintis, H., Heyns, B., & Michelson, S. (1972). *Inequality: A reassessment of the effect of family and schooling in America.* New York: Basic Books.

Jensema, C. (1975). *The relationship between academic achievement and the demographic characteristics of hearing-impaired children and youth.* (Series R, No. 2). Washington, DC: Gallaudet Research Institute Center for Assessment and Demographic Information.

Kelly E. A. (1980). *Improving school climate.* Reston, VA: National Association of Secondary School Principals.

Kluwin, T. N. (1990). Consumer motivated research to development: The rationale for the national research to development network. In D. F. Moores & K. Meadow-Orlans (Eds.), *Research in the educational and developmental aspects of deafness* (pp. 137–153). Washington, DC: Gallaudet University Press.

Kluwin, T. N., & Gaustad, M. G. (1991). Predicting family communication choices. *American Annals of the Deaf, 136*(1), 28–34.

Kluwin, T. N., & Moores, D. F. (1989). The effects of integration on mathematics achievement of hearing-impaired adolescents. *Exceptional Children, 52,* 153–160.

Lezotte, L. W., Edmonds, T., & Ratner, G. (1974). *A final report: Remedy for school failure to equitably deliver basic school skills.* East Lansing: Michigan State University, Department of Urban and Metropolitan Studies.

Miller, S. K., Cohen, S. R., & Sayre, K. A. (1985). Significant achievement games using the effective schools model. *Educational Leadership, 42,* 28–43.

Moores, D. F. (1991). *Dissemination of a model to create least restrictive environments for deaf students.* (Final Report to NIDRR, United States Office of Special Education and Rehabilitation Services. Project No. 84133). Washington, DC: Gallaudet University.

Moores, D. F., Kluwin, T. N., & Mertens, D. M. (1985). *High school programs for deaf students in metropolitan areas.* (Monograph No. 3). Washington, DC: Gallaudet College, Gallaudet Research Institute.

Mortimer, P., & Sammons, P. (1987). New evidence on effective elementary schools. *Educational Leadership, 45,* 4–8.

Mortimer, P., Sammons, P., Stoll, L., Lewis, D., & Ecob, R. (1988). *School matters: The junior years.* Somerset, MA: Open Books.

National Study of School Evaluation. (1988). *Teacher Opinion Inventory.* Falls Church, VA: Author.

Pukey, S. C., & Smith, M. S. (1983). Effective schools: A review. *Elementary School Journal, 84*(4), 427–452.

Reich, C., Hambleton, D., & Houldin, B. (1977). The integration of hearing impaired children in regular classrooms. *American Annals of the Deaf, 122*(6), 534–539.

Scheerens, J. (1990). Process indicators of school functioning. *School Effectiveness and School Improvement, 1,* 61–80.

Schildroth, A. (1988). Recent changes in the educational placement of deaf students. *American Annals of the Deaf, 133*(3), 61–67.

Slavin, R. E. (1987). Ability grouping and student achievement in elementary schools: A best-evidence synthesis. *Review of Educational Research, 57*(3), 293–336.

Smith, S. J. (1975). *The relationship between organizational climate and selected variables of productivity-reading achievement, teacher experience, and teacher attrition.* (ERIC Document Reproduction Service No. ED 126 495).

van de Grift, W. (1990). Educational leadership and academic achievement in elementary education. *School Effectiveness and School Improvement, 1,* 26–40.

Walberg, H. (1984). Improving the productivity of American schools. *Educational Leadership, 41*(8), 19–27.

Wolk, S., Karchmer, M., & Schildroth, A. (1982). *Patterns of academic and non-academic integration among hearing impaired students in special education.* (Series R, No. 9). Washington, DC: Gallaudet University, Gallaudet Research Institute.

CHAPTER 11

The Career Development of Young People with Hearing Impairments

SUZANNE KING

"Blessed is he who has found his work; let him ask no other blessedness."

—Thomas Carlyle

Work, and work that is satisfying, is important to the psychological well-being of all people. According to Freud, work is what binds an individual to reality. Thus, an undemanding job for which one is overqualified, overtrained, and underpaid can lead to dissatisfaction with life itself. Our schools are predicated on the belief that a compulsory education will create a nation of young people ready to make the transition from childhood to adulthood, from life as student to life as worker.

However, reviews of the success of legislative efforts designed to facilitate the transition of handicapped students from school to work are mixed at best. Brolin and Gyspers (1989) have suggested that, despite the new laws, the school-to-work transition of students with disabilities is no better now than it was 10 years ago. In fact, the President's Committee on Employment of Persons with Disabilities reports that, while the national unemployment rate was at 7% in 1984, 65% of working age persons with disabilities were unemployed and the remaining third worked only part time (Fagan & Jenkins, 1989). Unless one accepts the assumption that most handicapped adults are not capable of full-time, competitive employment, these findings indicate that, in light of national priorities, something is amiss in our attempts to render all young people, with and without handicaps, employable and self-sufficient.

All of us in the business of educating deaf youngsters share in the responsibility of providing these young people with the skills they need to meet their vocational potentials. With that goal in mind, the purpose of this chapter is to introduce the reader to the career development literature, to summarize theories about career development, to present the career development research relevant to the deaf, and to discuss the implications for educators.

CAREER DEVELOPMENT THEORY

By far the most encompassing theory of career development is that of Donald Super (Super, 1953, 1980; Super et al., 1957; Super & Overstreet, 1960). His ideas expanded the concept of career development beyond the simple selection of a first occupation. In Super's view, a career is a lifetime of activities related to work and leisure. Super constructed his theory of career development using ideas from self-concept theory and developmental theory. Expanding on self-concept theory, Super suggests that an individual chooses an occupation and makes career decisions based on the match he or she sees between beliefs held about certain occupations and beliefs held about the self. Thus, the choice of an occupation is guided by the assumption that the chosen career is one that is most likely to permit self-expression, and the person with accurate information about him- or herself and about the world is likely to make sound career decisions.

The second major influence on Super's career development theory was the developmental psychology of Buehler (1933), who described the natural progression of human development through distinct stages. Building on her ideas, Super suggested that the vocational self-concept develops and shifts throughout the lifespan as one acquires information about, and experience with, a variety of people and occupations. Role playing and reality testing, which begin early in life, are a large part of this developmental process.

According to career development theory, there are three basic principles guiding an individual's career development. First, it is hypothesized that career behavior proceeds from random and undifferentiated activity to goal-directed, specific activity. Next, the progression is in the direction of increasing awareness and orientation toward reality. Third, the individual moves from dependence toward increasing independence (Lerman, 1976). Crystallization, the formulation of ideas about work, most often occurs between the ages of 14 and 18, although it can happen at any time during the life cycle.

The concept of vocational exploratory behavior (Jordaan, 1963) is a useful complement to Super's theory. As the adolescent explores the world and his or her own abilities, and gains knowledge about himself or herself, he or she will be faced with information that will threaten the previously established self-concept. Personal growth is most likely to occur if the individual reconciles the discrepancy between established beliefs and reality by modifying the self-concept appropriately. A willingness to tolerate the discomfort associated with change, and a family atmosphere that encourages independence, may facilitate exploratory behavior.

As for factors seen as influencing career development, Super feels that parental socioeconomic status, one's own mental abilities, personality characteristics, and the opportunities to which one is exposed all play an important part in defining an individual's career development.

Career Development During Adolescence

The normal developmental process takes young people through a stormy period during the teen years. These years can best be characterized as a competition between two rival needs: the drive to be a distinct and separate person in one's own right, and the need to see continuity between one's current and past selves while recognizing the similarities between the self and others. According to Erikson, adolescence is the time during which the individual's primary task is that of resolving this most central identity crisis (Schlesinger & Meadow, 1972). On the vocational scene, this task translates into an "orientation to the need to make educational and vocational choices including acceptance of responsibility for choosing and planning, and a planning and information-getting approach to the orientation and choice process: it is, essentially, planfulness" (Westbrook, 1983, p. 150).

Families can help adolescents to develop planfulness. Roe's (1957) theory suggests that the process by which adolescents come to make career decisions is influenced by parental acceptance. Hesser's (1981) research indicates that a nondirective, supportive home atmosphere that features high interest has the most positive influence on a child's career planning.

CAREER MATURITY

According to Crites (1984), the concept of career maturity was first developed as a result of Super's so-called Career Pattern Study (Super et al., 1975). In brief, the term "describes the differential ability of an individual to meet the tasks in life that deal with vocational matters" (Osipow, 1975, p. 11). As reflected in Super's Career Development Inventory (Super, Thompson, Lindeman, Jordaan, & Myers, 1981), career maturity comprises four basic qualities in two underlying domains: career attitudes (planfulness and exploration) and career knowledge and skills (decision making and information about the world of work). Thus, career maturity is one's readiness and ability to make realistic, informed decisions about one's vocational future.

There are many ways to evaluate the progress that an individual has made in the course of his or her career development. Besides assessing career maturity, one might evaluate career aspirations or career choices. Career maturity, however, involves fewer biases and assumptions than do other outcome constructs. If we accept the fact that we cannot know for certain how high any one individual should set his or her career goals, or in which occupation they are likely to be satisfied and successful, the most we can hope for is that young people be mature in their planning for the future. Career maturity is an age-normed construct. Thus, since we all compete to a certain extent with our age-mates for the available jobs, the use of career maturity measures to gauge a person's progress in career development is intuitively appropriate. Research results support the importance of career maturity during adolescence. Empirical evidence suggests that measures of career maturity in high school can predict longer-term outcomes. A 10-year follow-up of the Career Pattern Study (Super, Kowalski, & Gotkin, 1967) found that career maturity, measured in the ninth grade, was a good predictor of career satisfaction, self-improvement, and occupational satisfaction at age 25.

While career aspirations, occupational choice, and occupational attainment are measured on absolute scales, career maturity is a relative characteristic; the career maturity of a 21-year-old college graduate and a 10-year-old fifth grader are not measured on the same scale, although their career aspirations (to be a lawyer, for example) may be equivalent. Whereas the younger person may only daydream about courtroom drama, the older person will be expected to have selected university courses and to have worked for high grades in order to increase the chances of being admitted to law school. Both individuals can be said to be highly career mature relative to their places in the life cycle.

THE IMPACT OF HEARING IMPAIRMENT ON CAREER DEVELOPMENT

Significant hearing losses can have profound implications for students' transition from school to work. The impact of the hearing loss on career development may be mediated by the influence of the impairment on communication skills, the self-concept, family dynamics, and the school setting.

Communication

Lerman and Guilfoyle (1970) concluded from their study of career development in adolescents with hearing impairments that, for such a youngster, career maturity "is primarily an outgrowth of his own language competence and of the cultural stimulation provided for him by his parents" (p. 63). This suggests that while the ability to understand and communicate is critical, it is worthless without information to absorb. By the same token, abundant career information will not benefit the child incapable of acquiring it.

The role that deafness-related communication deficits can play in shaping all aspects of a child's development is clearly monumental. By influencing social relationships, academic achievement, imaginary play, self-concept, and all other aspects of his or her life, the impairment has profound implications when it comes time for the young person to take actions necessary to become a working, independent adult (Meadow, 1980). Because most of what normally hearing young people learn about the world is acquired serendipitously and because a deaf child in a hearing environment cannot pick up career-related information casually, a marked hearing loss may severely stunt early career development (McHugh, 1975). Growth through the awareness of occupations and exploration must, then, come primarily as a result of planned educational experiences.

Self-Concept

As mentioned above, as one's understanding of the self and of working environments develops, vocational choices can be made that are based on realistic perceptions. McHugh (1975), putting the situation in terms of Super's theory, states that a communication handicap will influence the self-concept of a person with a hearing impairment "because it affects his ability to successfully or profitably navigate the exploratory stages of life in the normal way" (p. 6) and that the resulting self-concept is then "built upon inadequate information, and often misinformation, from a society and an environment that cannot adequately communicate with him" (p. 7).

The identity formation of children with hearing impairments seems to be influenced by the hearing status of the parents. The self-image of students with deaf parents is significantly more positive than that of students with hearing parents (Meadow, 1980). This difference may be due to the positive role model provided by the deaf parent who is employed, and by the child's ability to communicate with family members early in life through sign language. For the deaf child of hearing parents, however, certain questions about his or her very nature and future in the world may arise (Schlesinger & Meadow, 1972).

The unresolved identity crises of adolescence do not just go away during young adulthood. As stated by Schlesinger and Meadow (1972), "many of our young adult deaf patients give evidence of identity diffusion" because they "have become separated from the rather protective settings of most school situations, and they find the world quite difficult" (p. 24).

Family Dynamics

As noted earlier, the ability to communicate with the environment is an advantage only if the environment contains information worth absorbing. The family environment ought naturally to be a source of vital stimulation related to life in the outside world. Here again, however, the hearing status of the parents can play an important role in the family atmosphere and resultant cultural stimulation. In the case of the deaf child of hearing parents, the young person emerges into adolescence with his or her adolescent crises relatively unresolved (Schlesinger & Meadow, 1972). It is at this same time that the parents may be experiencing certain crises of their own: The goals that they initially set for their perfect infant must now be compared with the emerging reality of their imperfect child's limitations (Schlesinger & Meadow, 1972). Deaf parents, on the other hand, are less likely to see their child's hearing impairment as a personal tragedy, and thus the family integration is less likely to be threatened as a result of the hearing loss (Schlesinger & Meadow, 1972).

The way in which the dynamics in a family with hearing parents can act to limit the career development of a child with a hearing impairment involves exposure to age-normed activities and responsibilities. Stinson (1974, 1978; cited in Meadow, 1980) found that the mothers of hearing boys respond to the pressures, burdens, and restrictions of child rearing by increasing the demands on their children; the mothers of children with hearing impairments, however, respond by relaxing demands. By denying their children age-related opportunities to explore the world and their own capabilities, hearing parents may hamper their children's career development and successful transition from school to work.

The most obvious way in which the hearing status of the parents can influence the child's career development is through communication difficulties: The inability to communicate easily can lead to family tension and, at times, dysfunction (Schlesinger & Meadow, 1972; Spradley, 1978). The child with a handicap may potentially be drawn into marital discord, playing the role of scapegoat or bone of contention, which will further hindering his or her emotional and, consequently, career development.

School Setting

Meadow's (1980) findings suggest that residential school students are less socially mature than those who interact daily with hearing peers. Lacey (1975) describes some of the consequences associated with placement in a residential setting:

> The evolution and maintenance of this restricted life space has these outcomes: fewer exposures to the work lives of parents and significant adults; reduced opportunities for investigation and imitation of appropriate work roles; a high degree of security in a safe and predictable environment; and limited access to and familiarity with the customs, laws and institutions of the larger, host community. (p. 300)

Although McHugh (1975) agrees that students in residential schools are more isolated from the world of work, he suggests that staff in residential schools, who are more likely to communicate well in sign language and who may have more information about careers for the deaf, are better prepared to communicate with deaf students about the outside world than are the staff in regular schools. Students in residential schools might, therefore, not only have more opportunities to absorb career information, but might also be exposed to a greater number of working adults who themselves have hearing impairments and who can act as appropriate role models.

Comparisons with Hearing Peers

In general, students with hearing impairments tend to be less career mature than their hearing peers. At the second-grade level, there is already a modest difference between the number of occupations a hearing student can spontaneously name ($M = 54$) and the number a deaf student can list ($M = 38$) (Chubon & Black, 1985). In fact, in second grade, deaf students have difficulty distinguishing what is work and what is play. By the eighth grade, the gap between the deaf and the hearing students has widened significantly: Hearing students can name an average of 83 occupations, while deaf age-mates can name only 37 (Chubon & Black, 1985).

The results of Lerman and Guilfoyle's (1970) study of deaf adolescents and their hearing siblings suggest that adolescents with hearing impairments are less career mature than their hearing siblings, specifically in the following characteristics: awareness of the social aspects of work, general occupational information, specific job information, commitment to occupational preference, reality of the preference, and the consistency of the preference.

ANTECEDENTS OF CAREER MATURITY IN THE HEARING IMPAIRED

Given that the development of career maturity ought to be the goal of career development programs for high school students, particularly those in programs for the deaf, it would be useful to know how young people become career mature. In addition, one may wish to know which of the factors that influence career maturity are open to intervention on the part of educators. In the following sections, empirical data relevant to the explanation of variance in career maturity will be presented. Then a statistical model of career maturity of the hearing impaired will be presented and discussed.

Background Factors

A consistent result of many career development studies is that females tend to score higher than males on measures of career maturity such as the Career Development Inventory (Hesser, 1981; Lokan, Boss, & Patsula, 1982; Neely & Johnson, 1981), the Career Maturity Inventory (Burkhead & Cope, 1984), and others (Super & Nevill, 1984; Westbrook, 1983). In addition, several studies have concluded that career maturity increases with age for both hearing impaired (Lerman & Guilfoyle, 1970) and hearing subjects (Lokan, Boss, & Patsula, 1982; O'Neil, et al., 1980; Super & Overstreet, 1960).

The child's age at the onset of hearing impairment and the degree of hearing loss are frequently discussed as important predictors of adjustment for hearing impaired individuals (Burkhead & Cope, 1984; Cowan, 1965; Karchmer, Malone, & Wolk, 1979; Lacey, 1975; Lerman & Guilfoyle, 1970; Overs, 1975). But these two variables are inconsistent in their ability to demonstrate their empirical associations with various measures of development (Karchmer, Malone, & Wolk, 1979, p. 97; Virginia Council for the Deaf, 1980). Any effect that the degree of hearing loss and the age at onset would have on career maturity would likely be through the language factor: The earlier the loss occurred and the less the individual is able to hear, the less able the individual is to pick up information and attitudes from the hearing world.

The socioeconomic status (SES) of an adolescent's parents appears to play an important role in the development of career maturity. Both Super and Overstreet (1960) and Hesser (1981) found correlations of about .30 between parental SES and adolescent career maturity.

Family Environment Variables

Hesser (1981) concluded from his study of 262 nonhandicapped high school seniors that it is the parents who have the greatest influence on their children's occupational aspirations and career maturity. Both he and Khan and Alvi (1983) found significant correlations between parental expectations for the child's occupational attainment and the child's career maturity.

Perhaps related to the family's SES is the quality of the cultural stimulation provided for the child in the home. Cultural participations included the number and types of educational and recreational materials and equipment available to household members. Super and Overstreet (1960), studying ninth-grade boys, and Lerman and Guilfoyle (1970), studying deaf adolescents and their siblings, found that cultural participation correlated significantly with career maturity.

Related to family dynamics, Hesser (1981) concluded from his study of hearing high school students that a "family's tendency to form coalitions [dyadic allegiances] is negatively associated with career exploration" (p. 185). Super and Overstreet (1960) included a family cohesion, or closeness, measure in their study and found a correlation of .18 with career maturity.

The ability of parents and children to communicate freely may have an important impact on a child's developing sense of the world, the self, and of personal control. However, it has been estimated that, in the population, fewer than half of all parents of deaf children learn to communicate in the child's most natural language of signs (Virginia Council for the Deaf, 1980). When parents and deaf children do communicate, it is not likely to be at a very abstract level (Schlesinger & Meadow, 1972).

Locus of Control and Career Maturity

As an individual experiences a variety of situations, he or she gradually builds expectations about receiving reinforcement and draws conclusions about the relationship between behaviors and outcomes (Rotter, Chance, & Phares, 1972). An *internal locus of control* is the belief that one is in control of one's fate. The alternative is to have the expectation that outcomes are determined primarily by forces outside one's control, such as fate, luck, or chance, and is termed an *external locus of control*. Social learning theory predicts that persons with an internal locus of control are more likely to be goal-seeking, while those with an external locus of control tend to allow life to happen to them passively. One's belief in the control of reinforcement is related to career development, with a more internal locus of control being associated with greater career maturity in both able and disabled populations (Bernadelli, Stephano, & Dumont, 1983; Blevins, 1984; Gellatt, Varenhorst, Carey, & Miller, 1973; Khan & Alvi, 1983; Lokan, Boss, & Patsula, 1982; Phillips, Strohmer, Berthaume, & O'Leary, 1983). Deaf adolescents may have learned that, in fact, there is much in their world that is beyond their personal control but that nonetheless has an important impact on their lives. Perhaps for this reason, adolescents with hearing impairments tend to be more external in their locus of control than nondisabled peers (Blanton & Nunnally, 1964; Dowaliby, Burke, & McKee, 1983; King, 1988).

Educational Variables and Career Maturity

As mentioned earlier, there is some debate as to whether a deaf child's career development would be encouraged more by education in a residential setting or in a mainstreamed setting. Empirical evidence from at least one source (Fitzsimmons & Butson, 1986) suggests that, in deaf adults between the ages of 18 and 50, greater vocational knowledge was associated with education alongside nondisabled peers.

A THEORY- AND RESEARCH-BASED MODEL OF CAREER MATURITY FOR THE HEARING IMPAIRED

Figure 11.1 illustrates a causal model of career maturity based on theoretical considerations and on the empirical literature with hearing and with deaf samples. The variables in the model were arranged according to a logical, temporal order. The first variables in the sequence are those for which no particular cause is postulated; that is, the adolescent's sex and age, and the parent's socioeconomic status, as well as the degree and age at onset of the hearing loss. These background variables are hypothesized as having an effect on five family variables:

1. The parents' aspirations for their child's occupational attainment,
2. The degree of family cohesion as rated by the child,
3. The cultural participation in the home as indicated by the parents,
4. The quality and quantity of mother-child communication, and
5. The quality and quantity of father-child communication.

The background and family variables in the model are assumed to have an influence on the personality and schooling of the child— that is, his or her locus of control, achievement level (reading and math achievement), and placement in either a residential or mainstreamed school setting. Finally, the background, family, person-

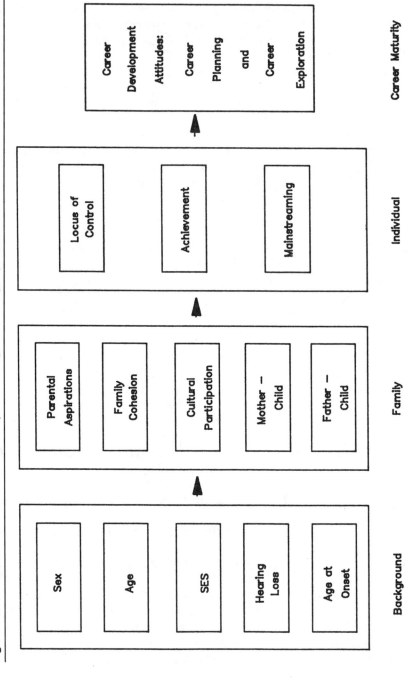

Figure II.I. Causal model of career maturity for hearing and hearing impaired adolescents

ality, and educational variables are all presumed to influence the child's degree of career maturity.

Testing the Model

To test this causal model, King (1988) collected data from 71 male and female high school students in programs for the deaf in Virginia and Washington, DC. The deaf participants were selected on the basis of their reading level, which had to be at a 3.5 grade equivalent or better. Hearing losses ranged from mild (9% of sample) to profound (65% of sample).

Three instruments were administered to the students in groups ranging in size from 5 to 30. Information on the subjects, instruments, and procedures is presented in greater detail elsewhere (King, 1990). The Career Planning and Career Exploration Subscales of the Career Development Inventory (Super, Thompson, Lindeman, Jordaan, & Myers, 1981) yield a composite score on the Career Development Attitudes Scale, this study's measure of career maturity. The Attitudes scale reflects the type and extent of career planning in which the student has engaged, the student's self-reported degree of knowledge possessed about the kind of occupation the student currently believes he or she might like to choose, the student's judgment about the quality of career information already obtained from a variety of human and media sources, and the student's beliefs as to which of these sources he or she would go for help.

Students also completed the Different Situations Inventory (Gardner & Warren, 1978), which measures locus of control orientation. High scores represent an internal locus of control, while low scores indicate an external locus of control.

The third student measure was the Family Adaptability and Cohesion Evaluation Scales (FACES III)(Olson, Portner, & Lavee, 1985). Scores on the Cohesion scale reflect disengagement (extreme interpersonal distance) at the low end of the continuum and enmeshment (extreme closeness) at the high end.

Finally, standardized reading and math achievement scores were obtained from school records and were combined to create the achievement variable.

A questionnaire was mailed to the students' parents. This instrument was used to obtain background information about the student and his or her family as well as an estimate of the parents' aspirations for their child's occupational attainment (professional or nonprofessional). Each mother and father was also asked to indicate the degree of complexity they were capable of when communicating with their deaf child and to estimate the amount of time each spent communicating with the child on days when both were at home. Also included in the packet was a 29-item version of the Cultural Participation Scale (Super, Kowalski, & Gotkin, 1967). Scores on this instrument indicate the number of different kinds of material read by the student as well as the number of different kinds of educational and recreational equipment available in the home.

The advantage of a path analytic model is that the relationship between any two variables can be freed from the confounding effects of other variables in the model. The results of the path analysis are presented in graphic form in Figure 11.2 (showing only significant and near-significant effects that relate to career maturity). The results suggest that this model explains 31.3% of the variance in career maturity scores in high school students who have hearing impairments ($p < .10$).

In the explanation of career maturity scores in this sample, only family cohesion and academic achievement had significant direct and total effects: Greater ratings of family cohesion by the student were associated with greater career maturity. Higher achievement scores were associated, surprisingly, with lower career maturity levels. Once all the other variables in the model are controlled for, however, mainstreaming has no significant effect on career maturity ($B = .039, p > .10$).

When one variable has an effect on a second variable by influencing a third, intervening variable, this is called an indirect effect. The results from the current study suggest that there was one significant indirect effect in this model: the effect of mother–child communication on career maturity. This indirect effect may manifest itself in two different ways. First, the higher the quality of the mother–child communication, and the more internal the child's locus of control, the greater his or her career maturity scores tend to be. Second, better mother–child communication was associated with lower academic achievement, which, in turn, was associated with higher career maturity scores.

In short, then, the results of this path analysis suggest that the most important variables in the explanation of career maturity in adolescents with hearing impairments are the following:

1. Academic achievement (which is negatively related),
2. The child's perception of cohesion in his or her family,

Figure 11.2. Significant and near-significant paths in causal model

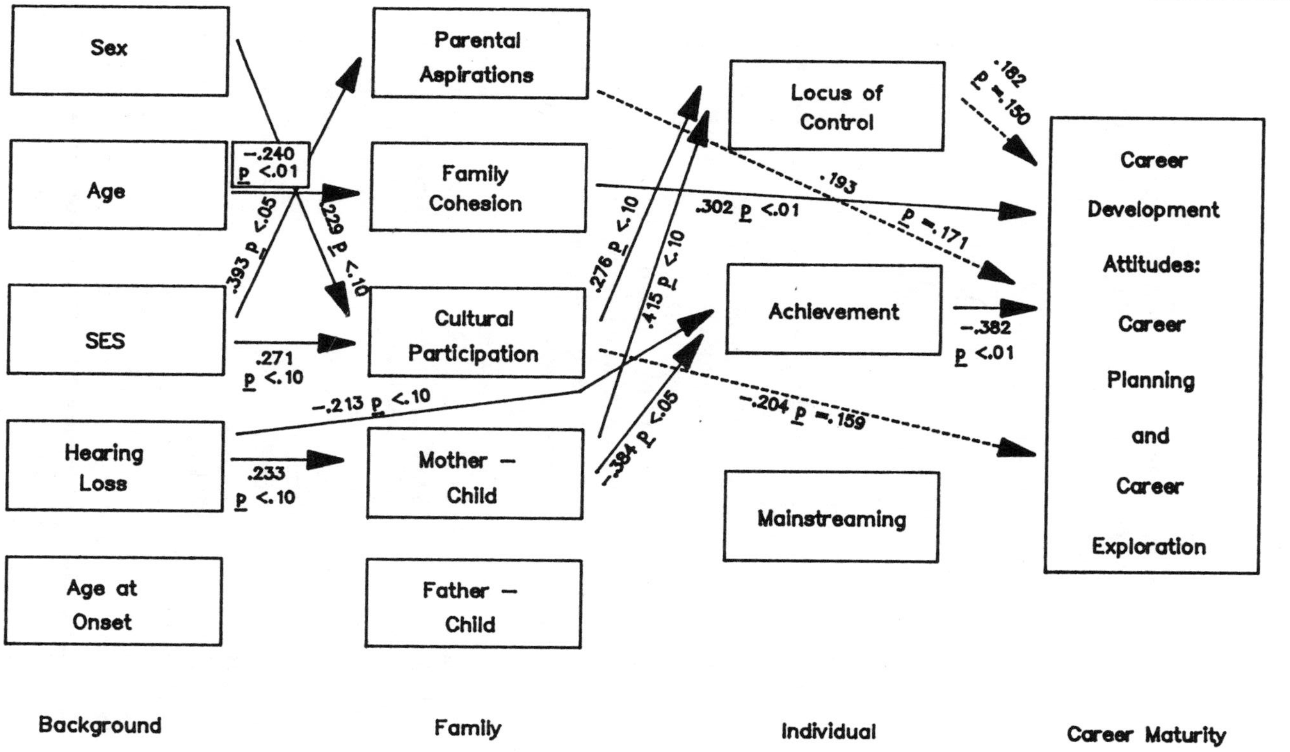

3. An internal locus of control,
4. Parental aspirations for the child's occupational attainment, and
5. The quality of mother–child communication.

Mainstreaming, the degree and age at onset of the hearing loss, and the parents' SES all had negligible total effects on career maturity for this group of youngsters.

Implications for Educators and Counselors

In light of the data on career development in adolescents, Super (1953) has suggested that educators not take too seriously the career aspirations expressed by high school students but rather work on improving the self-concept of young people and on guiding them through vocational tasks such as crystallization. The goal of such counseling efforts is to develop career maturity, particularly a sense of planfulness in the young person.

Given that the development of career maturity ought to be the goal of educators concerned about the school-to-work transition of deaf students, what do the results of this path analysis indicate about where efforts ought to be focused? The strong, negative effect of academic achievement on career maturity is puzzling and difficult to interpret, particularly since achievement has a near-zero association with career maturity in hearing peers (King, 1990).

The direction of the achievement effect for the deaf may be explainable by programming decisions. Since a child with a hearing impairment will pick up only career-related information that is presented explicitly in a way that he or she is able to absorb, career education must be as important an aspect of education for the academically gifted as for those less able academically. The results of these analyses may suggest that career education is a greater component of daily class instruction in the lower academic tracks than it is in the higher academic tracks. It may be that the first mandate of educators should be to ensure that all hearing impaired students receive career education programming. Alternatively, there may be some other difference between higher and lower achievers that would explain the negative direction of the achievement effect; they may differ in the extent to which they are interested in the career information with which they are presented, for example.

The results presented here may suggest that the mainstreaming debate is irrelevant to the development of career maturity in students with hearing impairments. While decisions to mainstream appear to be related to the degree of the impairment and to the extent of language acquisition before the onset of the loss, there appears to be little reason to believe that, all else being equal, one form of education is superior to the other in the development of career maturity.

The importance of an internal locus of control to career maturity suggests a possible point at which the career maturity of hearing impaired students can be enhanced. Research suggests that the locus of control and career maturity of adolescents with hearing impairments can be improved through intervention in a school setting (Blevins, 1984).

The child's perception of the cohesion in his or her family is a strong predictor of career maturity. The parents' aspiration for the child's occupational attainment and the quality of mother–child communication are moderate predictors. Although there is little an educator can do to encourage family cohesion, efforts can be made to help parents develop realistically high aspirations for their children by informing parents of occupational opportunities available to their children and by assisting parents in their efforts to learn to communicate more easily with their deaf children. The realization that a sense of family cohesion is important to the development of career maturity may help a counselor understand a given student's readiness to make career decisions, even though that factor is beyond the counselor's sphere of influence.

The most direct effort to improve career maturity is through career education. Since deaf adolescents appear to have difficulty even naming a variety of occupations (Chubon & Black, 1985), they can hardly be in a position to consider and evaluate the range of occupations for which they may be suited. Before career counselors or parents attempt to acquaint hearing impaired adolescents with the gamut of occupations to consider, however, parents and educators may need some education of their own. It appears that both parents and teachers have a tendency to advise deaf young people into so-called "deaf occupations" (Cook & Rossett, 1975; DeCaro, Dowaliby, & Maruggi, 1983; Farrugia, 1982; Lacey, 1975).

Even if deaf students are career mature and well trained in an occupation of their choice, this may not ensure their ability to maintain employment success. One well-known fact among rehabilitation counselors is that approximately 70% of jobs that are lost are not lost due to lack of ability but rather for social-motivational reasons. This can be particularly important for the worker with a hearing impairment who is already likely to have less well-developed social skills than his or her hearing coworkers. Troop (1966) presents examples from his experience as a rehabilitation counselor.

> Time after time, I have seen good deaf workers fired from their jobs for reasons which are not understandable unless you understand the total background of the deaf: stopping to eat lunch when he became hungry rather than waiting for the official lunch hour; occupying someone's 'paid-for' parking spot with the rationalization, "Well, he wasn't here"; walking away from the job when it appeared that someone was talking about him or reprimanding him. (p. 4)

An important aspect of career education programs for the deaf must be, then, training in the social, nonoccupational work behaviors that can ensure success and acceptance in the workplace. Brolin and Gyspers (1989) describe several career guidance programs that include daily living skills and personal-social skills in their curricula, including the Life-Centered Career Education Curriculum. Gardner and Warren (1978) describe a career education program for disabled students that emphasizes the development of a work personality and an internal locus of control.

CONCLUSIONS

What research tells us is that it is neither the degree of the hearing loss nor the age at onset of the loss nor even the setting in which one is educated that makes the difference between a career mature and a career immature deaf adolescent. Career education in a language the deaf adolescent can understand, in conjunction with a supportive and nondirective family willing to explore the full range of vocational possibilities in a culturally stimulating environment, is our best bet in the struggle against the national, and personal, hardship of un- and underemployment. Given the profound personal implications of a hearing loss and a communication deficit, career development cannot be left to chance alone.

REFERENCES

Bernadelli, A., Stephano, J., & Dumont, F. (1983). Occupational information-seeking as a function of perception of locus of control and other personality variables. *Canadian Counselor, 17,* 75–81.

Blanton, R. L., & Nunnally, J. C. (1964). Evaluational language process in the deaf. *Psychological Reports, 15,* 891–894.

Blevins, B. A. (1984). The effects of career decision-making skills intervention on locus of control and career maturity of adolescent deaf students. Doctoral dissertation, Virginia Polytechnic Institute, Blacksburg.

Brolin, D. E., & Gyspers, N. C. (1989). Career education for students with disabilities. *Journal of Counseling and Development, 68,* 155–159.

Buehler, C. (1933). *Der menschliche Lebenslauf als psycholo-gisches Problem.* Leibzig: Herzel.

Burkhead, E. J., & Cope, C. S. (1984). Career maturity and physically disabled college students. *Rehabilitation Counseling Bulletin, 27,* 142–150.

Chubon, R. A., & Black, B. L. (1985). A comparison of career awareness development in deaf residential school student and non-disabled public school students. *Journal of Rehabilitation of the Deaf, 18,* 1–5.

Cook, L., & Rossett, A. (1975). The sex role attitudes of deaf adolescent women and their implications for vocational choice. *American Annals of the Deaf, 120*(7), 341–345.

Cowan, E. (1965). Adjustment to auditory disability in adolescence. In U.S. Department of Health, Education and Welfare (Ed.), *Research on behavioral aspects of deafness: Proceedings of a national research conference* (393–412). Washington, DC: Author.

Crites, J. O. (1984). Instruments for assessing career development. In N. C. Gyspers (Ed.), *Designing careers* (pp. 248–294). San Francisco: Jossey-Bass.

DeCaro, J. J., Dowaliby, F. J., & Maruggi, E. A. (1983). A cross-cultural examination of parents' and teachers' expectations for deaf young regarding careers. *British Journal of Educational Psychology, 53,* 538–563.

Dowaliby, F. J., Burke, N. E., & McKee, B. B. (1983). A comparison of hearing-impaired and normally-hearing students on locus of control, people orientation, study habits, and attitudes. *American Annals of the Deaf, 128*(1), 53–59.

Fagan, T. K., & Jenkins, W. M. (1989). People with disabilities: An update. *Journal of Counseling and Development, 68,* 140–144.

Farrugia, D. L. (1982). Deaf high school students' vocational interest and attitudes. *American Annals of the Deaf, 127*(8), 753–762.

Fitzsimmons, G., & Butson, S. (1986). Vocational knowledge testing of a deaf and hard of hearing population. *Canadian Journal of Counseling, 20,* 104–113.

Gardner, D. C., & Warren, S. A. (1978). *Careers and disabilities: A career education approach.* Stamford, CT: Greylock.

Gellatt, H. B., Varenhorst, B., Carey, R., & Miller, G. P. (1973). *Decisions and outcomes: A leader's guide.* New York: College Entrance Examination Board.

Hesser, A. (1981). *Adolescent career development, family adaptability and family cohesion.* Unpublished doctoral dissertation, Virginia Polytechnic Institute, Blacksburg.

Jordaan, J. P. (1963). Exploratory behavior. The formulation of self and occupational concepts. In D. E. Super (Ed.), *Career development: Self-concept theory* (Research Monograph No. 4). New York: CEEB.

Karchmer, M. A., Malone, M. N., & Wolk, S. (1979). Educational significance of hearing loss at three levels of severity. *American Annals of the Deaf, 122*(2), 97–109.

Khan, S. B., & Alvi, S. A. (1983). Educational, social, and psychological correlates of vocational maturity. *Journal of Vocational Behavior, 22,* 357–364.

King, S. (1988). Modeling the career maturity of hearing and hearing-impaired adolescents. *Dissertation Abstracts International, 49*(5), 1063A. (University Microfilms No. 88–04, 409)

King, S. (1990). Comparing two causal models of career maturity for hearing-impaired adolescents. *American Annals of the Deaf, 135*(1), 47–63.

Lacey, D. (1975). Career behavior of deaf persons: Current status and future trends. In J. S. Picou & R. E. Campbell (Eds.), *Career behavior of special groups* (pp. 237–263). Columbus: Charles E. Merrill.

Lerman, A. (1976). Vocational development. In B. Bolton (Ed.), *Psychology of deafness for rehabilitation counselors* (pp. 57–73). Baltimore: University Park Press.

Lerman, A. M., & Guilfoyle, G. R. (1970). *The development of prevocational behavior in deaf adolescents.* New York: Teachers College Press.

Lokan, J. J., Boss, M. W., & Patsula, P. J. (1982). A story of vocational maturity during adolescence and locus of control. *Journal of Vocational Behavior, 20,* 331–334.

McHugh, D. F. (1975). A view of deaf people in terms of Super's theory of vocational development. *Journal of Rehabilitation of the Deaf, 9,* 1–11.

Meadow, K. P. (1980). *Deafness and child development.* Berkeley: University of California Press.

Neely, M. A., & Johnson, C. W. (1981). The relationship of performance on six scales of the Career Development Inventory to sex, father's education and father's occupation. *Educational and Psychological Measurement, 41,* 917–921.

Olson, D. H., Portner, J., & Lavee, Y. (1985). FACES III: *Family Adaptability & Cohesion Evaluation Scales.* St. Paul: University of Minnesota.

O'Neil, J. M., Ohlde, C., Tollefson, N., Barke, C., Piggot, T., & Watts, D. (1980). Factors, correlates, and problem areas affecting career decision making of a cross-sectional sample of students. *Journal of Counseling Psychology, 27,* 571–580.

Osipow, S. H. Theories of Career Development (2nd ed.) New York: Appleton-Century-Croft.

Overs, R. P. (1975). Career behavior of the physically and mentally handicapped. In J. S. Picou & R. E. Campbell (Eds.), *Career behavior of special groups* (pp. 177–198). Columbus: Charles E. Merrill.

Phillips, S. D., Strohmer, D. C., Berthaume, B. L., & O'Leary, J. C. (1983). Career development of special populations: A framework for research. *Journal of Vocational Behavior, 22*, 12–29.

Roe, A. (1957). Early determinants of vocational choice. *Journal of Counseling Psychology, 4*, 212–217.

Rotter, J. B., Chance, J. E., & Phares, E. J. (1972). *Applications of a social learning theory of personality*. New York: Holt, Rinehart & Winston.

Schlesinger, H. S., & Meadow, K. P. (1972). *Sound and signs*. Berkeley: University of California Press.

Spradley, T. S. (1978). *Deaf like me*. New York: Random House.

Super, D. E. (1953). A theory of vocational development. *American Psychologist, 8*, 185–190.

Super, D. E. (1980). A life-span life-space approach to career development. *Journal of Vocational Behavior, 16*, 282–298.

Super, D. E., Crites, J. O., Hummel, R. C., Moser, H. P., Overstreet, P. L., & Warnath, C. F. (1957). *Vocational development: A framework for research*. New York: Teachers College Press.

Super, D. E., Kowalski, R. S., & Gotkin, E. H. (1967). *Floundering and trial after high school*. (Cooperative Research Project No. 1393). New York: Teachers College Press.

Super, D. E. & Nevill, D. D. (1984). Work role salience as a determinant of career maturity in high school students. *Journal of Vocational Behavior, 25*, 30–44.

Super, D. E., & Overstreet, P. (1960). *The vocational maturity of ninth grade boys*. New York: Teachers College Press.

Super, D. E., Thompson, A. S., Lindeman, R. H., Jordaan, J. P., & Myers, R. A. (1981). *Career Development Inventory*. Palo Alto, CA: Consulting Psychologist Press.

Troop, H. W. (1966). Provision of services. In Department of Health, Education and Welfare (Ed.), *The vocational rehabilitation of deaf people* (pp. 87–94). Washington, DC: Rehabilitation Services Administration.

Virginia Council for the Deaf. (1980). *Virginia's hearing-impaired children: A needs assessment*. Richmond: Author.

Westbrook, B. W. (1983). Career maturity. The concept, the instruments, and the research. In W. B. Walsh & S. H. Osipow (Eds.), *Handbook of vocational psychology* (pp. 263–303). Hillsdale, NJ: Erlbaum.

The Collision of Reality and Expectations

DONALD F. MOORES

There are a number of recurring themes throughout this part of the book. For me, the greatest impact comes from the apparently overpowering influence of deafness on every aspect of a child's functioning—social, academic, linguistic, and emotional. Those who believed that mere placement of deaf children in contiguity to hearing peers would solve all the problems of deafness, and that in some magical way hearing children would provide behavioral and linguistic models, have been sadly mistaken. The expectation of automatic assimilation was naive. Conversely, those who feared that the trend from residential to local public school education would be an unmitigated disaster for deaf children have not seen their fears realized. Regardless of the environment, the education of children with severe and profound hearing losses is a difficult process, and the greater the hearing loss the greater the obstacles to be surmounted.

The increased placement of deaf children in local public schools was never met with the resistance and hostility that racial and ethnic minorities frequently have had to face in the American public school system. Perhaps this is due somewhat to the fact that the numbers of deaf children are so small, as well as to the reality that the increase in the numbers of deaf children born in the mid-1960s due to a worldwide Rubella epidemic coincided with the end of the post-World War II baby boom and a subsequent decline in school enrollment. Quite simply, for the first time in more than a generation there were empty classrooms in American public schools. On the other hand, although there was no resistance to the presence of deaf and other categories of handicapped children, there was little in the way of positive change in public school programs or procedures to facilitate the incorporation of deaf children as full-fledged members of the school community. To a large degree, deaf children were allowed entry to the schools and allocated space as well as varying degrees of access to regular classrooms through interpreters. Aside from that, few accommodations were made. The deaf children were expected to adapt to the school, not vice versa.

To some extent, at least until recently, deaf children constituted one more minority moving through the schools. This was brought home to two of the editors of the present volume (Moores and Kluwin) at the beginning of our research program in 1982. Two of the large city high school programs for the deaf we visited were located within racially and ethnically mixed regular high schools. In each case, during lunchtime the cafeteria was largely segregated and one of the groups in which there was significant ethnic and racial mixing was identified as consisting of deaf students. It was ironic that the staff did not think of the deaf students as segregated because they formed a multi-ethnic/multiracial cluster. However, the self-segregation of deaf and hearing students was at least as pronounced as the self-segregation of black, white, and Hispanic students. This separation is highlighted by Stinson and Whitmire's observation that positive interaction rarely occurs between deaf and hearing students in the unwritten curriculum of riding on school buses and interacting in hallways, cafeteria, and sports.

In addition to the problems of communication, the issue of transportation and accessibility is a major factor. Because deafness is such a low-incidence condition, most children in a centralized program for the deaf do not live in a school's usual catchment area and typically travel to and from school by special bus or van. This raises two problems. First, the deaf child is not familiar with the school environs and neighborhood. Second, the deaf child, because of transportation requirements, may have little opportunity to participate in school sports and other extracurricular activities. In addition, as Stinson and Whitmire point out, since deaf children generally live some distance from each other, their nonschool social activities are also restricted. Given this perspective, the description of minimal to nonexistent interaction of deaf and hearing peers presented by Gaustad and Kluwin should come as no surprise.

Stewart and Stinson's report that there has been a decreasing emphasis on physical education concomitant with increasing interest in interscholastic athletics has serious implications for the enculturation of deaf students. Stewart and Stinson stress the importance of interscholastic competition in residential schools for the deaf, not only with schools for the hearing but also the system of regional competitions and tournaments with other schools for the deaf. However, the opportunities for participation in interscholastic athletics is much more limited for deaf students in local public schools. First, enrollments tend to be much larger, implying a higher level of competition. Second, in team sports deaf students may face obstacles in communication that might limit their effectiveness, especially in "skill" positions. The most obvious example would be in football, where a quarterback might call "audibles" to change a play in which the assignments of other members of the team would be altered. Even here, however, some outstanding deaf athletes can compensate. For example, the quarterback on the Gallaudet University football team in the late 1980s had played quarterback for a "hearing" high school football team. His speech was good enough to call audibles for his hearing teammates in high school. In college he used signs to call "audibles." There are several examples of such outstanding athletes, but they are exceptional cases.

The picture of minimal deaf and hearing peer interaction, of course, is not monolithic. Although the patterns of class placement, extracurricular participation, and social interaction appear to be similar, there are also some differences. Socially, we may think of roughly four groups. The first, which according to Gaustad and Kluwin's data from 12 high schools may account for roughly 10% of deaf students, have highly developed oral skills and interact essentially through speech with both deaf and hearing peers. These students may be thought of as socially enculturated. As a group, they also may have relatively little need for additional services in the form of interpreters, counseling, and tutoring. These are the types of students who might have been integrated prior to the enactment of PL 94–142, the group that constitutes those students traditionally classified as "oral successes."

The second group, somewhat more than one-third of the sample, relied predominantly on oral communication with hearing peers and manual communication with deaf peers, reflecting a flexibility in communication strategies. Most educators of the deaf might think that this group would comprise the majority of deaf public school children, those who could function in both hearing and deaf environments. Although the numbers are relatively large, these children in reality represent a minority of public school deaf children.

The third group, somewhat less than one-third of the sample, interacted with both deaf and hearing peers but relied on manual communication. This suggests that at least some hearing students are willing and able to develop a degree of manual communication skill to accommodate deaf students with few usable oral skills.

Finally, there is a group of about one-sixth of the deaf sample that interacts only with deaf friends and only signs. The extent to which this group is different from the previous one is unclear. One might expect that students within this category would communicate with some hearing peers through manual communication, but this does not appear to be the case. These students may have little or no motivation to interact with hearing peers, and there also may be program factors at work. Regarding program influences, of particular interest is the finding by Gaustad and Kluwin that in 3 of the 12 schools, no deaf students reported the use of speech only, suggesting that more is involved in the selection of a mode of communication by deaf students than hearing loss alone. Perhaps the differences in interaction reflect attitudinal differences to some extent.

The data from various chapters in this section indicate that manual communication has been effective in bringing deaf students to both self-contained and mainstream classes in public schools, with interpreters playing significant roles in placing deaf and hearing students in contiguity in academic classes and in athletics. This effectiveness has not extended to the same degree to the social realm, where deaf and hearing students in general do not interact frequently. The issue to a large extent concerns what the role of public schools should be in the education of deaf children. If it is primarily academic, then lack of social interaction, no matter how lamentable, is of secondary importance. If it is to integrate deaf children into all aspects of the hearing world, then the criteria for success should reflect this. If the goal is somewhere in between—to develop academic skills to as high a level as feasible while trying to prepare the deaf student to move comfortably between deaf and hearing environments—then program structure, academic content, and the criteria for success should be modified. The formal and supportive school structures needed to accomplish the various goals are quite different.

King's chapter on career development presents yet another picture. Most striking is her conclusion that it is neither the degree of hearing loss nor socioeconomic status nor the age of onset of the loss nor even the setting in which one is educated that makes the difference between a career mature and a career immature adolescent who happens to be hearing impaired. It appears that type of placement per se has no effect on career maturity of deaf adolescents, and thus King concludes that any mainstreaming debate is irrelevant to the development of career maturity. This would be acceptable if career maturity were uniformly high, but since the indications are deaf children in all educational placements are being poorly served in the area of career development, training should be improved across the board.

King's causal model of career maturity presents some interesting findings and raises a number of intriguing questions. To a large degree the results are as one might expect. Some of the most important variables in the explanation of career maturity are the student's perception of cohesion in his or her family, the student's internal locus of control, parental aspirations for the child, and the quality of mother–child communication. Completely unexpected, at least to me, was the finding that academic achievement was negatively correlated with career maturity in deaf adolescents. This is shocking, given King's quote of Osipow (1975, p. 11) that career maturity "describes the differential ability of an individual to meet the tasks in life that deal with vocational matters" and her statement that career maturity is one's readiness and ability to make realistic, informed decisions about one's vocational future. In other words, deaf students with higher academic achievement are less ready to make informed decisions about their vocational future and are less prepared to meet the tasks in life that deal with vocational matters. King's speculation that career education for deaf children may be a greater component of daily class instruction in the lower academic tracks than in the higher academic tracks is a matter worthy of serious investigation. If this proves to be the case, it must be rectified. As in so many chapters in this section, the complex reality of deaf children's public school attendance is far different from the simplistic expectations of professionals seeking easy answers.

Conclusion: Some Reflections on Defining an Effective Program

THOMAS N. KLUWIN

Whether it was three little girls walking between ranks of bayonets to get into school or Medgar Evers surrounded by the state police, educational integration began with the necessity of establishing the legal principle that all children have the right to an education. However, integration cannot function on a day-to-day basis at the point of a bayonet. Over time the structural integration of separate systems evolved. Today we have legal integration, if not racial harmony, because it is no longer legal to discriminate on a formal basis. However, we cannot expect that because at one point we proclaim the right of all deaf children to participate in American society when they are adults, that that is a guarantee for the future. If Chapter 1 shows anything, it shows that values can change. Vigilance, and with it controversy, will continue to mark the field.

In the education of the deaf, the point of the bayonet has been replaced in many programs by the shoehorn (see Chapter 1). Some school programs are attempting to fit the deaf child into the school system and into hearing society one at a time. The IEP, which should be an individual educational bill of rights, has become a device for not responding to the larger issues of the integration of deaf individuals into society. Racial integration occurs in public schools in this country not because individual minority children have educational plans that require certain degrees of contact, but because public school administrative and instructional systems do not tolerate separate programs. The shoehorn is no better than the bayonet because both are temporary solutions. The starting point for the racial integration of children in schools must be the structural and legal integration of the adults who are the educational system. Since the first casualties of political turf battles in educational systems are the children, the legal and structural integration of educational programs must be the starting point for effective public school programs for deaf and hard of hearing children. Before we can expect deaf children to be integrated with their hearing peers, the adults responsible for these programs must create systems that promote formal interaction between adults.

THE PROBLEM IS THAT THE SOLUTION IS A PROBLEM

American education has a long history of such apparent contradictions, the inheritance of trying to promote a pluralistic democracy. The education of deaf children in public school programs cannot avoid these tensions.

Being a Member of a Family

An indirectly addressed, but implicit, assumption in this book is the value of being a member of a family. Chapter 4 ties family processes to school achievement. More important, a motivation for the local public school education of deaf children is the maintenance of the child within his or her own family and within a local community. Both are assumed to be good in and of themselves.

However, because deafness is a low-incidence condition, it is difficult to collect sufficient numbers of deaf children within an area to operate a program. This has resulted in some instances in isolated, disconnected, and inadequately supervised staff; incomplete service provision for children; and the absence of a deaf community or even deaf adult contact for the children.

An alternative has been to create regional schools in urban areas. This solves some of the problems but creates others (see Chapter 8). Transportation, particularly long bus rides, becomes a critical psychological, social, and economic consideration. While a critical mass of deaf children is accumulated to form the nucleus of a deaf peer group, the long transportation times involved militate against participation by these children. Since hearing peers are outside of the deaf child's community, meaningful contact with them is difficult. The ultimate irony is that, because of the distances and time involved, such programs can erode family contact and local neighborhood involvement.

Improving Achievement

One of the early claims of the mainstreaming movement was that mainstreaming would improve the educational achievement of deaf children. However, as Carlberg and Kavale (1985) showed, mainstreaming is a mixed academic blessing in that some children, such as the mildly mentally retarded, benefit, but others, such as the emotionally disturbed or the learning disabled, do not. Repeated studies of the achievement of deaf children, as outlined in Chapters 8 and 9, show that mainstreaming per se is not a solution to improving the academic achievement of deaf students, since effective instruction is possible for deaf students in special classes as well as for mainstreamed deaf students. Ultimately, the question is not where but how well.

The problems that mainstreaming have produced include the necessity for and the cost of interpreters, the frequent social isolation of individual deaf students in mainstream classes, and the often unquestioned assumption of how good mainstream instruction is.

Supporting Individual Needs

In one of the early studies that preceded much of the work presented in this book, Donald Moores and I gave a communication practices questionnaire to 185 deaf students in three public secondary school programs (Moores, Kluwin, & Mertens, 1985). We asked the students how they communicated with members of their families. By the time we put together the number of different family relationships and the number of different modes of communication, we had 176 unique sets of communication situations. If we had taken any other combination of educationally significant factors such as ethnicity, gender, academic ability, or degree of hearing loss, we could quickly have generated nearly as many unique combinations. Essentially, nearly every deaf student, in a public school program or a residential school, is a unique population. While this is the basis for special education's emphasis on individualizing education, it produces problems for practitioners.

The resources of school systems are finite, even in the most affluent areas; consequently, decisions have to be made about the allocation of those resources. The term *resources* has to be understood to include not just the local tax base, but the availability of qualified staff (see Chapter 10). Even affluent school districts cannot always attract qualified staff if the staff simply do not exist. Consequently, decisions have to be made about the allocation of resources to meet the demands of the various educational constituencies, and those decisions will limit individual options.

Living with Uncertainty

Simply advocating the return to residential schools will not make any of these problems go away. There are competing claims in the education of deaf children, but there are also competing values in American education, such as the constant battle between egalitarianism or equity versus quality or achievement. Given this view of trying to balance the conflicting demands of a complicated system of competing values as well as the need to create formal systems to guarantee the integration of deaf and hard of hearing children into American education and ultimately into American society, we can describe some steps toward an effective program.

TOWARD DEFINING AN EFFECTIVE PROGRAM

Adequate Student Population

To have an effective program, both for the sake of administrative requirements such as special personnel and for a nucleus of a deaf community as well, the administrative unit should consist of at least 125 to 150 students, sufficiently homogeneous in their abilities to be concentrated in age-appropriate sites. In other words, this number does not include hard of hearing students who function in regular classrooms, unless the administrative system permits the counting of these children in formulae for the provision of appropriate services at the site schools. A program with fewer than 25 students with educationally significant hearing loss at a single site will experience problems in providing adequate services (see Chapters 9 and 10).

Regionalization

Regionalization is a solution when transportation and political barriers can be overcome (see Chapter 8). If the modal deaf students are spending more time on the bus than the hearing students in that district, then the deaf students may be objectively at a disadvantage. In other words, it may be possible to construct a regional district by requiring deaf students to spend 3 hours a day on the bus; but if the longest bus ride for a hearing student in that district is less than an hour both ways, then regionalization has become counterproductive.

Additionally, if regionalization permits the withdrawal of students from the regional program because of within-home-district political or economic changes, then the effort toward regionalization is counterproductive. The child cannot become a political football. In the establishment of regional programs, there needs to be state level guarantees for the integrity of the regional program to ensure the stability of children in school.

Administrative Integration

The effective program for the deaf will take place in an environment where the school principal has respect for the administrator of the program as a professional. Such respect is a personal matter, but it starts with the establishment of a clear relationship between the two.

The landlord–tenant model that many programs use—that is, the program for the deaf just takes up space—is a poor basis for operation. Just as the landlord–tenant relationship depends on the vagaries of personalities, so does the program relationship. Further, the mutual commitment is the same as in the landlord–tenant relationship. The landlord likes a tenant who does not damage the property and pays more rent than anyone else, but there is no commitment on the part of the landlord to support the tenant. At the same time, the tenant does not have to participate in any of the goals of the landlord.

An integrated model is more appropriate because the administrator of the program for the deaf has two responsibilities: to the total educational program and to ensure the provision of the best services to the deaf students. The commitment to the general education program is shown in the use of a title and a set of responsibilities by the administrator of the deaf program, such as assistant or associate principal. Since many large schools have specialized responsibilities, for example, curriculum or instructional supervision, for assistant or associate principals, such a system is not foreign. At the same time, this individual would share in the cross-building responsibilities of the other members of the administrative team.

An Effective Deaf Education Staff

There are three areas that the staff of the deaf education program must claim for themselves as their areas of expertise: knowledge of deafness, a unique ability to communicate with deaf students, and the capacity to work with individual deaf students better than anyone else can.

Knowledge of deafness needs to be defined positively (see Chapter 3). In the traditional coursework in deaf education, knowledge of deafness is the knowledge of disability: how to read an audiogram, speech pathology, social or psychological "problems" of deaf adults. This domain needs to be redefined to include the history of the deaf community in the United States, the capacity of ASL to produce unique and rewarding art forms, and the skills that are called for in order to live in two worlds. The effective staff will recognize the change in attitude toward deafness, and staff members will prepare themselves individually and as a group to function in this changed environment.

The unique ability to communicate does not depend on the advocacy of a single, preferred mode of communication at the staffing level; it rests, rather, on the staff's competence to communicate with all deaf or hard of hearing students in the mode most beneficial to each student. A competent staff will not be satisfied with minimal manual communication skills but will develop skills in the use of ASL. The competent administrator will encourage this through a "carrot and stick" approach. Financial rewards should be offered for higher levels of signing skill. For example, if the school district has a merit pay system, a special exception should be sought in the definitions of meritorious teaching to allow for signing skill improvement.

To work with individual deaf students to the fullest extent possible, deaf education must, as a field, explore more effective ways to provide instruction. For example, in special classes for the deaf, this will require more imaginative approaches to planning, more intelligent use of student time, and a greater variety of student monitoring. Traditional lesson planning should be eliminated in favor of computerized or "spreadsheet" approaches to planning for heterogeneous groups. Teacher time should be devoted less to administration and more to direct instruction of individual or small groups of children, with an emphasis on engaging students actively. Teachers do not have to burn the worksheets; they have to find ways to have the students think about and interact with what they are doing. Assessment needs to be frequent, informal, and varied. An emphasis on formal assessment ends up in a mind-numbing routine of paper checking, but varied forms of evaluation, including student projects, short essays, story performance, and so on, can be worked into a system of instruction, practice, and assessment.

The key to individualized instruction will be technologies that teachers can use to track individual students. These might range from paper and pencil "executive planners," where each student becomes a "project," to software systems on personal computers.

Reciprocal Inclusion

Reciprocal inclusion (Higgins, 1990) is based on the fundamental premise that to create understanding between groups of people each side must be involved in a direct way with the life of the other. In his book on making mainstreaming work, Higgins (1990) proposes several strategies whereby both deaf education and general education personnel can be involved with each other in a variety of informal ways.

However, reciprocal inclusion must start at the top and not at the bottom of the educational hierarchy. I have already mentioned administrative integration, but other steps are required. Teachers of the deaf must be integrated, formally and informally, into the operation of the overall educational program. It is not enough to have lunchroom acquaintances. Teachers of the deaf must sit on school-wide committees, participate in subject-matter departmental meetings, and support nondeafness-related, school-wide activities. This participation must be reinforced by the supervisory and evaluative system. At the level of individual deaf students, resources must be provided to them so that they can participate fully in all aspects of school life. A program for the deaf is underfunded and providing substandard educational benefits if the deaf child does not have the transportation and interpreting support required to voluntarily participate in school-wide activities.

Higgins (1990) offers a range of personal relations strategies as well as possible activities that programs for the deaf can institute to attract the interest of hearing students. However, the effective program for the deaf will not depend on the deaf child to make integration work. Successful integration must take place at all levels of the educational system.

Creating Options, Not Default Systems

The effective program will not be one that can say "money is no object"; that response means that the program is temporarily overfunded or is merely fiscally mismanaged. The effective program manager will look at the needs of his or her student population and at the available resources and make reasonable recommendations.

One traditional American educational system solution to problems is to wave technology at them and walk away. This inevitably fails to solve the problem because the proposed technological system is either too expensive or too complicated to be used in a school. A better starting point is to look at human beings and how they need to live. Then the educational planner can draw on available solutions in an organized fashion. For example, regionalization is an obvious solution to the problem of inadequate numbers of deaf students for a fully supported program, assuming that a large enough urban population and an adequate highway system are available.

Another low cost approach to creating options is to advocate the acceptance of ASL as a foreign language within the general curriculum. There is no particular reason why French, German, and Spanish have to be the only languages in the schools. Why not Japanese, Russian, or Chinese? Several reasons contributed to the rise of the three "modern" foreign languages, including the economic, scientific, or cultural prestige of the language, or the competition of that language with English in a specific locale as immigrant students were brought into the public school system. Although there has been comparatively little interest in Native American languages in American schools—primarily as a result of the dominance exerted over Native Americans in this country—there is no reason why effective lobbying at the state level cannot achieve the status of an "academic language" for ASL. This would permit deaf students to meet a "foreign" language requirement and hearing students to become more conversant with some of their peers.

Hearing impaired magnet classes are also an alternative to creating permanent, more costly school structures to aid in integration. Since some deaf or hard of hearing students will have to be taught in special classes for the deaf and some trained teachers of the deaf will have to be in a school building to teach them, magnet classes to attract hearing students could be created. These classes would be small and their focus would be on the quality of the interaction between the teacher and the individual students. There are many parents of hearing children who would be willing for their children to be in class with deaf children if it meant smaller classes and more individual attention. These classes would follow the regular curriculum and pace, thus putting pressure on the deaf students to keep up, but would offer unique instructional approaches to attract hearing students.

Nurturing a Child in Two Worlds

The first world, the hearing world, is not difficult to provide in a public school setting. Usually, the provision of this world is overwhelming. The solution is to mediate rather than "soften" exposure to this world. The second world, the deaf community, must be specifically provided to students in public school through regular contact with peers at residential schools, access to deaf adults as members of the staff and as regular nonstaff participants, and the organization of deafness-related events (see Chapter 3). Access to peers in the deaf community can come through joint participation with residential programs, where possible.

Deaf adults must be employed as professionals in deaf education programs. In states where "competency" tests mediate against the employment of deaf adults in schools, the deaf education programs have a responsibility to lobby for exceptions or adjustments that would permit the employment of deaf teachers in public school programs. The discrimination against deaf adults as preschool or elementary school aides as "poor speech models" must end. An effective program would recognize that sign language models and adult role models are also part of the early educational experience (see Chapter 4).

Another way to involve deaf adults is to make use of the local system of deaf clubs or to contact the National Association of the Deaf for references (see Chapter 7). For example, in units about the family, deaf children need to meet and interact with elderly deaf. If hearing children can have "foster grandparents," why can't deaf children? As deaf children approach adolescence and learn about work, local deaf workers and professionals should be made available to the children, a point made by King (Chapter 11). Deaf adults can also be used as coaches or club advisors, and, as Stewart and Stinson (Chapter 7) point out, the system of deaf sports clubs suggests a ready supply of coaches.

Schools, particularly high schools, have Future Farmers, Future Teachers, Junior Achievement, Distributive Education Clubs of America (DECA), and a variety of other organizations that give children exposure to adult activities. An effective program for the deaf would be expected to have a chapter of the Junior National Association of the Deaf as well as to develop affiliations with some of the local deaf adult organizations as a way to provide a transition into that community.

Anyone who expects that it will be easy to include deaf children meaningfully into American public schools is at least self-deluded and at worst a menace to those children. But saying that something is not easy is not the same thing as saying it is impossible or undesirable. Legal racial integration was not accomplished easily and even today is a fragile proposition; social integration recedes from us every time the economy dips or a new "problem" such as cocaine abuse arises. However, progress has been made: a black man is governor of Virginia and a deaf man is president of Gallaudet University.

By substituting the lessons of history and a concern for our common humanity for the easy dogmatism of the past, steps can be taken toward a system in which deaf children will be educated in a humane way so that they may take their place in the two worlds that it is their right to occupy. And, in the process, draw the two worlds closer together.

REFERENCES

Carlberg, C., & Kavale, K. (1985). The efficacy of special versus regular class placement for exceptional children: A meta-analysis. *The Journal of Special Education, 14*(3), 295–309.

Higgins, P. C. (1990). *The challenge of educating deaf and hearing youth together.* Springfield, IL: Charles C. Thomas.

Moores, D., Kluwin, T. N., & Mertens, D. (1985). *High school program for deaf students in metropolitan areas.* (Monograph No. 3). Washington, DC: Gallaudet College, Gallaudet Research Institute.

Osipow, S. H. *Theories of Career Development* (2nd ed.). New York: Appleton-Century-Croft.

About the Contributors

Thomas N. Kluwin is a professor in the Department of Educational Foundations and Research and a research scientist in the Center for Studies in Education and Human Development at Gallaudet University, Washington, D.C.

Donald F. Moores is a professor in the Department of Educational Foundations and Research and Director of the Center for Studies in Education and Human Development at Gallaudet University, Washington, D.C.

Martha Gonter Gaustad is an associate professor in the Department of Special Education at Bowling Green State University, Bowling Green, Ohio.

Valerie J. Janesick is an associate professor in the Department of Curriculum and Instruction at the University of Kansas, Lawrence, Kansas.

Suzanne King is a researcher in the Psychosocial Research Unit at the Douglas Hospital Research Centre, Montreal, Quebec, Canada.

Angela O'Donnell is an assistant professor in the Department of Educational Psychology at Rutgers University, New Brunswick, New Jersey.

Joe D. Stedt is an assistant professor in the Department of Education and Psychology of Cameron University, Lawton, Oklahoma.

David A. Stewart is an associate professor in the Department of Counseling, Educational Psychology, and Special Education at Michigan State University, East Lansing, Michigan.

Michael S. Stinson is a research associate and an associate professor in the Department of Educational Research and Development at the National Technical Institute for the Deaf, Rochester, New York.

Kathleen Whitmire is a speech and language specialist for the Board of Cooperative Educational Services of Monroe County, New York.

Index

TEXAS A&M UNIVERSITY-TEXARKANA